Re-thinking Leisure in a Digital Age

Digital worlds and cultures—social media, Web 2.0, YouTube, wearable technologies, health and fitness apps—dominate, if not order, our everyday lives. We are no longer 'just' consumers or readers of digital culture but active producers through Facebook, Twitter, Instagram, YouTube and other emerging technologies. This book is predicated on the assumption that our understanding of our everyday lives should be informed by what is taking place in and through emerging technologies given these (virtual) environments provide a crucial context where traditional, categorical assumptions about the body, identity and leisure may be contested. Far from being 'virtual', the body is constituted within and through emerging technologies in material ways. Recent 'moral panics' over the role of digital cultures in teen suicide, digital drinking games, an endless array of homoerotic images of young bodies being linked with steroid use, disordered eating and body dissatisfaction, Facebook games/fundraising campaigns (e.g. for breast cancer), movements devoted to exposing 'everyday sexism'/metoo, Twitter abuse (of feminists, of athletes, of racist nature to name but a few), speak to the need for critical engagement with digital cultures. While some of the earlier techno-utopian visions offered the promise of digitality to give rise to participatory, user generator collaborations, within this book we provide critical engagement with digital technologies and what this means for our understandings of leisure cultures.

This book was originally published as a special issue of *Leisure Studies*.

Michael Silk is a professor and Deputy Dean (Research & Professional Practice) in the Faculty of Management, Bournemouth University, UK. His research and scholarship is interdisciplinary and focuses on the relationships between sport and physical activity (physical culture), the governance of bodies, mediated (sporting) spectacles, identities and urban spaces.

Brad Millington is a lecturer in the Department for Health, University of Bath, UK. His research is focused on how technology has helped shape sporting practices in different historical eras, in sport and physical activity policy, and in the meanings people ascribe to their sport and physical activity experiences.

Emma Rich is a reader in the Department for Health, University of Bath, UK. Her research examines sport, physical activity and physical/health education with a specific interest in digital health technologies (e.g. mobile and digital health, big data, wearable technologies).

Anthony Bush is a senior lecturer in the Department for Health, University of Bath, UK. He is an interdisciplinary scholar specialising in issues concerning the physically active body in a myriad of spaces and sites including, but not limited to, the elite sporting context.

Re-thinking Leisure in a Digital Age

Edited by
Michael Silk, Brad Millington,
Emma Rich and Anthony Bush

LONDON AND NEW YORK

First published 2019
by Routledge
2 Park Square, Milton Park, Abingdon, Oxon, OX14 4RN, UK

and by Routledge
52 Vanderbilt Avenue, New York, NY 10017, USA

First issued in paperback 2020

Routledge is an imprint of the Taylor & Francis Group, an informa business

British Library Cataloguing in Publication Data
A catalogue record for this book is available from the British Library

ISBN 13: 978-0-367-58497-9 (pbk)
ISBN 13: 978-1-138-32541-8 (hbk)

Typeset in Minion Pro
by RefineCatch Limited, Bungay, Suffolk

Publisher's Note
The publisher accepts responsibility for any inconsistencies that may have arisen during the conversion of this book from journal articles to book chapters, namely the possible inclusion of journal terminology.

Contents

Citation Information

The chapters in this book were originally published in *Leisure Studies*, volume 35, issue 6 (December 2016). When citing this material, please use the original page numbering for each article, as follows:

Foreword
Lively devices, lively data and lively leisure studies
Deborah Lupton
Leisure Studies, volume 35, issue 6 (December 2016), pp. 709–711

Chapter 1
(Re-)thinking digital leisure
Michael Silk, Brad Millington, Emma Rich and Anthony Bush
Leisure Studies, volume 35, issue 6 (December 2016), pp. 712–723

Chapter 2
Young people, digital media making and critical digital citizenship
D. McGillivray, G. McPherson, J. Jones and A. McCandlish
Leisure Studies, volume 35, issue 6 (December 2016), pp. 724–738

Chapter 3
Video games and the political and cultural economies of health-entertainment
Brad Millington
Leisure Studies, volume 35, issue 6 (December 2016), pp. 739–757

Chapter 4
Exploring online fitness culture and young females
Stephanie T. Jong and Murray J. N. Drummond
Leisure Studies, volume 35, issue 6 (December 2016), pp. 758–770

Chapter 5
Be who you are and be proud: Brittney Griner, intersectional invisibility and digital possibilities for lesbian sporting celebrity
Megan Chawansky
Leisure Studies, volume 35, issue 6 (December 2016), pp. 771–782

Chapter 6
Towards typologies of virtual maltreatment: sport, digital cultures & dark leisure
Emma Kavanagh, Ian Jones and Lucy Sheppard-Marks
Leisure Studies, volume 35, issue 6 (December 2016), pp. 783–796

Chapter 7
(Re)constructing the tourist experience? Editing experience and mediating memories of learning to dive
Stephanie Merchant
Leisure Studies, volume 35, issue 6 (December 2016), pp. 797–808

Chapter 8
Immaterial labour in spaces of leisure: producing biopolitical subjectivities through Facebook
Jeff Rose and Callie Spencer
Leisure Studies, volume 35, issue 6 (December 2016), pp. 809–826

Afterword
A new digital Leisure Studies for Theoretical Times
Steve Redhead
Leisure Studies, volume 35, issue 6 (December 2016), pp. 827–834

Notes on Contributors

Anthony Bush, PhD, is a lecturer in the Department for Health at the University of Bath, UK. His research is interdisciplinary, focusing on issues concerning the physically active body in a myriad of spaces and sites including, but not limited to, the elite sporting context.

Megan Chawansky is currently a senior lecturer at the University of Brighton, UK, in the School of Sport and Service Management. Her academic work has appeared in the following journals: *Sociology of Sport, Qualitative Research in Sport, Exercise and Health, Sport in Society* and *International Review for the Sociology of Sport.*

Murray J. N. Drummond is professor in Sport, Health and Physical Education in the School of Education at Flinders University, South Australia. He is the director of the SHAPE research centre. His primary research interests revolve around masculinities, health and sport.

Ian Jones is associate professor in Sport at Bournemouth University, UK. His teaching and research interests focus upon aspects of sport, identity and consumption. He is author of *Research Methods in Sport Studies* and co-author of *Qualitative Research in Sport and Physical Activity.*

J. Jones is currently the project coordinator for the Big Lottery Funded Glasgow 2014 Legacy project 'Digital Commonwealth'. She is a part-time researcher, completing a PhD on major events with a focus on citizen journalism, ethnographic methods using social media data and digital literacies. She is a digital media practitioner who has delivered digital materials, training and resource support for a number of education, third sector and cultural organisations.

Stephanie T. Jong is a PhD candidate in the School of Education at Flinders University, South Australia. Her research focuses on the influence of social networking sites on the health practices of young females, explicitly the subsets of fitness and exercise. Stephanie is also interested in the innovative use of methods for research.

Emma Kavanagh is a lecturer in Sports Psychology and Coaching Sciences at Bournemouth University, UK. Her research interests are within the disciplines of psychology and sociology. Current projects include an examination of humanisation and dehumanisation in high performance sport and its impact on athlete well-being, understanding human rights in elite sport and an exploration of virtual and face-to-face maltreatment in high performance environments.

Deborah Lupton is Centenary Research Professor associated with the News & Media Research Centre in the Faculty of Arts and Design, University of Canberra, Australia. Her research and teaching is multidisciplinary, incorporating sociology, media and communication, and cultural studies. Deborah has previously held academic appointments at the University of Sydney, Charles Sturt University and Western Sydney University. She is a Fellow of the Academy of the Social Sciences of Australia, the co-convenor of the national Digital Data & Society Consortium, and the director of the Smart Technology Living Lab at UC.

A. McCandlish is a PhD candidate in Cultural Planning at the University of the West of Scotland, UK, with a background in creative media, town planning and heritage conservation. Her research interests centre around community engagement using digital and artistic methods and heritage management. She writes a weekly newsblog for the Institute of Historic Building Conservation.

D. McGillivray's research focuses on a critical reading of the contemporary significance of events and festivals (sporting and cultural) as markers of identity and mechanisms for the achievement of wider economic, social and cultural externalities. His current research focuses on the value of digital media in enabling alternative readings of major sport events. He is co-author of *Event Policy: From Theory to Strategy* (2011), co-editor of *Research Themes for Events* (2013) and has published extensively in *Leisure Studies*, *Journal of Policy Research in Tourism*, *Leisure and Events* and most recently in *Urban Studies* and the *Annals of Leisure Research.*

G. McPherson leads and works on a wide range of research and knowledge exchange projects within the School of Media, Culture and Society at the University of the West of Scotland, UK. She is a member of the European Cultural Parliament and teaches at the Institute of Cultural Diplomacy in Berlin, Germany.

Stephanie Merchant is a lecturer in the Department for Health at the University of Bath, UK. Her research focuses on visual methodological innovation and philosophically informed analyses of the tourist and leisure experience. More specifically, her work has built on and critiqued traditional conceptualisations of both the spatial and embodied elements of the adventure tourism encounter. Notable publications include 'The Body and the Senses: Visual Methods, Videography and the Submarine Sensorium' in *Body and Society* (2011) and 'Negotiating Underwater Space: The Sensorium, the Body and the Practice of SCUBA-Diving' in *Tourist Studies* (2011).

Brad Millington, PhD, is a lecturer in the Department for Health at the University of Bath, UK. His research is focused on health and fitness technologies, with consideration given to the production, representation, regulation and consumption of devices such as fitness training apps.

Steve Redhead is professor of Cultural Studies in the Faculty of Education, Humanities and Law, Flinders University, South Australia, working in the School of Humanities and Creative Arts, and Flinders Law School. He is also an adjunct professor of Cultural Studies in the Faculty of Graduate Studies, York University, Ontario, Canada. He is a council member of the National Rural Law and Justice Alliance of Australia. He has published 16 books including *Football and Accelerated Culture: This Modern Sporting Life* (Routledge, Research in Sport, Culture and Society Series, 2015), *We Have Never Been Postmodern: Theory at the Speed of Light* (Edinburgh University Press, 2011), *The Jean Baudrillard Reader* (Edinburgh University Press/Columbia University Press, European Perspectives Series, 2008) and *Paul Virilio: Theorist for an Accelerated Culture* (Edinburgh University Press/University of Toronto Press, 2004). He is the editor of the *Subcultural Style* book series for Bloomsbury and a member of many editorial boards of journals including *Sport in Society*, *fusion*, *i-M* and *International Journal of Child, Youth and Family Studies.* He is a member of the international advisory boards of the Teesside Centre for Realist Criminology (TCRC) and the *Entertainment and Sports Law Journal.* His personal website is at www.steveredhead.zone.

Emma Rich, PhD, is a reader in the Department for Health at the University of Bath, UK. Her research draws upon the sociology of education, pedagogy, the body and physical culture to explore how learning about and through the body (body pedagogies) take places in relation to different physical cultures, spaces and sites.

Jeff Rose is a visiting assistant professor in the Department of Environmental Studies at Davidson College, USA. With a focus on public space, place attachment and non-normative behaviors, his research interests are in the use of qualitative methods to examine systemic inequalities displayed through race, class, political economy and relationship to nature.

Lucy Sheppard-Marks is a lecturer in Sport and Physical Activity at Bournemouth University, UK. Her research interests include crime and sport, transitions and leadership. She is currently completing her PhD exploring the experiences of athletes who commit crimes (this PhD is supported and aided by the Dame Kelly Holmes Trust).

Michael Silk is a professor and Deputy Dean of the Faculty of Management, Bournemouth University, UK. He is also director of the Sport and Physical Activity Research Centre at Bournemouth University. His research and scholarship are interdisciplinary and focuses on the relationships between sport and physical activity (physical culture), the governance of bodies, mediated (sporting) spectacles, identities and urban spaces.

Callie Spencer is a lecturer at Eastern Washington University, USA. Her research interests include leisure and new media, performance studies and the construction of subjectivities in transmedia leisure spaces. She employs qualitative methods that trouble notions of traditional epistemologies in her work in order to tilt systems of power both outside and within the academy.

Foreword: lively devices, lively data and lively leisure studies

Deborah Lupton

In the countries of the Global North, each person, to a greater or lesser degree, has become configured as a data subject. When we use search engines, smartphones and other digital devices, apps and social media platforms, and when we move around in spaces carrying devices, they record our geolocation, or where there are embedded sensors or cameras recording our movements, we are datafied: rendered into assemblages of digital data. These personal digital data assemblages are only ever partial portraits of us and are constantly changing: but they are beginning to have significant impacts on the ways in which people understand themselves and others and on their life opportunities and chances. Leisure cultures and practices are imbricated within digital and data practices and assemblages. Indeed, digital technologies are beginning to transform many areas of life into leisure pursuits in unprecedented ways, expanding the purview of leisure studies in several interesting dimensions.

These processes of datafication can begin even before birth and continue after death. Proud expectant parents commonly announce pregnancies on social media, uploading ultrasound images of their foetuses and sometimes even creating accounts in the name of the unborn so that they can ostensibly communicate from within the womb. Images from the birth of the child may also become publicly disseminated: as in the genre of the childbirth video on YouTube. This is followed by the opportunity for parents to record and broadcast many images of their babies' and children's lives. At the other end of life, many images of the dying and dead bodies can now be found on the internet. People with terminal illnesses write blogs, use Facebook status updates or tweet about their experiences and post images of themselves as their bodies deteriorate. Memorial websites or dedicated pages on social media sites are used after people's death to commemorate them. Beyond these types of datafication, the data generated from other interactions online and by digital sensors in devices and physical environments constantly work to generate streams of digital data about people. In some cases, people may choose to generate these data; in most other cases, they are collected and used by others, often without people's knowledge or consent. These data have become highly valuable as elements of the global knowledge economy, whether aggregated and used as big data-sets or used to reveal insights into individuals' habits, behaviours and preferences.

One of my current research interests is exploring the ways in which digital technologies work to generate personal information about people and how individuals themselves and a range of other actors and agencies use these data. I have developed the concept of 'lively data', which is an attempt to incorporate the various elements of how we are living with and by our data. Lively data are generated by lively devices: those smartphones, tablet computers, wearable devices and embedded sensors that we live with and alongside, our companions throughout our waking days. Lively data about humans are vital in four main respects: (1) they are about human life itself; (2) they have their own social lives as they circulate and combine and recombine in the digital data economy; (3) they are beginning to affect people's lives, limiting or promoting life chances and opportunities (for example, whether people are offered employment or credit); and (4) they contribute to livelihoods (as part of their economic and managerial value).

These elements of datafication and lively data have major implications for leisure cultures. Research into people's use of digital technologies for recreation, including the articles collected here and others previously published in this journal, draws attention to the pleasures, excitements and playful dimensions of digital encounters. These are important aspects to consider, particularly when much research into digital society focuses on the limitations or dangers of digital technology use such as the possibilities of various types of 'addiction' to their use or the potential for oppressive surveillance or exploitation of users that these technologies present. What is often lost in such discussions is an acknowledgement of the value that digital technologies can offer ordinary users (and not just the internet empires that profit from them). Perspectives that can balance awareness of both the benefits and possible drawbacks of digital technologies provide a richer analysis of their affordances and social impact. When people are using digital technologies for leisure purposes, they are largely doing so voluntarily because they have identified a personal use for the technologies that will provide enjoyment, relaxation or some other form of escape from the workaday world. What is particularly intriguing, at least from my perspective in my interest in lively data, is how the data streams from digitised leisure pursuits are becoming increasingly entangled with other areas of life and concepts of selfhood. Gamification and ludification strategies, in which elements of play are introduced into domains such as the workplace, health care, intimate relationships and educational institutions, are central to this expansion.

Thus, for example, we now see concepts of the 'healthy, productive worker', in which employers seek to encourage their workers to engage in fitness pursuits to develop highly achieving and healthy employees who can avoid taking time out because of illness and operate at maximum efficiency in the workplace. Fitness tracker companies offer employers discounted wearable devices for their employees so that corporate 'wellness' programmes can be put in place in which fitness data sharing and competition are encouraged among employees. Dating apps like Tinder encourage users to think of the search for partners as a game and the attractive presentation of the self as a key element in 'winning' the interest of many potential dates. The #fitspo and #fitspiration hashtags used in Instagram and other social media platforms draw attention to female and male bodies that are slim, physically fit and well-groomed, performing dominant notions of sexual attractiveness. Pregnancy has become ludified with a range of digital technologies. Using their smartphones and dedicated apps, pregnant women can take 'belfies', or belly selfies, and generate time-lapse videos for their own and others' entertainment (including uploading the videos on social media sites). Three-D printing companies offer parents the opportunity to generate replicas of their foetuses from 3D ultrasounds for use as display objects on mantelpieces or work desks. Little girls are offered apps which encourage then to perform makeovers on pregnant women or help them deliver their babies via caesarean section. In the education sector, digitised gamification blurs leisure, learning and physical fitness. Schools are beginning to distribute heart rate monitors, coaching apps and other self-tracking devices to children during sporting activities and physical education classes, promoting a culture of self-surveillance via digital data at the same time as teachers' monitoring of their students' bodies is intensified. Online education platforms for children like Mathletics encourage users to complete tasks to win medals and work their way up the leaderboard, competing against other users around the world.

In these domains and many others, the intersections of work, play, health, fitness, education, parenthood, intimacy, productivity, achievement and concepts of embodiment, selfhood and social relations are blurred, complicated and far-reaching. These practices raise many questions for researchers interested in digitised leisure cultures across the age span. What are the affordances of the devices, software and platforms that people use for leisure? How do these technologies promote and limit leisure activities? How are people's data used by other actors and agencies and in what ways do these third parties profit from them? What do people know about how their personal details are generated, stored and used by other actors and agencies? How do they engage with their own data or those about others in their lives? What benefits, pleasures and opportunities do such activities offer, and what are their drawbacks, risks and harms? How are the carers and teachers of children and young people encouraging or enjoining them to use these technologies and to what extent are they are aware of the possible harms as well as benefits? How are data privacy and security issues recognised and managed, on the part both of those who take up these pursuits voluntarily and those who encourage or impose them on others? When does digitised leisure begin to feel more like work and vice versa; and what are the implications of this?

These questions return to the issue of lively data, and how these data are generated and managed, the impact they have on people's lives and concepts of selfhood and embodiment. As I noted earlier, digital technologies contribute to new ways of reconceptualising areas of life as games or as leisure pursuits that previously were not thought of or treated in those terms. In the context of this move towards rendering practices and phenomena as recreational and the rapidly changing sociomaterial environment, all social researchers interested in digital society need to be lively in response to lively devices and lively data. As the editors of this special issue contend, researching digital leisure cultures demands a multidisciplinary and interdisciplinary perspective. Several exciting new interdisciplinary areas have emerged in response to the increasingly digitised world: among them internet studies, platform studies, software studies, critical algorithm studies and critical data studies. The ways in which leisure studies can engage with these, as well the work carried out in subdisciplines such as digital sociology, digital humanities and digital anthropology, have yet to be fully realised. In return, the key focus areas of leisure studies, both conceptually and empirically – aspects of pleasure, performance, politics and power relations, embodiment, selfhood, social relations and the intersections between leisure and work – offer much to these other areas of enquiry.

The articles published in this special issue go some way to addressing these issues, particularly in relation to young people. The contributors demonstrate how people may accept and take up the dominant assumptions and concepts about idealised selves and bodies expressed in digital technologies but also how users may resist these assumptions or seek to re-invent them. As such, this special issue represents a major step forward in promoting a focus on the digital in leisure studies, working towards generating a lively leisure studies that can make sense of the constantly changing worlds of lively devices and lively data.

Disclosure statement

No potential conflict of interest was reported by the author.

(Re-)thinking digital leisure

Michael Silk, Brad Millington, Emma Rich and Anthony Bush

4D ibabyscans, wearable baby gro's/monitors incorporating movement-based technologies and provide real-time video on your iPhone while your baby sleeps, speak to a dazzling assemblage of digital technologies, products, commodities, platforms, materialities and virtualities that enculturate, envelop and are embodied on/in the contemporary corporeality of young people, almost from conception. Play – commodified in the form of soccertots, rugbytots, waterbabies, turtletots, tumbletots, bunnies (gymnastics), musicbugs, and now digitised and quantified (real time ipad feedback during toddler swimming lessons) – is, we are told due to concerns over safety, the loss/privatisation of open space in our communities and multiple other 'risks', not something that can or should be done outside or alone. Tablets, phones, computers, consoles and touch screens in reception classes have become the new techno-pedagogic (Rich & Miah, 2014) devices through which the educative, leisured, consumptive and play elements of the everyday are filtered and organised. The capacity for mobile connectivity has blurred the boundaries between public/private/digitised leisure spaces. Our every step surveilled, logged, recorded and stored, as we engage in our neoliberal consumptive practices. Going to the cinema, eating out at a restaurant, taking a trip, shopping in themed malls part of a 'surveillant assemblage' (Haggerty & Ericson, 2000) predicated on an aegis of suspicion and a global climate of fear (see Bigo, 2011). Even Christmas is militarised and bought to us by NORAD. (Awkward) physical teenage relationships re-defined by shifting expectations brought about by the ubiquity of online pornography; bedrooms redefined as sexting production studios or as amateur porn streaming showrooms. Fitbit, Jawbone, Garmin, Microsoft Band, MiCoach, Strava, MapmyRun, RunKeeper, Runtastic, Nike+ FuelBand, Endomondo, Lose It!, Pokemon Go quantifying, shaping, sharing and augmenting our physical exertions, instructing us as we glide, plod, pedal, trot and chase.

We are living in a digital culture in which personalised data are amassed in great volume and variety and are exchanged with great velocity. Selfies, belfies (bottom or belly selfies), shelfies (of one's bookshelf), lelfies (legs) and even pelfies (female genitalia, with the dic-pic the male equivalent) over-determine (to differing intensities) a digitised and exacerbated visual youth leisure culture on a variety of social media platforms (from Facebook to Snapchat to Twitter to Instagram and everything else in between), in which the body (shaped, sculpted, manicured and governed) is displayed (publically, and not just to [virtual] friends).The leisure practices, experiences, structures and forms of young people (their everyday lives) are digitised and datafied unlike anything we ever experienced. As Deborah Lupton points out in the foreword to this volume, lively devices generate lively data that have considerable implications in our understandings of a lively Leisure Studies. The papers in this special issue aim to contribute to such debates, offering nuanced understandings of how various instances, experiences, practices and structures of digital leisure are embedded in complex inter-connections with the economic and political trajectories of neoliberal consumer capitalism, surveillance and the unequal power relations extant in all leisure practices (Spracklen, 2015).

A digital leisure assemblage

The 'digital turn' raises important questions, not least about the ways in which digitised 'leisure' practices are inflected with power relations, and shaped by sociocultural contexts (geographical, familial, spatial, religious, socio-economic and cultural). Popular media outlets amplify the (supposed) exacerbated relationships between the hyper-visibility of digitised celebrated/demonised bodies with pressing and contemporary social concerns – including, for example, disordered eating, cyberstalking, digital abuse, teen suicide, mental health issues, (classed, raced and gendered) politics of a normalised neoliberal bodily aesthetic, sexual norms and abuse, social and health inequalities (including unequal access to and engagement with social media), and, surveillance of (pathologised) citizens.

Further, our devices are more than digital extensions of our material bodies; the development in the design of mobile techniques means they are increasingly inserted and integrated into our fleshy sinews, disrupting traditional binaries between work/leisure, production/consumption, material/digital and human/non-human. As Gilmore (2015, p.2) suggests, it is the capacity to be tethered to the body that produces 'habitualization' of particular practices. Integrated, embedded, fleshy/digital 'lively' leisure forms, structures, experiences and practices complicate, if not render obsolete, established categories and bodies of work in our field, such as distinctions between serious, project or casual leisure (e.g. Stebbins, 2007), production and consumption. With Van Doorn (2010, p. 538), we simply cannot separate our (leisured) bodies

> from the technological networks that give them form and meaning. Conversely, media technologies cannot be apprehended without accounting for the embodied and gendered use cultures that imbue them with significance by mobilising them within larger everyday networks – both virtual and concrete.

Our everyday leisured lives are so interconnected – in a series of crabgrass-like entanglements – to digital cultural forms, products, services and economies that it has thus become impossible to understand leisure without considering digital culture. Indeed, to understand leisure (the everyday experiences, structures and forms of bodies in leisure) necessitates grasping the workings of digital cultures; our leisured selves are posthuman digitally mediated cyborgified bodies, hybrid techno-corpi (Braidotti, 2013; Haraway, 1991; Ringrose & Harvey, 2016), our (leisured) bodies are digital cyborg assemblages (Lupton, 2015). We live in a digital society that cannot be understood without the recognition that computer software and hardware devices not only underpin, they actively constitute selfhood, embodiment, social life, social relations and social institutions (Lupton, 2015). Leisure is no different, and somewhat modifying Lupton, Leisure Studies needs to make the study of digital cultures central; to explicitly make our point, failure to do so is a failure to understand contemporary leisure practices, experiences, institutions and subjectivities and the place of leisure in understandings of embodiment, power relations, social inequalities, social structures and social institutions.

And so, where is Leisure Studies as an academic discipline on these issues and developments? How has the field of study responded to such radical structural, material, cultural and technological shifts that have profoundly altered our everyday lives, our bodies, our leisured experiences? Within a world of fast-moving, interconnected and accelerated digitality, we would tentatively suggest the answer here is, initially at least, slowly.

Taking leisure seriously: a slow response to accelerated culture?

With notable exceptions (see below), digitality has not adequately – if not thoroughly – been conceptualised and theorised within Leisure Studies. This is perhaps of little surprise given the fast paced world of digital cultures, the relative slowness of academic publication, the availability of funding for such work and, (potentially) the place of gatekeepers and/or editors who shape the discipline. However, we need to enhance our understandings of what the articulations and inter-connections between/within digital cultures and leisure mean for our scholarship, impact, our pedagogy and, our understandings of our social worlds. This is not to say that these conversations have not occurred; indeed some of these conversations have occurred outside of the 'traditional' parameters of Leisure Studies. It is not, for example, uncommon to find discussions of the impact of various aspects of digital culture on leisure in allied and affiliated fields, with articles surfacing in outlets such as *Space & Culture*, the *International Journal of Cultural Studies*, the *European Journal of Communication, Media, Culture & Society*, or, *Television & New Media* and as the topic of a number of other articles in special issues elsewhere. Further, as pointed out in the foreword to this volume, and as 'leisure' expands into the workplace, health care, relationships and education, are new interdisciplinary areas (such as platform studies, internet studies, critical data studies and critical health studies) going to displace Leisure Studies as critical space in which to engage with such issues? Or, will Leisure Studies be 'consumed' within newer ('livelier') subdisciplines such as digital sociology, digital humanities or digital anthropology? The articles in this issue offer a timely and necessary contribution to these essential discussions. For, failure to engage with digital cultures, technologies, experiences and economies might well see the (further) entrenchment of the academic field of leisure into its (un-)comfortable traditional boundaries.

Leisure Studies, at least a relevant (and critical) Leisure Studies, needs to ensure it does not become stuck in an analogue world, one in which our understandings of leisure have been surpassed in other fields by scholars who in no way see themselves as leisure scholars (and perhaps who envision a post-disciplinary world). To avoid such an admittedly bleak and provocative picture suggests a need for the democratisation of leisure and of Leisure Studies, a call to re-invigorate the field, further enhance and utilise a critical and theoretical sophistication and be attuned to the fast-moving digital world with which leisure articulates. Indeed, with Redhead (2016a/2016b), as an academic 'discipline' Leisure Studies needs to 'catch-up' with accelerated culture. This would not only be a discursive/practical space (and one ground in a sophisticated, critical and relevant theoretical basis that perhaps to date has been all too absent) in which leisure – as a field of study – demonstrates its usefulness in relating to social problems, inequalities, issues and justice, but one in which the field is able to be meaningful, to make a difference and dare we say (whilst revising an established concept!), be taken 'seriously'. The articles in this special issue are one such attempt at so doing.

Whilst perhaps initially slow to react, there has been a (relatively) recent explosion in work in the field, published in leisure journals and by dedicated 'leisure' scholars, that has begun to push the boundaries in (re-)thinking leisure in a digital age. It is certainly the case that we build off these contributions in this article and hope to add to their accomplishments through this issue. Orton-Johnson (2014), for example, has argued that new social media technologies have become a reciprocal and interconnected aspect of knitting as leisure, one in which the distinctions between leisure and technology are increasingly dissolved and which has reshaped the consumption of leisure in rich and dynamic ways. Francombe (2014) points to how certain leisure activities – reading magazines, digital gaming, shopping for clothes, eating, engaging in physical activity, applying beauty products, makeup and hair styling – highlights a consumptive, embodied body politic not without consequence. In so doing, she begins to understand the digital/'real' worlds of young women by drawing out the ways in which young girls' body practices can shed light on the complex relationship between 'choice', agency, consumption and subjectivity (see also Crawford, 2005 and Delamere & Shaw, 2008 for discussions of the gendered nature of digital games). Nimrod (e.g. 2014, 2015) and Berdychevsky & Nimrod (2016) have pioneered netnography in Leisure Studies, addressing amongst other things the multiple roles of sex in older adulthood, mobile phone usage amongst older adults and the relationships between online communities and psychological well-being in elders' leisure use of the Internet. Meanwhile, McGillivray (2014) suggested that the emergence of social media forms has profound influence on the production and consumption of sport mega-events, arguing that ubiquitous digital technologies augment accelerated identities and offer alternative narratives to those offered by dominant media frames. These are important, and eclectic (demonstrating the breadth of digital/leisure entanglements), contributions that have begun to set the range of possibilities for a digitally informed Leisure Studies.

There are, of course, other examples (e.g. Bull, 2006; Lepp, Barkley, & Karpinski, 2014; Lincoln, 2012). Yet, perhaps the most telling, important and extensive forays into theorising digital leisure come from the work of Steve Redhead, Sandro Carnicelli and colleagues, Karl Spracklen and Tara Brabazon. All have embarked, as is the intent of this special issue, on (re-)thinking leisure within an increasingly banal digital moment. Carnicelli, McGillivary, and McPherson's (2016) collection builds from the 2014 Leisure Studies Association conference hosted by the University of West Scotland. They offer a significant contribution to our changing understanding of digital leisure cultures, reflecting on the socio-historical context within which the digital age emerged, while engaging with new debates about the evolving and controversial role of digital platforms in contemporary leisure cultures. They point, as above, to both the promise of the digital sphere as a realm of liberation, and the darker side of digital culture associated with control, surveillance, exclusion and dehumanisation. Importantly, this is not to suggest dichotomous thinking; indeed, we would argue that digitised spaces are many of these things simultaneously.

Spracklen (2015) covers an array of possibilities for (re-)thinking leisure, focusing on the ways in which the digitalisation of culture forces us to: reconceptualise our identities and (alternative) sub-cultural formations; re-think our engagement with, and ownership of, music; reconsider the ways in which we shop, gamble and consume sport content; and, the commodification of pornography/the pornification of popular culture. Indeed, the ubiquity of online pornography (as a leisure practice, see Spracklen, 2015) alters our understandings of the relationship between visceral sexual pleasures and real-world social interactions, and perhaps speaks more than anything to a sweaty, performative, affective, lively, orgasming digital/fleshy leisure assemblage. Indeed, with the emergence of virtual reality sex toys (such as Virtuadolls, the Autoblow 2 or FriXion that enables sex over distance using teledildonics combined with computer robotics) these could well be more sophisticated, sensual, pleasurable and lively leisure experiences than those depicted in Spike Jonze's film *Her* (2013). Further, Spracklen points to the compelling concerns related to the access we afford leviathans such as Google and Apple through our digital leisure footprints, an issue we pick up on below.

Redhead (2015, 2016a, 2016b) talks to the digitisation of previously analogue spaces (such as online football fandom, the organisation of football hooliganism or indeed fan protest online) as illustrative of chronic shifts in disciplines and in the material practices of everyday life. Like Carnicelli et al. (2016), Spracklen (2015) critiques the lack of sustained inter-disciplinarity in understanding digital leisure cultures, suggesting that to be multidisciplinary (while admirable and which has characterised much leisure research over the years) is simply not enough given the contingencies and complexities of the digital age; 'simply put, we have to engage in interdisciplinary studies of digital leisure because that is the most successful way of doing Leisure Studies' (Spracklen, 2015, p. 197).

Tara Brabazon (2016) argues the technical shifts to which we have been subject/that we have enabled point to a systemically different digital leisure culture; one qualitatively different from an analogue leisure culture. Brabazon suggests this is characterised by both disintermediation and deterritorialisation. For Brabazon, disintermediation points to the loss of chains in the production/consumption supply chain. Instead prosumption (Ritzer, 2015) – as opposed to 'mitigating steps' such as writers, editors, production editors and so on – at 'speed' (e.g. YouTube channels and stars such as, Charli's crafty kitchen, Hooplakidz, Mother Goose Club, Athenewins or McBarbie07) dominates and re-organises popular culture. Deterritorialisation on the other hand refers to how digitalisation has ridden us post-territorial, which in part has rendered material place obsolete given our bonds, affiliations, identities, fandom and so on can be defined in digital as opposed to spatial terms (e.g. the worldwide affiliations to Manchester United FC being lived out in blogs, social media, the net, satellite footprints, see e.g. Silk & Chumley, 2004).

These contributions are clearly re-shaping Leisure Studies; yet that shape (and we would expect it not to be static) is, as yet, undefined. Are we, as indicated by Redhead (2016a), moving away from 'fields' of study towards a post-disciplinary world; is this a scholarly world where we would expect a fragmented 'leisure' to be dispersed amongst a variety of scholarly areas and journals and one without perhaps a home or association? Or, especially given the recent and relative 'explosion' of scholarship, are we seeing the emergence of a 'digital Leisure Studies' (Redhead, 2016b) characterised by new (and older) critical theory, that re-shapes leisure as a discipline, bringing it up to 'speed' with the profound societal / technological changes that have come to characterise our present conjunctural moment? Indeed, is this a moment in which we become fully attuned to, and as a multi-disciplinary field are well positioned to take advantage of, the 'return of leisure' that a digital culture seems to suggest; one in which digitised popular cultural forms and experience can andragogically lead us – along with critical, sophisticated leisure theorising – forward (Brabazon, 2016). Such contestations are yet to fully materialise, nonetheless this is an exciting moment for 'Leisure Studies' in whatever form that may take in the future. For while we suggest that the 'field' has been initially slow to address an accelerated digital culture, this does seem like a moment in which there is clear trajectory and traction, with the emergence of a number of recent contributions attuned to (re-)thinking leisure in a digital age (and for more on this, see the Afterword to this special issue provided by Steve Redhead).

This special issue aims to contribute to these emergent debates, suggesting that to draw out the nuances, contradictions, complexities, tensions and possibilities of digital leisure necessitates a fluid interdisciplinary, theoretical and multi-methodological approach. This will enable us, as a field, to tease out the important constraints and possibilities enabled and suppressed through a digital leisure culture that can only be understood as relational to contemporary social formations and extant power relations.

These initial forays into theorising and conceptualising an increasingly accelerated and intensified everyday digital leisure experience – especially, although not exclusively, for young people who have been born into a digital society – have paved the way for a number of exciting avenues of future scholarship, research and thinking. Given the nature of the nascent academic study of digital leisure cultures, there are a multitude of avenues that are worthy of critical exploration; some of which are explored through this special issue and others for which we propose are important in realising a critically engaged, theoretical and impact-oriented Leisure Studies that can 'make a difference' (Grossberg, 1996; cf. Silk & Andrews, 2011). Within this introduction and indeed the special issue as a whole, we will not be able to address, or provide a sophisticated and nuanced agenda; what we hope to achieve however is to draw together important articles, point towards certain trajectories, engage with work from allied disciplines and begin to comprehend the challenging task at hand for Leisure Studies, so as to contribute towards important and critical conversations about the impact of digital cultures on understandings that have heretofore been taken for granted/unchallenged. In this regard, we hope, through the special issue, when held together as a cohesive entity, to be able to contribute to an understanding of leisure as digitally reconstituted in a number of ways and raise some key questions for future research agendas of Leisure Studies. The task at hand is, perhaps, to think carefully about the contributions and understandings that Leisure Studies can provide, the 'solutions' to pressing social problems, concerns and issues embedded within the convergence of digital culture/our leisured lives, the impact on policy, practice and everyday life such theorising and critical engagement might prosper and, given the intensification of an accelerated and seemingly ubiquitous digital world, the ways in which Leisure Studies can position itself as central – as opposed to on the scholarly peripheries – to understandings of contemporary/everyday life.

Our leisured data doubles

One such 'touching point' concerns thinking about the intensified political and economic interests in digitising leisure, and indeed the turn to theorising such interests. Said another way, and recognising that technology use has long had leisurely dimensions, and vice versa, there is much at stake for companies ranging from Nike, Adidas and Under Armour to Apple, Nintendo, Microsoft and Facebook in remaking leisure activities as necessarily 'digitised' activities. In this sense, it is essential for such companies to ensure the consumer's Sunday morning run, once an ephemeral feat aside from its health, is 'datafied', archived and most of all shared. The same is true of book purchases on Amazon, downloads on iTunes, film selections on Netflix and statements of one kind or another on Facebook. Our 'real' selves have always been valuable to industry for our capacity to spend – whether on televisions, video games, magazines, books, bicycles, trainers, swimming costumes, gym memberships, or other goods and services. Our leisured 'data doubles' (Deleuze, 1995) are now highly valued as commodities as well.

The point here is not that some sinister motive necessarily underpins the digitising of leisure. Certainly, there exists a profit-oriented desire to improve product performance and thus consumer experience. The need to innovate in perpetual fashion is a key theme in Brad Millington's article in this special issue. Millington examines the political and cultural economies of Nintendo's recent adoption of health and fitness motifs, and the company's growing interest in appealing to older consumers. These are deemed parts of Nintendo's quest for a 'blue ocean'–which is to say an environment free from competition. So, rather than byzantine motives (although perhaps at the extremes of consumer capital's propensity to consume, well, itself, such motives exist), the point instead pertains to the fact that digitising leisure activities – from one's choice of reading material to one's changing heart rate in navigating that Sunday morning run – creates economic value out of leisure, and is thus a trend unlikely to reverse course anytime soon. Indeed, the very notion of production/consumption is blurred in contemporary leisure practices. As Ritzer (2015) observes, consumption and production have never been mutually exclusive. We are in an age marked by the increasing 'interpenetration of the digital and the material' (Ritzer, 2015, p. 4) in which active prosumers digitally (re-)produce the fabric of everyday life (from the creation/production of images of a terror attack to the news media, reviews of a holiday destination, instruction on the latest kettleball or battle ropes workout, through to social media campaigns for terror groups and transnational corporations). In this special issue, focusing on the prevalence of the everyday use of these technologies, Stephanie Merchant provides insight into the ways in which commodified digital technologies are literally editing out 'memories' of tourist place and leisure practice, reconceptualising understandings of alternative leisure realities and points to the ways in which post-tourists are increasingly the auteurs – or prosumers – of their leisure experiences. Prosumption, datafication, archiving and sharing dominate our everyday leisured lives, and create valuable data doubles. Jogging whilst wearing a fitness tracker or having sex whilst logging calories (using devices such as the Sex Calculator or the penis pedometer 'SexFit'), for example, create data (all designed for optimal sharing on social media) that might be sold onto third-party advertisers and attest to Ritzer's point. Such political/economic considerations offer but one important point of departure for a 'lively' digitised Leisure Studies.

Further, leisure is increasingly tied to the wider Big Data movement whereby data are generated on a greater scale (volume) and scope (variety) and are exchanged at greater speed (velocity) than ever before. This raises pressing questions about surveillance and privacy in leisure cultures. Indeed, whereas in the mid-2000s, Wakefield (2004) described a process of 'people watching people' in sites like leisure complexes by means of foot patrol and closed circuit television, surveillance in leisure cultures increasingly takes the form of 'people watching people's data' as well. At the same time, the question here is of leisure fuelling, and not simply reflecting, a wider culture of Big Data and surveillance. For example, Ellerbrok (2011) highlights the 'function creep' of face recognition (surveillance) technology from militarised uses to consumer uses via photo organising software. For Ellerbrok (2011), in this transition, play – so central to many leisure pursuits – holds the capacity to obfuscate and/or normalise otherwise controversial technological functionalities.

For leisure participants, then, the digitising of leisure in the first instance presents new responsibilities – for example, to know how one's data are collected and used. Given that data prosumption and surveillance are matters of consumer rights and protection, the political economic side of digital leisure puts the role of governments in the spotlight as well. For example, the notion that companies can extract value out of ever-expanding forms of data collection (in leisure contexts and beyond) sits uncomfortably against the principle of 'data minimisation', which stresses that only 'necessary' data should be collected (and in North America is part of the Federal Trade Commission's Fair Information Practice Principles). Balancing consumer protection and industry innovation/growth is no doubt challenging in neoliberal contexts where governments face pressure to create conditions for the latter to thrive in particular; yet, we would aver, this is an important consideration for an increasingly engaged and democratic digital Leisure Studies.

A celebrated/pathologised digital leisure body politic

Production, consumption, prosumption and surveillance are of course more than just about data protection and consumer rights; they speak to the reproduction of extant power relations and the possibility that power relations might be challenged as well. That is, a contextually based understanding of digitised leisure practices is inseparable from comprehension of the corporeal practices, discourses and subjectivities through which active bodies become organised, represented and experienced in relation to the operations of social power. As scholars, and following Silk and Andrews (2011), we thus need to be attuned to the role that digitised leisure cultures can play in reproducing, and sometimes challenging, particular class, ethnic, gender, ability, generational, national, racial and/or sexual norms and differences. Indeed, we would suggest that this in and of itself is not enough for a burgeoning, critical and politically relevant Leisure Studies in a digital age. Rather, through the development and strategic dissemination of potentially empowering forms of knowledge and understanding, as a field we can work to illuminate, and intervene into, sites of injustice and inequity engrained within digital leisure cultures.

Such an approach assumes that digital leisure cultures are uneven and imbued with power relations; it assumes that power can be 'limiting and productive: producing differences, shaping relations, structuring identities and hierarchies, but also enabling practices and empowering social subjects' (Grossberg, 1989). We believe our approaches to digital leisure cultures need to explore, understand and address how (and why) various dimensions of leisure in a digital age represent moments at which such social divisions are imposed, experienced and at times contested. Such a motivation also enforces an unequivocal 'commitment to progressive social change' (Miller, 2001, p. 1), and points us towards the production of the type of knowledge that can intervene into the broader social world, make a difference, engage in social transformation and thereby further reinforce the import of the discipline of Leisure Studies.

As our leisure becomes both, at one and same, fleshy and digital (Francombe, 2010, 2014; Francombe-Webb 2016; Francombe-Webb & Silk, 2016), as it becomes impossible to separate the monitoring and scuplting of our digitised bodies and footprints (as leisure) from the surveillance and monitoring of the physical self, we need to understand how digital leisure cultures control, govern and regulate citizens and their bodies. Obsessive self-surveillance, policing, monitoring and re-shaping of the body via social media sites, dating and rendezvous apps (e.g. Snapchat, Instagram, Facebook, Twitter, Tinder, Tumblr, Down [formerly Bang with Friends], Grindr and 3ndr), sexting, the ubiquitous presence and accessibility of online pornography (some produced, some 'prosumed'), fitspiration, thinspiration, 'Neknominate' (binge-drinking) suggest a *hypervisibility*, like never before, of the (normally, but not exclusively, hyper-feminine) digital/fleshy body, signalling norms, excesses, compartmentalisation, sexualisation, competitiveness (measured in 'likes') individualisation and post-humanism. How do such leisure practices celebrate or pathologise? Which bodies matter (and which do not) to a hyper- or uber-sexual, digital culture? And what are the physical health, well-being and social wellness implications of such digital leisure cultures and the impact they have on the everyday lives, social interactions and relationships of young people? These processes are clearly evident in the contributions to this special issue from Megan Chawansky and from Emma Kavanagh, Ian Jones and Lucy Sheppard-Marks, who to differing degrees and intensities unpack the 'accepted' and normalised body politic (via celebrities as emblematic subjectivities of such politics) inherent in contemporary digital cultures. Stephanie Jong and Murray Drummond (this issue) add knowledge here, exploring the biopedagogies of fitness information on social networking sites (and trends such as thinspiration and 'pro-ana') with respect to the entrenchment of neoliberal responsibility, the promotion of idealised images of emaciation and, the governance and control of the body related to weight loss 'health' behaviours of young women.

Leisure, digitality & public pedagogy

As is clear in our discussion above of the political economy of digital leisure and in the reproduction of social inequality, conceptual definitions of 'leisure', of 'public' and of 'bodies' are undergoing radical transformations through the development of digital technologies in and through virtual public spaces. It is becoming of evident importance to consider not only what needs to be investigated in these contexts, but also to consider which theoretical lenses might be able to best capture the complexity of new digital leisure practices. It is likely here that a messy, oft contradictory, assemblage of theoretical sensibilities will be best able to conceptualise, contextualise and explain any given moment of 'leisure' in a digital age (see also Redhead, 2016a). Indeed, the papers in this issue speak to some of these complexities, deploying differing theoretical approaches and perspectives to understand digital leisure cultures to explicate, for example: the conflation of public/private spaces; the recognition of digital leisure practices as resistance/activism; and, the relationship between digital practices and everyday social contexts.

Furthermore, as the digitisation of leisure questions the presumed, taken for granted, boundaries between 'public' and 'private'; it reveals how 'politics and leisure are historically and dialectically tied' (Arora, 2015, p. 56). Thus, whilst blogging, social media and other digital sites and platforms are considered to be active sites of leisure practices, at the same time they are emerging as territories of resistance and protest (see Arora, 2015; also Lamond & Spracklen, 2014). Most obviously, through new digital networks of communication, political mobilisation can occur through virtual protests and cyberactivism focused on global issues such as the environment, economy, conflict and terrorism (one has to think, for example, of how Facebook users have changed their profile pictures to the Tricolore in the context of the Paris terror attacks in November 2015 or of the LGBT rainbow flag relational to the attack on Orlando's Pulse Nightclub in June 2016 or the role digital technologies played in the Arab Spring uprisings).

In this regard, given the potential for subversion and activism, digital leisure spaces might be read as sites of resistance that are now recognised as forms of public pedagogy (see Rich & Miah, 2014). As Burdick, Sandlin and O'Malley (2014: 2) observe, 'public pedagogy has been largely constructed as a concept focusing on various forms, processes, and sites of education and learning occurring beyond or outside of formal schooling'. This lens offers leisure researchers an opportunity to examine public pedagogies as spaces for resistance and identify enactments of public pedagogy that are capable of mobilising resistance and creating productive spaces within which to question and disrupt (Sandlin, Burdick, & Rich, 2016). Yet, despite the growth in scholarship exploring these enactments there has been a limited body of work exploring the public pedagogies of technologically mediated spaces (Freishtat & Sandlin, 2010). The digitising of leisure can be considered part of a complex assemblage of institutions, bodies and discourses through which differing meanings come to be constituted but so too resisted; and a relevant Leisure Studies should be active within these spaces.

We are only beginning to understand how the introduction of digital technologies within, or as, leisure/Leisure Studies can bring about possibilities for social transformation. Rose and Spencer in this special issue offer one such example, considering ways in which Facebook can be politicised and can counter various problematic hegemonic global structures, and can foster a form of resistance and 'publicness' (Biesta, 2012) against global neoliberal capitalism. In so doing, they partially define their roles as 'leisure scholars as reshaping (or partially demolishing and rebuilding and alternative to) individuals' social media leisure experiences'. Chawansky (this issue) suggests that the image-based mobile social networking platform, Instagram, provides opportunities for unique forms of 'digital activism that challenges the intersectional invisibility of black lesbian sporting celebrities' and which opens up all too invisible discussions about domestic abuse within LGN relationships. McGillivary et al. (also in this special issue) point to the ways in which major sporting events can, in part, impact upon the digital literacies of young people within a complex, digitally mediated world and provide spaces for cultivating pedagogies that can disrupt established institutional practices and facilitate opportunities for young people to develop critical digital citizenship.

Building on these contributions in very different spaces and contexts, many online video games, virtual communities and social media present differing opportunities for the perpetuation of extant power relations, yet they also provide opportunities for users to form alliances and networks that can also foster negotiation and resistance. For example, the real-time involvement of audiences at leisure events (e.g. virtual reality streamed court or pitch side seats or augmented tourism realities) or in gaming environments can influence those very events and their discursive framing and may complicate assumed boundaries between public and private leisure spaces in ways that can challenge inequalities. Furthermore, we might examine how gaming and social media environments act as 'sites of resistant public pedagogy' where young people engage in 'critical learning experiences' (Sandlin, Wright, & Clark, 2013). Further, digital technologies present the possibility of 'sousveillance' as well – that is, 'inverse' surveillance whereby those in traditionally powerful roles are watched 'from below' (e.g. citizens recording andlinencounters with police via mobile phones – Mann, Nolan, & Wellman, 2003). If 'surveillance of the surveillers' is now affecting the dynamics of social control in general, it is certainly relevant to leisure contexts in particular, such as sporting mega-events (see for example the work of the collective of academics and activists at gamesmonitor.org.uk).

This relationship between leisure spaces and resistance is not new (e.g. Wearing, 1998); Arora (2015, p. 56) draws similarities between digital networks as sites of political mobilisation and 'publics parks as a spaces, that in a similar fashion, were designed for leisure and consumption but also appropriated as sites of resistance, extending the spatial history of digital politics'. However, given the trends towards prosumption, digital leisure practices raise interesting questions about the negotiation between different sites and values sets, such as the 'negotiation between commercial and community interests' (Barta & Neff, 2016). In (re-)thinking a Leisure Studies that embraces the ethos and practices of public pedagogy, we raise possibilities for 'enacting political and cultural questions' (Sandlin et al., 2016). In the interests of critical public intervention, we need more nuanced understandings of the critical potential of emerging digital leisure assemblages.

If the 'field' of Leisure Studies is to understand these practices and insights, then novel digital tools for research will increasingly feature in future studies, and if we are to retain the 'critical promise of the pedagogical' this may mean moving beyond the 'lenses, tools and languages of institutionally based frameworks and methodologies' (Sandlin et al., 2016). With Thorpe (2016, p. 22), we believe there are 'valuable opportunities' to include social media and digital technologies (e.g. drones, 'go-pro' cameras) as part of our methods. Indeed, across the papers in this special issue, newer (innovative), forms of research methodology combined with critical theorising have been deployed – ranging from netnography, through articulation, critical readings of body texts, the conceptual development of typographies and the synthesis of digital leisure cultures with, for example Hardt & Negri's multitude as a form of hopeful resistance, or critical political economy to explore the technology enhanced reconceptualisation of health as a consumption-based experience. Leisure Studies requires a sophisticated and nuanced methodological and conceptual bricolage – incorporating the types of approaches inherent in these articles as well as a further array of visual, digital and narrative methodologies – in order to keep apace of the intensification of digital leisure cultures and their impact upon everyday lives. Indeed, there will be increasing need to capture and understand online conversations around leisure practices oriented, for example, towards activism (e.g. Knitivism or Slutwalk). Likewise, there might well be a need for us, as Leisure Studies scholars, to cross borders (Giroux, 2001) between the cossetted world of the academic and that of the artist, activist and yet to be imagined (and maybe, strange) alliances. With Giroux (2001), this might be a space for Leisure Studies scholars to break down the artificial barriers, the separate spaces and the different audiences that are supported through the infrastructure of disciplinary and institutional borders that 'atomise, insulate and prevent diverse cultural workers from collaborating across such boundaries' (p. 7). The irony that such meetings, interventions and spaces are increasingly manifest (e.g. blogs) or organised in digital spaces is not lost upon us; indeed, it may be that by inhabiting (or indeed, reclaiming) digital cultures, Leisure Studies might be in a position to make its most productive social change, impact and further develop a praxis-orientation.

Finally, it is necessary also to be vigilant of the populations that are still absent from these digital environments and the inequalities and disparities (Castells, 2007) of leisure opportunities; much as we are aware of our white, middle-class positionalities that shape our discussions within this article. In this sense, it is unlikely that *our* (historical and present) leisure practices and experiences really matter, and that we should (as a field) be far more attentive to the lives, leisure and patterns of inclusion/exclusion of those in far less privileged positions (e.g. of migrants, of those demonised and marginalised by contemporary neoliberal trajectories, of those in states torn apart by internal conflict and simply unable to connect, or indeed of those who choose not to connect/engage in (ephemeral) digital detox. At this juncture, we do not yet know enough about how different social groups access, negotiate and incorporate (digitised) leisure practices into their everyday lives, nor specifically how they might resist the neoliberal systems of dataveillance described above. Some emerging work is beginning to signpost some of the complexities. For example, Barta and Neff (2016, p. 528) identify the quantified self movement (using self-tracking data to improve the self/everyday life) as a site for 'soft resistance' to big data practices 'allowing the community to be aligned with commercial purposes at times and to the individual control and autonomy over data at others'. Elsewhere, Jethani (2015, p.39) argues that there is 'creative and political energy within practices of self-tracking' within the 'latencies' of the technological production of self-knowledge. As such, our work needs to be attuned to exploring how different geographical, familial, socio-economic, spatial and cultural factors shape, limit or provide opportunity for the digital leisure practices.

Coda

And so, by way of brief, temporary closure, we feel it important to reiterate both the concerns and possibilities for the academic study of leisure. As indicated above, our current conjunctural moment is a digital moment. To understand leisure in this moment necessitates understanding digital culture and the ways in which digital forms, structures and platforms have seismically shifted leisure practices, cultures and experiences. Yet, as a 'field'/'discipline'/loose amalgamation of scholars, the academic study (and we would aver, our research led-pedagogies) of a 'lively leisure' is not apace – at least not in traditional scholarly outlets – with an accelerated, consumerised, digitised, datafied, technologised, lively world. For 'leisure' scholarship to speak in an informed manner, to the complexities, nuances and contradictions of everyday leisured lives, and, to be relevant, meaningful and to contribute to policy, academic and public debates, necessitates a turn to the digital (and it might be that we populate digital spaces, such as [existing] academic blogs, to do so). Failure to do so would most likely be a failure of the possibilities of leisure scholarship. It would decry the possibilities for 'leisure scholars' to feature more fully in the debates about digitality currently led by cognate disciplines of sociology, cultural studies, critical health studies (and so on), to make a difference and to inform debate – leisure would (continue to) exist on the academic peripheries engaged in insular conversations with ever dwindling advocates and subscribers.

We do not wish to be overly pessimistic, in fact and whilst it might not seem like it, we are increasingly optimistic that the digital turn can bring leisure back to the centre of academic life (see also Redhead, 2016a) and that the nexus between digital leisure research and (it follows, we hope) research led-teaching can (re-)assert the importance of the field in an increasingly difficult, and often brutal, Higher Education system that sees 'leisure' as a soft-target. A relative and recent explosion of work on digital leisure (cf. Carnicelli et al., 2016; Redhead, 2016a, 2016b; Spracklen, 2015) speaks to the potential of an engaged, critical, interdisciplinary and crucial 'field' of study, a field perhaps poised to pounce and (re-)assert its import. We offer but one tentative contribution to these exciting debates and have pleasure in introducing the papers in this special issue, all of which, to differing degrees, develop the types of argument we have presented herein. Our hope, our intent, is that this will foster further debate and proffer a resurgence of a meaningful, relevant, 'lively', and socially just 'Leisure Studies'.

Acknowledgement

We are exceptionally grateful to Dr Jayne Caudwell and Professor Heather Gibson for their generous feedback on earlier drafts of this paper.

Disclosure statement

No potential conflict of interest was reported by the authors.

References

Arora, P. (2015). Usurping public leisure space for protest: Social activism in the digital and material commons. *Space and Culture., 18*, 55–68.

Barta, K., & Neff, G. (2016). Technologies for sharing: Lessons from quantified self about the political economy of platforms. *Information, Communication & Society, 19*, 518–531. doi:10.1080/1369118X.2015.1118520

Berdychevsky, L., & Nimrod, G. (2016). Sex as leisure in later life: A netnographic approach. *Leisure Sciences*,. doi:10.1080/01490400.2016.1189368

Biesta, G. (2012). Becoming public: Public pedagogy, citizenship and the public sphere. *Social & Cultural Geography, 13*, 683–697.

Bigo, D. (2011). Security, exception, ban and surveillance. In L. David (Ed.), *Theorizing Surveillance The Panopticon and Beyond* (pp. 46–68). Devon: Willan Publishing.

Brabazon, T. (2016). Afterword: (Digital) physcial cultural studies? In M. Silk, D. Andrews, & H. Thorpe (Eds.), *The routledge handbook of physical cultural studies*. London: Routledge.

Braidotti, R. (2013). *The Posthuman*. Chichester: Wiley.

Bull, M. (2006). No dead air? The ipod and the culture of mobile listening. *Leisure Studies, 24*, 343–355.

Burdick, J., Sandlin, J., & O'Malley, M. (2014). *Problematizing Public Pedagogy*. London: Routledge.

Carnicelli, S., McGillivary, D., & McPherson, G. (2016). *Digital leisure cultures: Critical perspectives*. London: Routledge.

Castells, M. (2007). Communication, power and counter-power in the network society. *International Journal of Communication, 1*, 238–266.

Crawford, G. (2005). Digital gaming, sport and gender. *Leisure Studies, 24*, 259–270.

Delamere, F., & Shaw, S. (2008). "They see it as a guy's game": The politics of gender in digital games. *Leisure/Loisir, 32*, 279–302.

Deleuze, G. (1995). Postscript on control societies. In G. Deleuze (Ed.), *Negotiations, 1972–1990* (pp. 177–182). New York, NY: Columbia Press.

Ellerbrok, A. (2011). Playful biometrics: Controversial technology through the lens of play. *The Sociological Quarterly, 52*, 528–547.

Francombe, J. (2010). 'I cheer, you cheer, we cheer': Physical technologies and the normalized body. *Television & New Media, 11*, 350–366.

Francombe, J. (2014). Learning to leisure: Femininity and practices of the body. *Leisure Studies, 33*, 580–597.

Francombe-Webb, J. (2016). Critically encountering exer-games and young femininity. *Television & New Media, 17*, 449–464.

Francombe-Webb, J., & Silk, M. (2016). Young girls' embodied experiences of femininity and social class. *Sociology, 50*, 652–672.

Freishtat, R. L., & Sandlin, J. A. (2010). Conquering the technological frontier: Understanding the educative aspects of Facebook's construction of the digital world. *Educational Studies, 46*, 503–523.

Gilmore, J. N. (2015). Everywear: The quantified self and wearable fitness technologies. *New Media and Society*, 1–16, doi:10.1177/1461444815588768

Giroux, H. (2001).Cultural studies as performative politics. *Cultural Studies ↔ Critical Methodologies*, 1, 5–23.

Grossberg, L. (1989). The circulation of cultural studies. *Critical Studies in Mass Communication, 6*, 413–421.
Grossberg, L. (1996). Identity and cultural studies: Is that all there is? In S. Hall & P. Du Gay (Eds.), *Questions of Cultural Identity* (pp. 87–107). London: Sage.
Haggerty, K., & Ericson, R. (2000). The surveillant assemblage. *British Journal of Sociology, 51*, 605–622.
Haraway, D. (1991). *Simians, cyborgs and women: The reinvention of nature*. New York, NY: Routledge.
Jethani, S. (2015). Mediating the body: technology, politics and epistemologies of self. *Communication, Politics & Culture, 47*, 34–43.
Lamond, I., & Spracklen, K. (2014). *Protests as events: Politics, activism and leisure*. Lanham, MD: Rowman & Littlefield.
Lepp, A., Barkley, J., & Karpinski, A. (2014). The relationship between cell phone use, academic performance, anxiety, and Satisfaction with Life in college students. *Computers in Human Behavior, 31*, 343–350.
Lincoln, S. (2012). *Youth Culture and Private Space*. London: Palgrave MacMillan.
Lupton, D. (2015). *Digital Sociology*. London: Routledge.
Mann, S., Nolan, J., & Wellman, B. (2003). Sousveillance: Inventing and using wearable computing devices for data collection in surveillance environments. *Surveillance & Society, 1*, 331–355.
McGillivray, D. (2014). Digital cultures, acceleration and mega sporting event narratives. *Leisure Studies, 33*, 96–109.
Miller, T. (2001). What it is and what it isn't: Introducing … Cultural Studies. In T. Miller (Ed.), *A companion to cultural studies* (pp. 1–20). Malden, MA: Blackwell.
Nimrod, G. (2014). The benefits of and constraints to participation in seniors' online communities. *Leisure Studies, 33*, 247–266.
Nimrod, G. (2015). The hierarchy of mobile phone incorporation among older users. *Mobile Media & Communication, 4*, 149–168.
Orton-Johnson, K. (2014). Knit, purl and upload: New technologies, digital mediations and the experiences of Leisure. *Leisure Studies, 33*, 305–321.
Redhead, S. (2015). *Football and accelerated culture*. London: Routledge.
Redhead, S. (2016a). Digital leisure studies. Podcast Retrieved from https://secure-hwcdn.libsyn.com/p/7/8/9/7899d6e79ccc2f16/Digital_leisure_studies.mp3?c_id=10663761Z&expiration=1466542985&hwt=69ad53e1539297b46f5282c62ed783db
Redhead, S. (2016b). Gigs will tear you apart: Accelerated culture and digital leisure studies. In S. Carnicelli, D. McGillivary, & G. McPherson (Eds.), *Digital leisure cultures: Critical perspectives* (pp. 13–25). London: Routledge.
Rich, E., & Miah, A. (2014). Understanding digital health as public pedagogy: A critical framework. *Societies, 4*, 296–315. doi:10.3390/soc4020296
Ringrose, J., & Harvey, L. (2016). Digital mediation, connectivity and affective materialities. In Silk, M., Andrews, D., & Thorpe, H. (Eds). *The Routledge Handbook of Physical Cultural Studies*.
Ritzer, G. (2015). Prosumer capitalism. *The Sociological Quarterly, 56*, 413–445.
Sandlin, J., Wright, R., & Calrk, C. (2013). Reexamining theories of adult learning and adult development through the lenses of public pedagogy. *Adult Education Quarterly, 63*, 3–23.
Sandlin, J., Burdick, J., & Rich, E., (2016). Problematizing public engagement within public pedagogy research and practice, *Discourse: Studies in the Cultural Politics of Education*, doi:10.1080/01596306.2016.1196343
Silk, M., & Andrews, D. (2011). Toward a Physical Cultural Studies. *Sociology of Sport Journal, 28*, 4–35.
Silk, M., & Chumley, E. (2004). Memphis united: Diasporic identities, s(t)imulated spaces and consumption economies. In D. Andrews (Ed.), *Manchester united: Sporting diaspora and simulated consumption* (pp. 249–264). London: Routledge.
Spracklen, K. (2015). *Digital leisure, the internet and popular culture*. London: Palgrave MacMillan.
Stebbins, R. A. (2007). *Serious leisure: A perspective for our time*. New Brunswick, NJ: Transaction.
Thorpe, H. (2016). Action sport, social media and new technologies: Towards a research agenda. *Communication and Sport*. doi:10.1177/2167479516638125
Van Doorn, N. (2010). The ties that bind: the networked performance of gender, sexuality and friendship on MySpace. *New Media and Society, 12*, 583–602.
Wakefield, A. (2004). The public surveillance functions of private security. *Surveillance & Society, 2*, 529–545.
Wearing, B. (1998). *Leisure and Feminist Theory*. London: Sage.

Young people, digital media making and critical digital citizenship

D. McGillivray, G. McPherson, J. Jones and A. McCandlish

A range of recent academic, policy and practice-focused work in the UK and internationally has identified a need for more focused attention on the role of digital literacies in enabling young people to more effectively navigate their way through an increasingly complex, digitally mediated world. In this article, we explore the main debates taking place around the prevalence of digital media in the early twenty-first century, with emphasis on the role of pervasive digital media in educational settings. Focusing on the practice-based project, Digital Commonwealth, a series of critical insights are drawn, highlighting the difficulties facing educational authorities and young people in dealing with the opportunities and threats brought about by digital media. We conclude that a critical digital citizenship agenda needs to be embedded in educational narratives, where young people are, through practice, asked to ponder how digitally mediated publics operate in the school setting and beyond. Integrating 'making' and 'thinking critically' about the benefits and dangers of pervasive digital media in and outside of school is imperative. Our study suggests that there remain significant inequities in terms of provision across schools, access to suitable infrastructure and equipment, and the presence of qualified and confident staff with the requisite digital leadership attributes to enable digital media projects to be integrated into everyday learning practices. Major events, like the Commonwealth Games, can precipitate and accelerate uptake of new approaches and innovative thinking but they do not represent a panacea for the systemic development of critical digital citizenship over time.

Introduction

> I do really believe that they should be in control of what they're putting out and it shouldn't all be filtered through me or through the school, I feel really strongly about that … I think it's really important that they're creators and not just consumers. (Head Teacher, Island School)

A range of recent academic, policy and practice-focused work in the UK and internationally has identified a need for more focused attention on the role of digital literacies in enabling young people to more effectively navigate their way through an increasingly complex, digitally mediated world (Gauntlett, 2011; Johnson et al., 2014). At a time when spreadable media (Jenkins, Ford, & Green, 2013) makes predefined boundaries between the inside and outside of school, between public and private, and leisure and work increasingly difficult to sustain, it is important to explore how young people experience and make sense of these environments. In possession of powerful mobile technologies and with easy access to a plethora of platforms (Gillespie, 2010; van Dijck, 2013) with both educational and entertainment functions, young people can now learn and play interchangeably in a fashion impossible only a few years previously. The emergence of the social Web (including Web 2.0 services) has further eroded distinctions between media production and consumption creating space for the emergence of the prosumer (Ritzer & Jurgenson, 2010) who both creates and consumes online content. Moreover, the ready availability of smartphone mobile devices in the pockets of young people further challenges notions of the school as a space solely for formal learning. If pupils can surf the Web, share photographs with friends and engage in instantaneous messaging in the playground then the school effectively becomes a digital 'leisure' space. This is reinforced as schools seek to more effectively integrate 'the kind of learning that takes place at home' into the classroom (Johnson et al., 2014, p. 5), 'extending learning beyond the school day and in the home' (p. 11). Yet, in many respects, the school environment has also been a space of resistance to the onward march of digital leisure – erecting boundaries to prevent pupils using social platforms and tools to experience learning, justified on the grounds of risk avoidance.

This article, first, explores the main debates taking place around the prevalence of digital media in the early twenty-first century, discussing the currency of concepts including Do It Yourself (DIY) cultures, digital making and creative citizenship as they relate to the lives of young people. Second, specific attention is given to the role of pervasive digital media in educational settings, reflecting upon international, national and local (Scotland) perspectives and their implications for policy, leadership and practice inside and outside of schools. Focusing on the practice-based project, Digital Commonwealth, a series of critical insights are then drawn highlighting the difficulties facing educational authorities and young people in dealing with the opportunities and threats brought about by digital media. Finally, the implications for the study of leisure and digital cultures, especially for young people, are discussed.

Digital making, creativity and questions of citizenship

A glut of academic writing on the practices associated with the creation, circulation and distribution of digital media has emerged over the course of the last decade. Henry Jenkins has been to the fore with his work on *spreadable media* (Jenkins et al., 2013) proposing that new media literacy should be considered as an increasingly important social skill, especially for young people. Other commentators concur, arguing that the process of digital media making can be viewed as a productive, creative and even political act, 'which sees the public not as simply consumers of pre-constructed messages but as people who are shaping, sharing, reframing, and remixing media content in ways which might not have been previously imagined' (Jenkins et al., 2013, p. 2). In a similar vein, Gauntlett (2011) proposes that *making is connecting*, suggesting that the internet has made it easier for everyday publics to make media, share it and, in the process, connect with others in a meaningful and fruitful manner. Other terminologies have been coined to help make sense of the explosion in everyday creativity now possible with the Web. Ratto and Boler (2014) talk of DIY citizenship when referring to the do-it-yourself or do-it-together ethos made possible through digital making (and activism). Within their definition of DIY citizenship, they argue for a continuum, with 'one end representing the overtly political/interventionist and the other end representing those simply channelling creativity and a kind of poiesis into everyday practices' (p. 19). This focus on everyday creative practices is reflected in others using the moniker 'creative citizenship' to reflect on the use of cultural and creative activities where there is a social, political or civic element to the activities involved, however small (Lockton, Greene, Casey, Raby, & Vickress, 2014). Each of these perspectives broadly aligns with a cyber libertarian (Kelemen & Smith, 2001) perspective whereby the Web is viewed as a democratic space where user generated content is sovereign and popular creativity can flourish. Ritzer and Jurgenson (2010) use the term *prosumption* to denote a shift towards consumers being involved in the productive co-creation of content, 'driven by a desire for recognition, freedom and agency' (Zwick, Bonsu, & Darmody, 2008, p. 185).

However, accompanying discussions of the prosumer with their freedom to participate and create is the Foucauldian-inspired critique of the shift in citizenship towards individualised and responsibilised behaviour in the age of neoliberalism (Rose, 2000). In relation to narratives of digital creative citizenship and prosumption, it is relevant to draw on Paton, Mooney, and McKee's (2012) argument that we now live in a 'new era of 'consumer-citizenship' wherein individualised consumption, choice and responsibility are regarded as paramount … creating the more active consumer citizen in a moral and economic sense' (p. 1470). In this reading, citizenship is then only possible on the basis of a particular kind of conduct, with empowered citizens taking responsibility for their own life outcomes, self-governing behaviour which requires them to invest time and energy in enterprising their own lives. This critique is relevant to the apparently free and democratic space of Web 2.0, where users are encouraged to generate content and given the 'opportunity' to have it hosted on an open, neutral and egalitarian 'platform' (Gillespie, 2010) which gives the user the power to speak on an equal footing. Using the example of YouTube, Gillespie argues that it has successfully created a discourse around its 'egalitarian facilitation of expression, not an elitist gatekeeper with normative and technical restrictions' (p. 352). Yet, in an age of 'platform politics' (Gillespie, 2010; Hands, 2013), the rhetoric of the democratic, open and egalitarian Web has been subject to significant critique (Fuchs, 2014). As Ritzer and Jurgenson (2010) suggest, many people are unaware of the presence of corporate entities as owners of their favourite social platforms, accepting their terms and conditions unquestioningly and ignoring the concession of their personal data for free. Moreover, the platforms that many young people take for granted and use actively in their leisure lives are also infused with commercial imperatives and are therefore anything but neutral particularly as global conglomerates make choices 'about what can appear, how it is organised, how it is monetized, what can be removed and why, and what the technical architecture allows and prohibits' (Gillespie, 2010, p. 359). Whilst there are legitimate concerns expressed around the repositioning of citizenship in an age of neoliberalism, it is also important to reflect on the nuances of digital media use by young people. So, to what extent are young people's digital lives then framed by a wider responsibilisation agenda requiring upskilling in order to make the most of corporately owned 'social' platforms that demand their creative input, whilst at the same time compromising their freedom and privacy? This question requires a closer look at the social Web, its position in contemporary society and its use by young people.

Creating, sharing and networking through social media

Social media platforms have afforded digital making (e.g. video, audio and animation) a more prominent place in academic debates around citizenship and everyday creativity. As a form of leisure (and educational) culture, social media usage has seen an exponential increase over the last decade, in the form of social networks sites, video sharing tools, blogging and microblogging platforms 'that allow participants to create and share their own content' (Boyd, 2014, p. 6). Boyd (2014) views social media more akin to a 'cultural mindset' (p. 6) whereby younger people alter their behaviours, going online to interact with others in their community, blurring the lines between their online and offline social worlds. Her description of the cultural mindset aligns with Gauntlett's (2011) notion that making and connecting go hand in hand in the digital sphere and social media now provides (digital) makers with a platform to share, to be heard and to interact with others who follow similar interests but who may not share geographical proximity. In educational settings, teachers and other educators are also beginning to use social media to help enhance 'professional communities of practice, as learning communities' whilst, at the same time, taking learning outside the classroom through using it as 'a platform to share interesting stories about topics students are studying in class' (Johnson et al., 2014, p. 10). In this respect, social media usage has become normalised, to the extent that young people's online participation is 'not eccentric: it is entirely normal … social media plays a crucial role in the lives of networked teens' (Boyd, 2014, pp. 4–5). This normalisation is not just about technology, either. Instead, social media represent a set of 'spaces' where people congregate, complementing or supplementing face-to-face encounters, both enhancing and disrupting conventional educational narratives.

Though there are many benefits available to young people from social media, these are by no means uncontested. A residue is left online when people share, collaborate, like and retweet, and this can produce tensions when recognising that 'the 'collective allotment' of Web 2.0 space … is not collectively *owned*' (Gauntlett, 2011, p. 212). Risk narratives abound over the threats posed by an uncritical acceptance of the benefits of digital devices and social media (Fuchs, 2014; Halpin, 2013; Hands, 2013; Miller, 2009). These risk narratives include a concern for the emotional wellbeing of users. Some commentators decry the pressure to be connected continuously (Crary, 2013; van Dijck, 2013), to take advantage of the plethora of ways to 'participate' digitally and not miss out on – or catch up – on the experiences available all day, every day. Turkle (2011) has been an outspoken critic of the *cult of connectivity*, where people create, analyse and perform their emotional lives through the medium of technology. This fear is reinforced by those promulgating the argument that privately-owned corporations (e.g. Google, Facebook and Twitter) now routinely take ownership of users' content and for free (Andrejevic, 2014; Fuchs, 2014; Gillespie, 2010; Halpin, 2013; Miller, 2009).

However, rather than labelling all users of the social Web as akin to cultural dupes, drawing on Gauntlett (2011) and Boyd (2014), we propose that users of social media platforms are more nuanced in their understanding of the realities of living in a period of platform politics (Hands, 2013) where the opportunity for unbounded creative self-expression online is always likely to be limited and relative. As Ritzer and Jurgenson (2010) have argued, exploitation is much more ambiguous on the social Web, making it difficult for capitalism to appropriate and monetise the efforts of prosumers. Kim (2014) concurs, arguing that users can bend social media platforms for their own purposes, continuing to use them as spaces for creation, discussion and debate 'whilst also thinking about how mediated publics function and what sort of affordances and limits this particular medium allows and also breaks down'. While young people, parents and teachers need to be aware of the limitations of social media and potential exploitations present in their design and ownership structures, there is also value in being exposed to the collaborative engagements, learning and access to global conversations possible within these dynamic environments (Kim & Kim, 2014). The concept of responsible citizenship is valuable when used to ensure young people are exposed to critically informed perspectives on digital platforms, their ownership and matters of privacy, security and persistent digital footprints. This requires a discussion of critical digital citizenship and what this might mean in and outside of educational contexts.

Towards a critical digital citizenship

Whilst there are legitimate concerns to voice about the 'darker' side of digital and social media (Gillespie, 2010; Halpin, 2013; Van Djick, 2013), it is even more important that young people are supported to develop a critical and informed attitude towards their digital capacities inside and outside the educational sphere (Livingstone, 2010). Rather than viewing the digital turn as a retrograde educational step, Gauntlett (2011) suggests that the world of Web 2.0 can actually play an important role in introducing a 'making and doing' (p. 8) rather than 'sit back and be told' culture within schools – contributing to the development of critically reflective thinkers. In the former, teachers set their learners challenges that invariably include collaborative working, finding creative solutions and using media artefacts as a vehicle for critically reflective learning. In the latter, learning is directed solely by teachers who input it into students' minds in a passive and instructional format. Gauntlett (2011) asserts that everyday creativity represents a crucial proactive choice to make rather than passively consume and that, in an educational context, is important because it 'helps to build resilience … and the creative capacity to deal with significant challenges' (p. 20). These challenges could include how to deal with possible exploitation, control and concession of personal data to organisations that promote themselves as acting in their interests.

There is a growing recognition, internationally that what we term critical digital citizenship needs to be more effectively embedded in the school curriculum to provide young people with the opportunity to design, create, make, remix and share their creative content using a range of digital tools and technologies (Johnson et al., 2014). Until recently, media literacy education has tended to focus on accessing, analysing and evaluating media artefacts as a consumer (Livingstone, 2004). However, understanding issues associated with the ownership of data, privacy, platform convergence and the space for creative reinvention are now necessary to underpin digital media usage in a networked society whilst facilitating movement across different media platforms and social networks, safely and with confidence.

Debates about the importance of (digital) media literacy are also gaining traction at European and national levels. In Europe, recent work by the European Association for Viewers Interests concluded that 'citizens must be equipped with the skills to utilise and benefit from media', requiring the acquisition of new competencies, including the development of critical thinking and citizen participation in public life through the media. In the UK, FutureLab (Grant, 2010) has undertaken extensive UK research in educational settings, and proposes that digital literacy needs to be viewed as an 'entitlement' for all young people in an increasingly digitally mediated culture, helping them to expand and extend their use of technology for creativity and self-expression. Crucially, they argue that schools need to develop the 'savvy-ness' to allow young people to participate meaningfully and safely as digital technology becomes more pervasive (Grant, 2010). They view the formal educational sphere as having a crucial role in preparing young people for the social and cultural practices of digital literacy as they participate in multiple interactions with digital technology and media.

Despite their being a demonstrable need for digital literacy within school settings, putting theory into practice is identified as a weakness within school settings, at primary and secondary levels (Grant, 2010). Teachers are often fearful of their own capability to teach digital literacy and require the mystique of technology use to be removed (Grant, 2010). Similarly, Ertmer, Ottenbreit-Leftwich, Sadik, Sendurur, and Sendurur (2012) identified first-order (resources of hardware and software, training and support) and second-order (teacher confidence levels or beliefs) barriers to the effective integration of technology into the curriculum. Others (Brill & Galloway, 2007; Collins & Halverson, 2010) have also identified significant obstacles to the effective integration of the digital into the activities of schools, producing a picture internationally, nationally and locally of uneven practice in embedding a critical attitude to digital literacy at the local level. The remainder of this article focuses on practice at a local level to further understand the nuances of how the digital both enables and constrains in the school setting.

Methodology

In exploring the role of digital media in young people's lives, this article draws on a case study from the participatory arts and media project, Digital Commonwealth, with a particular focus on its schools programme. Whilst most academic attention has been paid to the economic legacies of large-scale sporting events, there is also a growing group of interdisciplinary scholars interested in how these events can be leveraged for wider social good and make a positive contribution to social change (Chalip, 2006; Smith, 2014). The authors have made a contribution to this realm around the efficacy of large-scale sporting events in creating space for the everyday use of digital technologies in citizen media activity (McGillivray, 2013). The way large-scale sporting events are conceived, planned and reported is changing thanks to the mass availability of everyday digital technologies, which some commentators have argued democratises media making (Miah & Garcia, 2012). Integrated blogs, audio, video and social media can be used effectively to mobilise, organise and circulate information that would not appear in traditional media coverage of these global extravaganzas. Crucially, new digital infrastructures offer a broader range of people new ways of communicating, working together and make it easier for them to get involved (Bakardjieva, Svensson, & Skoric, 2012). The Digital Commonwealth project sought to provide a creative response to the 2014 Commonwealth Games, working with a diverse range of community groups and organisations from across Scotland. In total, the project worked with nearly 1000 participants, producing over 300 unique digital media artefacts, including video, audio, blogs and social media outputs. The project Digital Commonwealth focused on providing a platform for those voices marginalised in established media narratives to be heard, using participatory methods and exploiting networks (including in schools) to support the more widespread use of accessible tools, techniques and environments to tell stories, digitally.

Methodologically, Digital Commonwealth adhered to the principles and practices of action research in its participatory and democratic ethos, focusing on 'action and reflection, theory and practice, in participation with others, in pursuit of practical solutions' (Reason & Bradbury, 2001, p. 1). Creative practitioners were central to the delivery of the project and the authors were also actively involved in facilitating discussions as both participants and observers, supporting schools to define and amend their own project ideas and curating the final creative outputs on a project website. Practically, the Digital Commonwealth schools programme engaged with learners in primary and secondary school contexts across 23 of Scotland's local authority areas, delivering a structured (yet flexible) set of integrated digital media workshops to twenty learners in each cluster from January to October 2014. Workshops were supplemented by the production of an open access digital storytelling handbook available to schools beyond the completion of the project. The schools programme involved 585 learners, 57 teachers and 57 schools in total. Using creative research methods (Gauntlett, 2011), creative practitioners and the authors were actively involved in supporting young people to make digital artefacts and to explore the most appropriate place for these to be hosted online to ensure ownership resided with the pupils and their schools wherever possible. Beyond the creative content produced by learners, extended interviews with teachers and other ancillary staff also form part of the findings presented in the remainder of the article along with data generated from a formal evaluation of the schools programme conducted in the latter part of 2014. When referring to interview respondents, only role, school status (primary or secondary) and location are mentioned to ensure confidentiality.

Discussion

'Doing' critical digital citizenship

In its ethos and approach to delivery the Digital Commonwealth project sought to encourage and facilitate an everyday, practical form of critical digital citizenship. The ethos of the project adhered to Gauntlett's (2011) *making is connecting* ambition whereby participants learn 'by making the thing that they want to make, getting help where necessary' (p. 235). Each learning cluster proposed a thematic focus around broad Commonwealth themes that suited their own interests (e.g. place, people, culture or exchange). Clusters were afforded significant flexibility in terms of what digital artefacts they chose to make and why. Those writing about creative (Lockton et al., 2014) or DIY citizenship (Ratto & Boler, 2014) and everyday creativity (Gauntlett, 2011) emphasise the importance of allowing participants to be self-directed, and exploiting hybridised forms of learning where online and offline, at school and at home can be integrated. In-school workshops were designed with a focus on encouraging pupils (and teachers) to make use of an integrated set of digital storytelling skills – blogging, audio, video and social media – coproduced with creative practitioners who ensured the sessions were neither 'laborious or patronising' (Gauntlett, 2011, p. 235). Pupils brought in photographs, suggested people they knew for interview and used their own devices in class – highlighting the value of their non-school leisure experiences in informing wider educational experiences and outcomes.

The collaborative mode of learning adopted for the project utilised the digital realm as a disruptive device enabling cross-disciplinary and cross-institutional work – a core ambition of the new Curriculum for Excellence recently introduced to the Scottish educational system. The collaborative nature of digital media making (e.g. interviewing, editing and commenting) enabled pupils and teachers to work across the age range (e.g. primary and secondary), subjects and schools. Aligning with our desire to embed a critically informed attitude to digital media literacy, in-school workshops also emphasised the importance of content ownership and the appropriateness of the platform chosen to host the work they produced. Working with creative practitioners, learning clusters decided whether they were comfortable with their content going public on the project website and the use of social platforms to share their work with wider audiences. In different parts of the country, school clusters viewed, commented upon and shared the work of others. As one Principal Teacher commented, 'the collegiate working and working alongside other children throughout the whole of Scotland, certainly made it more exciting for the children' (Principal Teacher, Rural School).

The digital medium also helped eliminate some of the persistent boundaries between study and leisure practices, helping to produce creative responses that drew upon pupils' curricular and extracurricular activities. By means of illustration, one project in the Western Isles saw the participating school cluster interact with external community organisations and utilised pupils' interest in Minecraft to link class work onsite with online research and engagement. In another urban location, pupils produced a cookery show, made and designed a board game and then videoed the instructions to share widely. This school aggregated all their outputs on one blog platform, and used it to progress peer learning and collaboration. In a central Scotland local authority, pupils wrote and recorded rap lyrics and poetry about Commonwealth nations and made use of their schools' social media profile to share their outputs widely. In remote Highland communities, two small schools used the digital interface to reduce geographical distance and involved other Commonwealth island communities to compare experiences across nations and territories.

Each of these examples is illustrative of the expression of everyday practical creativity, enhanced, but not dependent on the digital medium. Crucially, the videos, audio clips, Minecraft worlds and tweets created by participants bore the marks of those that produced them (Gauntlett, 2011). Though acknowledging Gillespie's (2010) view that corporate platforms like YouTube and Flickr shape the contours of public discourse online, our work illustrated that this need not necessarily negate the value of small-scale creative endeavours that reflect the meaning of their makers. Moreover, although corporate social platforms also provide a space for professional media makers to promote their work, experience from the Digital Commonwealth school programme suggests that developments associated with Web 2.0 and spreadable media mean that small contributions can be networked up and reach out to a wider interest community, whether in schools or beyond. In one small rural school, a single tweet related to the Digital Commonwealth project generated 1441 retweets and demonstrated the power of networked publics (Boyd, 2014). Social platforms enable creators to share artefacts that they have made themselves with an immediacy (of circulation and response).

As young people's use of digital media is increasingly normalised (Boyd, 2014), their practices can also challenge established modes of professional practice. Specifically, pupil's comfort with the use of instant sharing of content via social platforms like Snapchat, Vine and Instagram, drawn from their leisure lives, impacted on their experience of learning in the educational setting. For example, when encountering a creative practitioner who delivered learning in a manner suited to high-end, professional practice, one Head Teacher commented that 'there is a need to challenge the 'expert' and that sometimes, tools and equipment can limit rather than enhance what you do' (Head Teacher, Island School). This school had embraced the use of creative technologies in learning, including encouraging pupils to bring their own devices and to challenge what they saw as outdated models of professional practice in teaching media production. They reflect what Boyd (2014) described as a cultural mindset around the use of digital and social media and, rather than lock down school infrastructure, they sought to exploit its potential to ensure their pupils were connected to others.

'The teacher says no': digital leadership

Experiences generated through the delivery of the Digital Commonwealth project across 23 local authorities in Scotland highlighted differential access to digital tools and technologies within school settings. Genuine disparities exist in access to audio and video equipment, tablets and smartphone devices and especially in relation to desktop computers for editing, surfing the internet or uploading media content. This finding aligns with Johnson et al.'s (2014) research which found that in the EU, 63% of the population's nine-year olds and 50% of 16-year olds attend schools that are missing important digital equipment and twenty percent of secondary school students have never – or almost never – used a computer in class. Availability of adequate digital equipment and being able to access the internet (legitimately) at school was recognised as a problem by almost all participants in the Digital Commonwealth project. However, more problematic still were issues relating to the leadership and practice of teachers to support the development of critical digital citizenship.

Digital leadership emerged as a significant challenge for the schools participating in Digital Commonwealth, with a broad spectrum of approaches and practices evident. There were examples of well-informed, inventive and progressive digital leadership in some settings, providing a supportive environment for digital media to be used in cross-curricular activities. In one participating small island school, a culture of openness, trust and empowerment of young people were evident. Examples include pupils being allowed to use their own mobile technology in and outside of taught classes and being able to access the school's wifi connection outside class for sharing videos and for publishing their schoolwork. The opening quotation in this article showed a Head Teacher actively promoting the importance of pupils owning the content they created and publishing it because she felt creation was more important than consumption – reinforcing the importance of the prosumer narrative (Ritzer & Jurgenson, 2010).

The same respondent felt that it was vital head teachers were able to exercise their own judgement in terms of what digital innovations could be justified according to sound pedagogical principles i.e. collaborative problem solving, self-directed learning, global awareness and critical thinking. In one peri-urban school, digital leadership was evident in the embedding of social media as a learning tool, meaning that several teachers were already using Twitter to talk about what was happening within the school. However, as Johnson et al. (2014) conclude, 'many teachers lack the skills or formal education they need to empower learners to pursue their own interests and free class time for more experiential forms of learning' (p. 24). The absence of skills, low levels of awareness and lack of confidence to contest institutional gatekeepers was particularly marked in a number of school contexts. This is perhaps unsurprising given Ertmer et al.'s (2012) findings on first and second order barriers to the integration of technology into the curriculum.

Whereas young people are increasingly comfortable with social platforms for creating, sharing and interacting, the educational setting they inhabit can be monolithic, working with standardised, industrial-like learning platforms that can disempower, deter and delimit creative expression. The Digital Commonwealth project came up against numerous examples of system requirements that were disabling. For example, the national virtual learning environment (VLE) for Scottish schools, Glow, required specialist knowledge from teachers and support services that dis-incentivised its use. Teachers had often not received adequate training and/or permissions to be able to use it as a classroom blog or communication device for the learners to work with. As a result, reliance on the VLE discouraged the production and sharing of publicly available and shareable media, instead favouring the 'private' gatekeeping function. The Digital Commonwealth project sought to challenge these system restrictions by providing support for schools to utilise other social learning environments, including Wordpress the blogging platform. However, even here, local authorities often restricted access to particular functions within this platform, allowing basic access but not enabling permissions so that staff could upload and share the audio, video or photographic content generated by pupils. Whilst we acknowledge and recognise the legal and ethical responsibilities of schools toward those under their charge, include exposing them to social platforms where privacy and security cannot be guaranteed, a failure to debate and discuss these issues within the school setting does little to advance the development of critical digital literacies. It is, in our view, more important to use, say, paper tweets to highlight the practice of micro-blogging in a safe space, than to ignore the presence of Twitter, Instagram and Snapchat in the lives of young people both inside and outside the school gates.

The obstacles described confirm Gauntlett's (2011) assertion that there continue to be significant issues about users having 'the skills, confidence, and awareness necessary to use available resources and tools in a fruitful manner' (p. 154). The Digital Commonwealth project highlighted a significant demand for more continuous professional development for teachers and other school employees to facilitate more effective use of digital media in learning. For example, one teacher commented that 'it was great having someone coming in who had greater expertise than we had – that was really helpful' (Teacher, Rural School). However, if the use of digital media is to be further embedded in learning to satisfy the growing expectations of pupils and parents then, 'digital learning should permeate teacher education at all levels' (Johnson et al., 2014, p. 24). At Scottish, UK, European or international level, this remains an ambition rather than a reality.

'The computer says no': disrupting institutionalisation

Atton (2014) argues that media production needs to be deprofessionalized, decapitalized and deinstitutionalized if the promise of 'democratic communication to people who are normally excluded from media production' (p. 343) is to come to fruition. Being able to create and communicate media in settings other than media institutions is also important so that 'such media will then have the potential to more closely reflect the everyday practices of decentralised, directly democratic, self-managed and reflexive networks' (p. 343). The Digital Commonwealth project sought to facilitate a disruption in the way that educational institutions thought about the possible uses of digital media in learning and how critical digital citizenship could be encouraged. The ambition was not to profess grand statements about social change or media activism but rather less ambitiously to enable pupils (and teachers) to participate in everyday cultural production (Atton, 2014) within the school setting, drawing on their leisure interests and practices. However, the realisation of this ambition was impeded by a number of factors relating to digital risk narratives, especially around publishing and the restricted mode of 'publicness' possible in educational settings. Whilst the VLE used in Scottish schools enabled the production, uploading and publication of learning content to internal school audiences, this platform also curtailed the range of possible publics that could encounter the creative outputs generated by pupils involved in Digital Commonwealth.

As a consequence of encountering closed systems, the project team created a solution for learners to host their content in an open and public way, not just behind the digital gates of their own school. For the Digital Commonwealth project, it was important that we were able to create a realistic environment in order to teach digital media literacy skills whilst adhering to the existing policies and procedures laid down by education authorities. Our project sought to advance the pace of change within schools, enabling primary school pupils to write blog posts, observe their upload to Wordpress and experience their own content being published in real time. They were also able to embed their short audio interviews with each other on Audioboom, and to watch back the videos they had made either at school or at home, building on the concept of re-mediation – where ownership and consent is made meaningful through involving creators and participants in reviewing final outputs. Using an integrated platform, parents, friends and other participating schools across the country were able to comment, share and learn from the experiences and stories of the pupils. Having an output for the work strengthened the resolve of the young people involved to engage with the learning. Moreover, this approach helped operationalise the original principles of the project to encourage those taking part to feel confident enough to make informed decisions to develop and share public content within a safe online environment. We recognised that young people need to know about 'who produces digital media, and how audiences ... receive and interpret it, or use it to create their own products and meanings' (Grant, 2010, p. 11). Exposure to audiences, beyond an internal one in schools was also important, as if 'they hadn't been publishing it – it just stayed within the school. So I think it's raised awareness of the possibility of finding a wider audience for the pupils and I think that's made a difference' (Head Teacher, Island School).

Whilst it remains imperative that risks are managed sensitively when working with young people in the school setting, there are important pedagogical issues to consider when systems create inertia and become the justification for avoiding creative and playful learning cultures. This problem is accentuated when institutional gatekeepers, rather than educators, define what is legitimate and what is not:

> I think people in the school might be quite happy to do it (use social media) but I think the barriers might be more with the sort of technical, the ICT support guys. Their job is to make sure that everything is locked down and secure. (Teacher, Urban School)

Whereas the project ethos encouraged learners to view themselves as potential publishers and creators of shareable content, system restrictions often placed them in the role of viewers, readers or consumers. One teacher reflected on the system restrictions in terms of social media:

> (the) Council network isn't really geared up for that spontaneity that you could get with social media, for example. I can't put something up on Twitter – the kids certainly can't do it, they don't have access to the school site – I'd have to take a picture of it and put the text together and then send it to my senior management team and then put it up – so it takes a bit of the momentum out of it. (Teacher, Urban School)

There was also absence of robust, yet nuanced, social media policies in participating schools to mitigate for genuine risk whilst at the same time encouraging creativity, understanding of networks and interaction with a wider public. Schools need to engage with these issues because outside of school, young people are well versed interacting with a Web 2.0 environment (Boyd, 2014; Johnson et al., 2014). If schools are to enhance young people's digital competencies to prepare them to be 'confident, critical, and creative' (Johnson et al., 2014, p. 26) users of digital technologies then they must embrace the fact that 'it's very much part of their life too – it's what they're used to (Head Teacher, Island School).

Across the Digital Commonwealth schools programme, there were examples of disruptions taking place in pedagogical terms, using digital media either as the vehicle or the outlet. Whether these are sustained and the obstacles identified are overcome is by no means certain, however there is already a number of examples that indicate incremental changes are taking place. In the formal evaluation of the project, most teachers reported enhanced digital skills from involvement in the project, providing concrete example of ongoing, sustainable initiatives beyond the temporary stimulus of the Commonwealth Games. One participating primary school has already used the audio skills they learnt to create radio broadcasts as part of a mock election campaign organised to learn about the European Parliament. Another participating primary school has continued to use video and audio as part of their school blog with classes using the technology as an integral part of their learning. There is also evidence that a more supportive environment is emerging that could enable creative, cross-curricular activities to take place on a more frequent basis. One teacher commented that 'although CfE has this big focus on cross-curricular, interdisciplinary work that made it more possible … I don't think a couple of years ago we would have been allowed to do something like this' (Teacher, Urban School). There is little doubt that the context of the Commonwealth Games and its high-profile media presence helped to generate interest in a project like Digital Commonwealth, including making available the resources to have it funded in the first place. However, there remains a need for a more systemic approach to embedding digital media into the curriculum. The power of the event pulse could quickly evaporate unless the capacity and confidence of teachers is enhanced and institutional inertia is continually disrupted.

Conclusion

This article began with a powerful quotation from an educator demanding that young people be given the opportunity to create and not simply consume media content. The Digital Commonwealth project sought to disrupt established institutional practices, enabling school children to 'make', digitally, their own creative mark using the context of a major sporting and cultural event as a catalyst. Working directly with young people, their teachers and associated educational actors, the project secured privileged access to gauge the state of digital media practice in Scottish schools. It is on the basis of the insights through this experience that we conclude with discussion of three main matters relating to critical digital citizenship and leisure for young people.

First, whilst there are legitimate concerns pertaining to the responsibilisation of individuals (including young people) accompanying the age of neoliberalism, with empowered citizens required to invest time and energy in enterprising their own lives, our study has advanced an alternative reading of this phenomenon. We have argued for the embedding of a critical digital citizenship agenda, where young people are, through practice, asked to ponder how digitally mediated publics operate and think carefully about matters of ownership, privacy, security and risk in the school setting and beyond. Integrating 'making' and 'thinking critically' about the benefits and dangers of pervasive digital media in and outside of school is imperative. Moreover, extending discussions of DIY, creative citizenship and prosumption, we contend that allowing pupils to draw on wider leisure experiences, including their absorption in the social Web and its interactive possibilities, enable them to make their mark on the outputs they produce, creating rather than consuming others' media passively.

Projects like Digital Commonwealth have disruptive potential, for educational authorities, pupils and for how we might think about conventional understandings of institutional spaces. Though we have to be careful not to promulgate technologically determinist narratives, it is likely that increasing mobility (in the sense of devices and their use) will shape the future of education. It is imperative that *pedagogies* align with *technologies* to ensure that young people and their educational guardians are adequately prepared to deal with the opportunities and threats brought about and intensified by the digitally mediated world. Our study suggests that there remain significant inequities in terms of provision across schools, access to suitable infrastructure and equipment, and the presence of qualified and confident staff with the requisite digital leadership attributes to enable digital media projects to be integrated into everyday learning practices. Major events, like the Commonwealth Games, can precipitate and accelerate uptake of new approaches and innovative thinking, but they do not represent a panacea for the systemic development of critical digital citizenship over time.

Finally, this study also contributes to debates about the growing importance of digital cultures in problematising the activities and spaces traditionally conceived as the sole preserve of leisure, work or education. The digital medium contributes to the creation of leaky, porous institutional contexts, bringing the outside in and vice versa. As the social Web creates the potential for simultaneous learning and leisure, both educational actors and young people have to adapt their pedagogical practices to deal with a collapsing of spatial and temporal boundaries of schooling and leisure.

Disclosure statement

No potential conflict of interest was reported by the authors.

Funding

This work was supported by the Big Lottery Fund [grant number SGD/1/010466723].

References

Andrejevic, M. (2014). Exploitation in the data mine. In C. Fuchs., K. Boersma., A. Albrechtslund, & M. Sandoval (Eds.), *Internet and surveillance: The challenges of Web 2.0 and social media* (pp. 71–88). London: Routledge.

Atton, C. (2014). Alternative media, the mundane and 'everyday citizenship'. In M. Ratto & M. Boler (Eds.), *DIY citizenship: Critical making and social media* (pp. 343–358). Cambridge, MA: MIT Press.

Bakardjieva, M., Svensson, J., & Skoric, M. (2012). Digital citizenship and activism: Questions of power and participation online, *JeDEM*, *4* (1), i–v.

Boyd, D. (2014). *It's complicated: The social lives of networked teens*. London: Yale University Press.

Brill, J. M., & Galloway, C. (2007). Perils and promises: University instructors' integration of technology in classroom-based practices. *British Journal of Educational Technology, 38*, 95–105.

Chalip, L. (2006). Towards social leverage of sport events. *Journal of Sport & Tourism, 11*, 109–127. doi:10.1080/14775080601155126

Collins, A., & Halverson, R. (2010). The second educational revolution: Rethinking education in the age of technology. *Journal of Computer Assisted Learning, 26*, 18–27.

Crary, J. (2013). *24/7 Late capitalism and the ends of sleep*. London: Verso.

Ertmer, P. A., Ottenbreit-Leftwich, A. T., Sadik, O., Sendurur, E., & Sendurur, P. (2012). Teacher beliefs and technology integration practices: A critical relationship. *Computers & Education, 59*, 423–435.
Fuchs, C. (2014). *Social media: A critical introduction*. London: Sage.
Gauntlett, D. (2011). *Making is connecting: The social meaning of creativity, from DIY and knitting to Youtube and Web 2.0*. London: Polity.
Gillespie, T. (2010). The politics of 'platforms'. *New Media & Society, 12*, 347–364.
Grant, L. (2010). *Connecting digital literacy between home and school*. Bristol: Futurelab.
Halpin, H. (2013). Immaterial civil war: The world wide war on the web. *Culture Machine, 14*, 1–26. Retrieved from http://culturemachine.net/index.php/cm/article/view/509/524
Hands, J. (2013). Introduction: Politics, power and 'Platformativity'. *Culture Machine, 14*, 1–9, Retrieved from http://culturemachine.net/index.php/cm/article/view/504/519
Jenkins, H., Ford, S., & Green, J. (2013). *Spreadable media: Creating value and meaning in a networked culture*. New York, NY: New York University Press.
Johnson, L., Adams Becker, S., Estrada, V., Freeman, A., Kampylis, P., Vuorikari, R., & Punie, Y. (2014). *Horizon report Europe: 2014 Schools edition*. Luxembourg/Austin, TX: Publications Office of the European Union/The New Media Consortium.
Kelemen, M., & Smith, W. (2001). Community and its 'virtual' promises: A critique of cyberlibertarian rhetoric. *Information, Communication & Society, 4*, 370–387.
Kim, D. (2014). *The rules of Twitter.* Retrieved December 5, 2014, from http://www.hybridpedagogy.com/journal/rules-twitter/
Kim, D., & Kim, E. (2014). *The #Twitterethics manifesto*. Retrieved December 5, 2014, from https://modelviewculture.com/pieces/the-twitterethics-manifesto
Livingstone, S. (2004). Media literacy and the challenge of new information and communication technologies. *The Communication Review, 7*, 3–14. doi:10.1080/10714420490280152
Livingstone, S. (2010). Media literacy and the challenge of new information and communication technologies. *The Communication Review, 7*, 13–14. doi:10.1080/10714420490280152
Lockton, D., Greene, C., Casey, A., Raby, E., & Vickress, A. (Eds.). (2014). *Creative citizens' variety pack: Inspiring digital ideas from community projects*. London: Royal College of Art.
McGillivray, D. (2013). Digital cultures, acceleration and mega sporting event narratives. *Leisure Studies, 33*, 96–109.
Miah, A., & Garcia, B. (2012). *The Olympics: The basics*. London: Routledge.
Miller, T. (2009). Cybertarians of the world unite: You have nothing to lose but your tubes. In P. Snickars & P. Vonderau (Eds.), *The YouTube readers* (pp. 424–440). Stockholm: National Library of Sweden.
Paton, K., Mooney, G., & McKee, K. (2012). Class, citizenship and regeneration: Glasgow and the Commonwealth Games 2014. *Antipode, 44*, 1470–1489.
Ratto, M., & Boler, M. (2014). Introduction. In M. Ratto & M. Boler (Eds.), *DIY citizenship: Critical making and social media* (pp. 1–22). Cambridge, MA: MIT Press.
Reason, P., & Bradbury, H. (2001). Introduction. In P. Reason & H. Bradbury (Eds.), *Handbook of action research: Participative inquiry and practice* (pp. 1–14). London: Sage.
Ritzer, G., & Jurgenson, N. (2010). Production, consumption, prosumption: The nature of capitalism in the age of the digital 'prosumer'. *Journal of Consumer Culture, 10*, 13–36.
Rose, N. (2000). Government and control. *British Journal of Criminology, 40*, 321–339.
Smith, A. (2014). Leveraging sport mega-events: New model or convenient justification? *Journal of Policy Research in Tourism, Leisure and Events, 6*, 15–30. doi:10.1080/19407963.2013.823976
Turkle, S. (2011). *Alone together: Why we expect more from technology and less from each other.* New York, NY: Basic Books.
van Dijck, J. (2013). *The culture of connectivity.* Oxford: Oxford University Press.
Zwick, D., Bonsu, S. K., & Darmody, A. (2008). Putting consumers to work: 'Co-creation' and new marketing govern-mentality. *Journal of Consumer Culture, 8*, 163–196.

Video games and the political and cultural economies of health-entertainment

Brad Millington

Focusing mainly on the company Nintendo, this paper examines the political economic and cultural forces underpinning the video game industry's recent interest in merging entertainment and health promotion. This is a trend best exemplified in sexagenarian actress Helen Mirren's endorsement of Nintendo's fitness-themed game *Wii Fit Plus*. In one sense, 'health-entertainment' is deemed a product of the coercive laws of competition that impress the need for reinvestment and innovation as a way of warding off industry rivals. Nintendo's turn to health promotion is from this perspective an extension of the 'console wars' that in the past drove gaming companies to pursue verisimilitude on screen in hopes of attracting (young male) consumers. In another sense, the present moment offers an ideal time to direct innovation towards the issues of health and healthy ageing in particular, as the cultural logics of healthism and the 'third age' both emphasise the virtues of 'healthy' and autonomous consumer activity. As such, Nintendo has pursued aesthetic simplicity but *kinaesthetic* realism as a way of extending the appeal of video gaming beyond the male youth demographic. In examining the implications of these developments, it is argued that health and entertainment, as independent constructs, are conceptually reimagined through their integration with one another. The pursuit of entertainment is made 'responsible', thereby remedying the concern that video gaming is an unhealthy activity. The pursuit of health, meanwhile, becomes a matter of playful, technology-enhanced and ultimately consumption-based experience.

'The brilliant thing about *Wii Fit Plus*: it's there, in your living room, sitting, looking at you, telling you, "Come to me Helen, come to me".' So begins famed actress Helen Mirren's online advert for the Nintendo *Wii Fit Plus* video game, a device designed to blend entertainment and health promotion in the confines of one's home. The ad, posted to the Nintendo UK YouTube channel, features Mirren's reflections on *Wii Fit Plus*' many merits: its simple set-up process, user-friendliness, entertainment value, and, most of all, its benefits in terms of health and fitness. Mirren's commentary on the last of these matters is punctuated by her playful ruminations on the typical barriers to exercise. The brilliance of *Wii Fit Plus*, she says, is its varied exercise offerings:

> Because I find exercise is a bit like meeting an old lover. You know, you're really pleased to see him, and you get tired of him really quickly. And you remember why you didn't like him in the first place, you know? … So with the Wii it's like having a new lover every day [laughs]. What could be better for a girl? (see Nintendo Wii UK, 2010)

That Mirren has in fact engaged with *Wii Fit Plus* is evidenced by short clips, spliced throughout the advert, of the actress standing on the game's 'Balance Board' – a motion-capturing platform that works in combination with the *Wii Fit Plus* software – so as to partake in 'virtual' activities like hula hooping and jogging. Never would she have imagined herself exercising through a video game console, Mirren says in conclusion. Doing so inspired feelings of youthfulness.

Helen Mirren is far from the lone celebrity to appear in video game marketing in recent years. The *Wii Fit Plus* itself was sold with the help of singer and television personality Louise Redknapp. More broadly, Brookey (2010) has charted in detail the emergent points of convergence between the video game and film industries. But video games are commonly associated with youth, and more specifically with young males. Mirren, by contrast, was 65 at the time of the advert's release. She herself signals these presumptions surrounding the 'proper' video game demographic in suggesting *Wii Fit Plus* had age-defying effects. And so this paper begins from a simple question: why would Nintendo seek an endorsement from a sexagenarian actress?

In fact, the question can be broadened further. As described herein, Nintendo has sought in recent years to expand its market share by appealing to consumers hitherto overlooked by mainstream gaming companies – older persons and women in particular. The Wii itself, the console with which *Wii Fit Plus* is compatible, was designed in part to fulfil this purpose. In simplifying the gaming experience, and in privileging a light-hearted, cartoonish aesthetic in many of its core games, the idea was to make factors like gender and age irrelevant in determining the make-up of the video game audience. Beyond the presence of Mirren and Redknapp in Wii marketing, commercials for this console emphasised its intergenerational appeal. As Deborah Chambers (2012) writes, against the themes of militarism and male heroism often found in video game marketing, 'the Nintendo Wii commercials accentuate kinship bonding by showing teenagers and younger children playing sport video games with parents and grandparents in domestic settings' (p. 73). Moreover, while games like *Wii Fit Plus* set the body in motion, in recent years 'non-traditional' gaming audiences have been targeted in the promotion of 'brain training' games as well – that is, computer and video game software aimed at improving cognitive functioning through tests of mental dexterity. Indeed, in that cognitive decline is deemed a concern for later life in particular, older persons have featured prominently in the promotion of games like Nintendo's *Brain Age*[2] (Millington, 2012, 2014).

The broader question is thus as follows: why has Nintendo, the world leader in video gaming, taken this 'sudden' interest in new consumer demographics? Why turn their attention not just to Mirren, but to women and (older) adults in general? The discussion that follows contributes to a tradition of critical analyses aimed at identifying and explaining the political and cultural forces at work in the video game industry (e.g. Brookey, 2010; Dyer-Witheford, 2001; Dyer-Witheford & de Peuter, 2009; Kline, Dyer-Witheford, & de Peuter, 2003). Political economy is understood herein as the processes and (power) relations involved in the production, distribution and consumption of resources – in this case communication resources (Mosco,

2009, p. 24; also see Hardy, 2014). As Vincent Mosco (2009) notes, political economic analyses are commonly attuned to historical change; the discussion below indeed historicises recent developments in video gaming as a way of explaining their significance. Cultural economy, meanwhile, is understood as the systems of meaning that inform and are informed by economic activity (see du Gay & Pryke, 2002). To be sure, political and cultural economies overlap – a point evidenced in Nintendo's recent offerings to consumers.

Indeed, the argument presented in this article is that the presence of Helen Mirren in Nintendo advertising has arisen from both the need for 'perpetual innovation' in the immensely competitive video game industry and from the contemporary salience of consumer-based solutions to the 'problems' of health and ageing. Said otherwise, while Nintendo is inherently driven towards innovation and corporate reinvention, wider cultural forces have made the present moment a better time than ever before to direct innovation towards the issues of health and healthy ageing in particular. The final section of the paper features reflections on the implications of these developments. Most notably, it is argued that Nintendo's turn to health-entertainment has important conceptual ramifications. In purposefully seeking to reimagine entertainment, the company is also helping to reimagine *health*, and is specifically reinscribing a neoliberal understanding of healthy living.

In making these arguments, the article strategically draws from a number of sources. These include existing analyses of recent trends in the gaming and health technology industries (e.g. Millington, 2009, 2012, in press; Brookey, 2010; Chambers, 2012; Jones & Thiruvathukal, 2012; Lupton, 2012, 2013), as well as materials such as news media reports and corporate documents recently released by Nintendo (e.g. Nintendo, 2014a, 2014b). The paper concludes with reflections on the need for further empirical enquiry to follow on from the conceptual account presented herein.

Political Economy: Console Wars and 'Ideal Commodities'

To assess the cycle of 'perpetual innovation' that lies at the core of the video game industry, it is useful to turn to Kline et al. (2003) influential book Digital Play. This is an instructive text both for its empirical and theoretical insights.

Summarising these authors' central argument, video games are said to be 'ideal commodities' for conditions of post-Fordism. This is a claim that follows from Lee's (1993) supposition that particular commodity forms can come to embody the economic, technological, social and cultural forces at work within a wider capitalist regime – that is to say, they can become contextually 'ideal' in comparison to others. Under conditions of Fordism, these criteria were best fulfilled by the car (as foretold by the name 'Fordism' itself) and by standardised housing. These commodities in the most direct sense reflected Fordism's production imperative: they were rigid, predictably structured and produced en masse for a 'massified' audience. More than this, however, and more than simply buoying the wider economy, the car and the standardised home 'were goods around which a whole set of social practices and values that were vital to the [capitalist] regime were arrayed' (p. 74). The automobile not only reflected a desire for mobility and privatised living away from the physical spaces where labour took place, it allowed for the empirical manifestation of what Williams (1974) famously called 'mobile privatisation'. The standardised home was the perfect space for the idealised nuclear family of the post-war years.

But *post*-Fordism's central logic is defined less by the principles of durability and massification and more by those of intensification and innovation; 'its typical commodities are instantaneous, experiential, fluid, flexible, heterogeneous, customised, portable, and permeated by a fashion with form and style' (Kline et al., 2003, p. 74). Kline, Dyer-Witheford, and de Peuter acknowledge that there are other candidates for the mantle of 'ideal' post-Fordist commodity. The Internet is one, for example, though its tendency towards open access as much as commodification is a complicating factor. Video games emerged from the same 'hacker culture' as the Internet but were quickly steered towards commercial development (p. 75). More to the point, in production, video games represent the contemporary divide between knowledge-based labour and manual production – as well as the tendency to situate the former in the Global North while exporting the latter to South American and Asian production zones. In consumption, video games are not merely engrossing in their storylines and spectacular aesthetics. They represent, as Chambers (2012) says of the Wii, the tendency to turn domestic spaces into consumer spaces while also allowing for portable media experience through hand-held equipment like Nintendo's DS console. Interactive gaming is also deeply reliant on sophisticated marketing schemes that appeal to niche audiences as opposed to a massified block of consumers. To appeal, via Helen Mirren, to older consumers is a clear example of this dynamic marketing imperative at work.

And yet, the very term 'ideal commodity' also need be reflexively scrutinised. It suggests a sort of harmony and simplicity – a vision of video game companies 'ideally' situated – whereas survival under post-Fordism is tantamount to 'riding chaos' (Kline et al., 2003, p. 76). That is to say, there is tension and anxiety even among those developing sought after technologies. Most of all, the transition from durable commodities with lengthy life cycles to personalised, experiential goods that quickly (and often intentionally) become obsolete is where the need for perpetual innovation rears its head. This is also where Kline et al. (2003) empirical insightfulness manifests.

The history of the video game industry is too lengthy to recount here (see Wolf, 2008). For these purposes, a key 'moment' worth reviewing came in the mid-1990s in the 'console wars' between Nintendo and its rival company Sega. Nintendo's rise to prominence had come a decade earlier. In the mid-1980s, the company Atari relinquished its position at the forefront of the home video game market. Video game developers at this time flooded the marketplace with games. Consumers, in turn, had trouble distinguishing between poor and high quality products at the point of purchase. As Kline et al. (2003) say, the image of unsold video game cartridges being bulldozed at landfill sites 'like the contaminated residues from some unspeakable industrial accident' (p. 106) would haunt the interactive game business for years to come. In North America, the home video game industry virtually disappeared.

As Dyer-Witheford (2001) recounts, however, Nintendo had Atari's overproduction crisis in mind in reviving the industry and, in the latter half of the 1980s, ascending to a quasi-monopolist position in the marketplace. Most importantly, the Nintendo Entertainment System (NES) console was a 'lock and key' device: a patented chip on the console (the 'lock') communicated with a patented chip on game cartridges (the 'key'). And so Nintendo could control not only console development but the 'flow' of new games as well; unlicensed game production violated the company's 'lock and key' patent. Nintendo's triumph, then, was largely one of intellectual property. That games like *Super Mario Bros.* and *Zelda* were fast-paced in their game-play, enthralling in their storylines, and strategically marketed also helped Nintendo's cause.

Yet the 'console wars' were not named without reason. In the 1990s, the company Sega emerged as a challenger to Nintendo. Specifically, they developed the Genesis console – one that, with its 16-bit graphics, outstripped Nintendo's 8-bit NES machine. This was supported with what Dyer-Witheford (2001) describes as an aggressively 'cool' TV advertising campaign aimed at older boys – 'a demographic targeting underlined by Sega's violent games, such as the notorious heart-ripping version of Mortal Kombat' (p. 969). Nintendo eventually countered with the 16-bit Super NES. From there, it was not long before console-based video gaming attracted the attention of the wider technology sector, including that of the companies Sony (makers of the PlayStation console) and Microsoft (producers of the Xbox). The crucial point, however, lies in the *nature* of competition as much as its outputs. 'With the time lag between new product cycles diminishing,' Kline et al. (2003) write, 'developing a new console, determining the timing of its launch, building attractive game libraries, and creating the requisite marketing buzz were to prove frantically exhausting missions' (pp. 138–139). *Perpetual* innovation, like the console wars, is aptly named.

At the root of all of this activity is a basic capitalist principle. Capital, Harvey (2010) remarks, is not a thing but a process. And while capital*ists* can in turn set this process in motion in different ways, 'production' capital has long been a dominant approach. Production capital is based on the 'coercive laws of competition' – laws that themselves operate on the basis of reinvestment. 'If I, as a capitalist, do not reinvest in expansion and a rival does, then after a while I am likely to be driven out of business. I need to protect and expand my market share. I have to reinvest to stay a capitalist' (p. 43). In the video game industry, reinvestment has largely taken the form of 'performance play': investing in labour power and means of production towards 'the development of a striking new technology that offers users substantial advantages over existing technology' (Shapiro & Varian, 1999, p. 205). This approach is particularly attractive to new entrants in a given industry, given their lack of a customer base and their lacking concern for 'backward compatibility' (i.e. making new technologies compatible with their predecessor devices). In the gaming industry, however, even established companies have made their new systems to not only outperform but to fully oust earlier offerings.

Thus, console makers moved from 8 to 16 to 32 to 64 to 128 bit consoles over time (Dyer-Witheford, 2001, p. 975), all in the name of protecting and expanding their market share. To be sure, a goal in making consoles that could accommodate ever flashier, faster-paced games was to attract new video game consumers. Those unimpressed with the 8-bit Nintendo Entertainment System might change their minds upon witnessing the advances contained in the 16-bit *Super* NES. But Dyer-Witheford's (2001) observations on the limitations in the gaming market near the turn of the century are important in this regard. Video games, he wrote in 2001, five years before the Wii's release, are 'boy toys':

> They are played mainly by teenage and preteen males, whose preferences are reflected and reinforced by the industry's concentration on fighting, strategy and sports genres … The game industry, conjured into being by technologically adept and culturally militarized men, made games reflecting the interests of its creators, germinating a young male subculture of digital competence and violent preoccupations. The industry then

> recruited new game developers from this same sub-culture, replicating its thematic obsessions and its patterns of female exclusion through successive generations. (p. 971; cf. Cassell & Jenkins, 1998)

This is a positive feedback loop whereby those targeted in production eventually become producers themselves. The imperative, at least compared to recent years, was more about satisfying than broadening the 'core' base of consumers.

This is not to suggest that female consumers have fully eschewed video gaming as a pastime, nor the complete absence of industry efforts at targeting female gamers over time. Nooney (2013) highlights the tendency to overlook female gamers and game designers in historical accounts of the gaming industry and, by contrast, the remarkable successes of Roberta Williams, co-founder of the computer game company Sierra On-Line. Williams, Nooney (2013) recounts, was an innovative figure – for example, she served as the lead designer on *King's Quest IV*, 'the first major graphical computer game with a recognisably human female avatar' and one that won the interest of roughly 200 000 female gamers upon its release. Justine Cassell and Henry Jenkins (1998) add that other gaming companies followed Williams' lead by offering one female in-game character for users to choose to control. 'This character was not always a draw for girls, but it was a nod in the direction of the female audience' (p. 10).

Indeed, as Nintendo and fellow gaming giants were mired in the console wars in the 1990s, a number of smaller firms set sights on developing a 'girls' market.' This, argue Cassell and Jenkins (1998), reflected both economic and political imperatives: the former in the sense that companies like HerInteractive and Girl Games needed to open new demographics for the sake of competitiveness; the latter in that there was simultaneously a commitment to feminism and female empowerment among key stakeholders in this initiative. Still, the positive feedback loop described by Dyer-Witheford (2001) whereby men created games for men and boys was firmly entrenched at the industry's centre. This came not simply at the cost of ignoring other demographics; it often brought an exceedingly narrow representational politics as well. Female characters, when present, commonly took up secondary roles, and were often highly sexualised in their appearances (e.g. see Consalvo, 2003; Dietz, 1998; Williams, Martins, Consalvo, & Ivory, 2009).

The Wii

It is at this point that the Wii becomes relevant, as its introduction marked a departure from existing mainstream logic when it came to style, marketing and video game content. Indeed, that the Wii was codenamed 'Revolution' prior to its 2006 release is suggestive of a break from earlier themes in the industry's cycle of perpetual innovation (Jones & Thiruvathukal, 2012).

The changes brought forward with the Wii first pertain to the 'style' in which gamers interact with this device and second to the on-screen aesthetics they encounter during game-play. That is to say, they are extra-diegetic and diegetic both. For the former, whereas video games had long required users to push buttons in sequence to control characters on screen, the motion-capturing Wii Remote changed this dynamic – often raising gamers up off the couch in the process. As Jones and Thiruvathukal (2012, p. 3) write:

> Compared to learning complicated button combinations while controlling analog sticks on a typical game-control pad, using the Wii is remarkably easy. The plain-white rectangular wand shaped like a television remote works by mapping the player's gestures to what's happening in the game world and how the game world is represented on the television screen. In this way, the mimetic interface shifts attention from the game world or what's on the screen to the player's body in physical space, out in the living room.

Thus, the Wii is based on a 'first person' style of gaming; an *embodied* style aimed at narrowing the gap between 'real' and 'virtual' kinaesthetics. Microsoft's Xbox Kinect – a rival to the Wii just as the Sega Genesis once rivalled the NES – functions on a similar basis. The Kinect, however, eliminates the controller altogether with the help of a motion-capturing camera. The accompanying advertising slogan, 'You are the controller' (Microsoft, 2010), suggests that the gap between people and technology has disappeared altogether.

In terms of on-screen representations, while some Wii games still press forward in the quest for realism, Wii software – especially that developed by Nintendo itself, such as the *Wii Sports* package – often casts verisimilitude aside in favour of *less* realistic aesthetics. Games like *Wii Bowling* have a cartoonish look; they are designed to be realistic only in their feel (Jones & Thiruvathukal, 2012). Technology writer Andy Robertson captures the historical significance of this development, referring along the way to the hand-held DS console and the Wii predecessor, the GameCube. 'A lot of this is gaming history now,' Robertson writes:

> but go back a few years and the idea of low-fi gaming was unheard of. Before the Wii and the DS broke onto the scene, everybody clamored for fidelity, resolution, and hardware features in new gaming consoles. Each new generation had to outgun the last and deliver previously unimagined graphical realism. Go back to the GameCube, though, and you can hear Nintendo quietly building its vision of games not dependent on horsepower. Its big idea: fun from ideas and implementations rather than processor speed, polygon count and frame rate. (The Escapist, 2010; also see Robertson, 2010)

Each new generation had to outgun the last. To succeed in the gaming industry was, for as long as the industry existed, to break new representational ground. With the Wii, perpetual innovation suddenly meant simplicity in appearances. Jones and Thiruvathukal (2012) go as far as to say that the Wii's 'revolutionary turn away from realistic graphics' was the primary goal in the making of this console (p. 15).

The question that persists, though, is why enact this 'revolutionary' turn? Consider again Chambers' (2012) description of Wii advertising:

> Nintendo Wii commercials share key features that signify the console's rightful place in the communal space of the living room. The activity, whether sport or quiz game, is staged in the heart of spacious, uncluttered middle class, suburban homes. These open plan display homes boast ample space for hand-held controls and bodies to be swung around by players and their observer–competitors. The game is performed by all members of a nuclear-style family, by parents, children and even visiting grandparents. (p. 74)

The goal then, is to *physically* move the gaming console from the (presumably male teenagers') bedroom to a more communal space in the household, and to *discursively* move the image of gaming in the public imagination to a place where 'everyone' is welcome to play. In the words of famed game developer Shigeru Miyamoto, Nintendo has effectively sought to 'break free of the stereotypical definition of what a gamer is, because until we do, we'll never be part of the national or worldwide culture' (Totilo, 2006; as cited in Jones & Thiruvathukal, 2012, p. 141). In other words, the company is ostensibly striving to undo the above-described positive feedback cycle whereby developers privilege games that would seemingly be of interest to young male audiences above all others. As discussed in the following section, health promotion factored into this quest to broaden the gaming audience as well.

The Wii's arrival, then, was in one sense shaped by political economic forces. The coercive laws of competition urged Nintendo to reimagine the video gaming experience in the name of warding off competitors. Now more so than ever, though, the strategy was to widen the video game market: rather than simply cutting a bigger piece of an existing pie, the pie might be altogether enlarged. As company President Satoru Iwata said in a recent corporate report: 'Our basic strategy is the *expansion of the gaming population*, which is to encourage as many people in the world as possible, regardless of age, gender or gaming experience, to embrace and enjoy playing video games' (Nintendo, 2013, emphasis in original). Brookey (2010) notes that the first five pages of the company's 2008 report contain ten photos featuring thirteen women and ten men, 'including middle-aged parents playing the Wii with their children and an older couple playing the console' (p. 125). As Brookey (2010) remarks, this is the manifestation of an underlying 'blue ocean strategy': an attempt to exit out from the competitive (or 'bloodied') 'red ocean' of the console wars and into unchartered commercial territory (cf., Kim & Mauborgne, 2005). 'The Wii advances technology not by enhancing the graphics but by changing the game interface and the way video games are physically played' (Brookey, 2010, p. 126). By the standards established in the industry, this was indeed a novel way of attracting attention.

Lest the arrival of Nintendo's new console be deemed perfectly frictionless, however, the company continues to 'ride the chaos' of the wider post-Fordist moment. On the consumption end, the Wii and its follow-up console, Wii U – a system that adds a 'GamePad' reminiscent of an iPad or other tablet – have raised concerns that Nintendo is alienating its core audience in its quest to appeal to 'everyone' (Lee, 2013; Kohler, 2011). Part of the issue in this regard pertains to 'third party' support from software developers. Nintendo and other console developers have long outsourced the game making process to companies like Electronic Arts – save, that is, for choice populist titles like *Super Mario Bros.* and the *Wii Sports* package. This can be a boon in that software development is expensive. But when support is not forthcoming console sales and/or customer allegiance can wane (e.g. see Totilo, 2013). On the production end, Nintendo did not escape the recent wave of criticism surrounding labour practices at Foxconn factories in Shenzhen, China, where devices ranging from Apple iPhones to the Wii U are made. This is not the first time the company has faced claims of labour malpractice. Dyer-Witheford (2001) documents the Maxi-Switch incident in Cananea, Mexico, in which labour conditions at a plant that produced the hand-held Nintendo Game Boy console were fraught to the point that local health officials reported making three or four ambulance trips daily for those collapsing on production lines. In Shenzhen, Nintendo of America's Senior Director of Corporate Communications acknowledged that underage workers had been employed in production (see Ashcraft, 2012). More broadly, Foxconn factories have been criticised for subjecting labourers to lengthy workdays, and poor living and working conditions (see Duhigg & Barboza, 2012; Millington, 2014). Knowledge and manual labour remain starkly divided in the making of post-Fordism's 'ideal commodities'.

Cultural economy: Health and Ageing in Neoliberal Times

Nintendo and its rivals are therefore inherently driven towards perpetual innovation. At the same time, the Wii's arrival can also be explained through an assessment of wider cultural conditions. Acknowledging that these cultural factors are too complex to exhaustively recount in this space, the focus of this section lies in particular with the contemporary politics of health and ageing.

It is useful first in this regard to look back at the historical perception of video games in the public imagination. That video games promote passivity and reflect misplaced priorities has for some time been a source of consternation. This is demonstrated in the very title of David Sheff's (1993) book, Game Over: How Nintendo Zapped an American Industry, Captured Your Dollars, and Enslaved Your Children, as well as the version of the book's cover that showed a young male consumer sat transfixed in front of a TV screen, presumably playing video games. This imagery is not out of step with the more specific view that video gaming is ultimately unhealthy from a biomedical perspective. For example, this position is marked out in a press release from 2002 – four years before the Wii's arrival – from the Public Health Agency of Canada. The Agency at this time summarised the position of several respected organisations:

> The Canadian Paediatric Society, the College of Family Physicians of Canada and the Canadian Teachers' Federation issued a joint call for action today urging parents, educators, politicians and policy-makers to act immediately to address the alarming rise in the incidence of child and youth physical inactivity and obesity …
>
> … Increased reliance on television, video games, and computer technology as pastimes for children, and the diminishing priority of physical education in Canadian schools, are cited by experts as the major reasons for the growing numbers of sedentary children and teenagers. (Public Health Agency of Canada, 2002)

Media consumption has furthermore been a concern in the scientific literature over time. For example, two years after the Public Health Agency of Canada's report, a study of nearly 3000 children aged 1–12 found that while television had no bearing on children's weight status, video games were in fact problematic in this regard (Vandewater, Shim, & Caplovitz, 2004). 'This may mean that video game play, but not television use, is indeed displacing the time children spend in more physically demanding pursuits' (p. 83). The point, for these purposes, does not pertain to the credibility of these findings; it is the *perception* that healthy living and video game consumption are at odds that is important.

To be more precise, it is the perception that healthy living and video game consumption are at odds *in a wider culture where health is construed as a 'super value'* that is most important for these purposes. This added caveat follows from the writing of Crawford (1980, 2006) and specifically his observation that, in the West at least, the pursuit of health and 'wellness' is now deemed paramount, and capable of subsuming all other concerns. That is to say, health is a super value in that the quest for a 'good life' is necessarily the quest for healthy living. In this regard, health becomes a question of *lifestyle* as much as (for example) medical diagnoses and treatments. These are cultural conditions that are furthermore ripe for *moralising* health – what Crawford terms 'healthism'. Through a moral lens, a healthy/unhealthy lifestyle becomes a matter of choice as much as, if not more so, than factors like genetics or one's surrounding environment. Healthism has furthermore been construed as a mechanism for class-based reaffirmation. As Deborah Lupton (2013) states, '[h]ealthism tends to be a discourse embraced by the socio-economically privileged, who are able to position "health" as a priority in their lives and have the economic and educational resources to do so' (p. 367).

The discursive gap between healthism and neoliberalism is minimal. For Crawford (2006), healthism helped establish the 'common sense' of neoliberalism's key tenets: deregulation, personal responsibility and consumer-citizenship among them. In his words, '[i]n contrasting a vision of autonomous, prudent and self-responsible individuals to images of the careless and the foolhardy, a link was easily made to the burden of social spending: the virtuous would have to pay taxes to provide medical care for those whose unhealthy lifestyles led to overutilization of medical care' (p. 410). Empirically, the gap is equally small. If neoliberalism in general privileges market-based solutions to social problems, healthism has helped flood the marketplace with goods and services for 'self-improvement'. For example, Lupton (2013) points to the arrival of web 2.0 technologies and mobile digital devices such as health-themed smartphone apps as a phenomenon that 'has allowed healthism to be promoted and promulgated in more detail and more intensely than ever before' (p. 367; also see Lupton, 2012).

Thus, it is not enough to say, as above, that the Wii was crafted as a tool for 'everyone' by way of its simplified aesthetics and 'first person' style of play. It is the console's link to an *active* style of play – and by extension, to *health* – that ushers the Wii to a wide audience as much as its other features. This is not an inference; it has been said explicitly by Nintendo spokespeople. To be relevant to 'everyone' in the household is to centre the concept of health – 'the very thing that video games were often blamed for ruining' (Jones & Thiruvathukal, p. 81). This logic crystallises most of all in the *Wii Fit* and its successors, the Mirren-favourite *Wii Fit Plus* and *Wii Fit U* for the Wii U console. In all cases, exercise is performed on a weight scale-sized platform called the Balance Board – a device capable of capturing movement in a way similar to the hand-held Wii Remote. On offer are both 'healthy' activities and *measures* of health. In this sense, gamers – the whole family – can partake not only in 'virtual' yoga, strength training, cardio and the like, they also can record and track measures like Body Mass Index, a weight-to-height ratio, to ensure they are improving. Nintendo developer Shigeru Miyamoto, a key architect behind *Wii Fit*, has spoken of the 'fun' of weighing oneself daily: 'I think that once you make weighing yourself with your family part of your daily routine, it'll be hard to imagine life without Wii' (Nintendo, 2014a). The game in this formulation becomes indispensable to the family as a whole.

Like Having a New Lover Everyday

The Wii can be perceived, then, as a device that articulates with the wider conditions of healthism. This is a personalised, consumerised 'solution' to the perceived problem of inactivity. But the question remains as to the purpose behind Helen Mirren's presence in marketing for *Wii Fit Plus*. This is certainly a function of the quest to appeal to 'everyone' in the sale of Nintendo's latest console. The claim forwarded here, however, is once again that wider cultural forces cannot be overlooked.

Specifically, Mirren's connection to the Wii can be viewed as the manifestation of 'third age' logic – a term that resonates in key ways with the healthism construct described above. The third age is both a descriptive and conceptual term. In a descriptive sense, it pertains to a stage in the life course – namely, the years preceding a 'fourth age' of frailty and often dependence but succeeding a 'second age' characterised by childrearing and/or workforce participation (Gilleard & Higgs, 2005; Higgs, Leontowitsch, Stevenson, & Jones, 2009; cf., Laslett, 1989). 'Third agers' from this perspective are swelling in their ranks: the onset of population ageing in many countries – the United States, the UK and Japan among them – means the proportion of the population that has surpassed their time in the workforce is on the rise. In conceptual terms, third age discourses imagine what life *should be* as one enters retirement. The image of later life that was long hegemonic – again, at least in the West – was of older persons disconnected from the wider society. Gilleard (2005) calls this the 'ghettoization' of age, a process that manifested across the Twentieth Century as youth culture flourished.

Third age discourses seek a reversal of these trends. The point is that older persons can remain empowered and active as they age – that their ghettoisation can be undone. Like healthism, the third age is a *lifestyle* construct as much as it is one that follows from (for example) improvements in medicine. The self is conceived as a project to be ameliorated through reflexive decision-making. Indeed, healthism and the third age overlap directly in that Higgs et al. (2009) situate the 'will to health' as a central component of the latter. The goal is to be perceived as actively and responsibly warding off the arrival of the fourth age. And so consumer products like make-up, pharmaceuticals and exercise technologies become tools for engaging in self-care, and perhaps for outwardly showing that one is doing so as well (e.g. see Millington, 2012; Katz & Marshall, 2003; Katz & Peters, 2008; Vincent, Tulle, & Bond, 2008; Williams, Higgs, & Katz, 2012).

The arrival of the third-age construct is historically significant. The unravelling of time-tested stereotypes of ageing should no doubt be welcomed. But the alliance of third age politics and neoliberalism is as clear as the affinity between neoliberalism and healthism. The rhetoric of empowering oneself in later life has arrived at the same time that social structures such as defined benefit pension plans have been criticised and even dismantled (e.g. see Kemp & Denton, 2003; Rudman, 2006). Like healthism too, the third age has been deemed a class-based construction. 'Indeed,' say Katz and Laliberte-Rudman (2004), 'for those individuals who lack the requisite economic resources, personal skills, and cultural capital to participate in consumer culture in successfully agential ways, or for those who suffer irreversible bodily decline or dependency on others, the new era of ageing creates a profound sense of personal failure and social marginalisation' (p. 49).

The Wii is relevant here once again. Mirren's very presence in Nintendo advertising is remarkable in itself, given that the video game industry was at least complicit in the 'ghettoising' of ageing over time. Her involvement in the promotion of *Wii Fit Plus* comes at the same time as an (anonymous) grey-haired man has appeared in other *Wii Fit* promotional materials (including on certain versions of the game's packaging) and, as said at the outset, as video and computer game companies have targeted adults and older adults in the selling of 'brain training' games like

Nintendo's *Brain Age*[2] (Millington, 2012). Near the time of the Wii's North American release, Nintendo also took its promotional efforts to Life@50+, an event sponsored by the AARP, an American non-profit group working in the interest of older persons. 'Nintendo has never gone after grandparents before,' a company spokesperson was quoted as saying in The New York Times. 'We're targeting this audience for themselves, not just their grandchildren' (Taub, 2006).

Yet more than simply targeting new demographics through Mirren's celebrity, among other tactics, the language used in Mirren's online advertisement is remarkable as well. Situated in a luxuriant domestic space, Mirren playfully ruminates on how an active exercise agenda is comparable to an active sex life. Exercise is like 'meeting an old lover': pleasant at first, tedious in the end. The Wii, by contrast, with its panoply of physical activities, is like 'meeting a new lover everyday': 'What could be better for a girl?' (Nintendo Wii UK, 2010). Apart from promoting sustained physical activity into later life, the arrival of third-age logic has brought a renewed understanding of sexuality in older adulthood – and with it, an 'endless chain' of possibilities for commercial/pharmaceutical intervention (Katz & Marshall, 2003, p. 13; also see Marshall, 2006). In *Wii Fit Plus* advertising, the two realms collide. Mirren's carnal imagery makes both sex and video gaming reasonable, even desirable, pursuits. Not long ago, they were both incompatible with the post-retirement stage of life. It is relevant in this regard that Mirren herself has been deemed a 'sex symbol' outside her promotion of active gaming. This title was bestowed on her, for example, by the AARP, the aforementioned ageing-focused American organisation (Newcott, 2014).

Thus, the Wii's unveiling articulates with the cultural logic of the third age in much the same way that it connects with the basic principles of healthism. Said otherwise, perpetual innovation was directed not simply towards a new style of play, but an ostensibly healthy, age-friendly style in particular. This was Nintendo's pathway towards its desired 'blue ocean'.

Again, however, perpetual innovation, and in this case the integration of health/healthy ageing and video gaming, is far from an uncomplicated process. In one sense, other gaming companies have ventured into the realm of 'games for health' as well. For example, Microsoft advertises the combination of its Xbox 360 console and Kinect motion tracking system as 'The future of fitness'. The game *Nike + Kinect* is promoted in terms that echo the description of the *Wii Fit* family of games: 'Whatever your level, whatever your goal, you can now experience personal training, at home. Using personalized, real time feedback and elite level coaching, Nike + Kinect Training delivers a personalized programme that evolves as you do' (Microsoft, 2014). In another sense, while Nintendo's turn to active gaming and health promotion was deployed as a 'blue ocean strategy', so too did it move the company into new competitive terrain. As suggested above, smartphones and tablets can now serve as health promotion technologies as much as entertainment and communication devices. 'Running programmes, for example,' notes Lupton (2012), 'can be downloaded to one's smartphone or tablet computer, which are able to record the number of kilometres run each session, the route taken, automatically report these details to one's followers on social media sites, suggest new routes and remind the user that she or he has not run for a few days' (p. 231; also see Millington, in press). Whereas Helen Mirren is confined to the household in using *Wii Fit Plus*, mobile health (or m-health) technologies like the apps described in Lupton's writing accompany the user both across space and over time. 'Via m-health technologies, the health promoter is able to insert her- or himself even more insistently into the private world of others, accessing them in any location in which their mobile device accompanies them' (Lupton, 2012, p. 241).

Competition is thus not so easily evaded. Even if the Wii has been a lucrative innovation on the whole – Nintendo has sold over 100 million units worldwide since the console's unveiling (Nintendo, 2014c), along with more than 20 million units of both *Wii Fit* and *Wii Fit Plus* (Nintendo, 2014d) – company President Satoru Iwata's above-stated claim from the company's 2013 annual report that Nintendo is seeking to expand the gaming population was accompanied by an admission that the company had posted an operating loss for the fiscal year ending March 2013 (Nintendo, 2013). Nintendo has in fact reported losses for three years running; as one commentator wrote, 'The company is fighting to attract new users to the Wii U as people spend more time on their smartphones and tablet computers' (Negishi, 2014).

Iwata has in turn suggested that, as a remedy, Nintendo will in one sense more thoroughly embrace the logic of health promotion. Nintendo's guiding purpose across Iwata's 12 years at the company's helm has been entertainment – something he previously defined rather nebulously as 'put[ting] smiles on people's faces' (Nintendo, 2014b). What he has pledged going forward is a mission to redefine entertainment's very meaning. At the centre of this initiative is the concept of 'Quality of Life', or QOL: improving people's lives in 'enjoyable ways', and in doing so 'tak[ing] a step forward in expanding our business areas.' The more specific jumping off point in this regard is health. But rather than joining the fray with m-health developers, Iwata suggests instead that the company will leverage its console expertise:

> … we wish to achieve an integrated hardware–software platform business that, instead of providing mobile or wearable features, will be characterized by a new area of what we like to call 'non-wearable' technology. When we use 'health' as the keyword, some may inevitably think about 'Wii Fit.' However, we are considering themes that we have not incorporated to games for our existing platforms. Including the hardware that will enable such an idea, we will aim to establish a blue ocean. (Nintendo, 2014b)

The integration of entertainment and health is construed as a key selling point in this fortified quest towards health promotion. Whereas consumers might typically cast aside healthy pursuits after a brief burst of activity, health-entertainment – what I have previously termed *bio-play* (Millington, 2014) – is imagined as a way of holding their interest, and presumably their willingness to spend, over time. The next 'blue ocean' lies not in abandoning health-entertainment, but in turning more sharply in its direction.

Ideal Commodities? The Implications of Health-Entertainment

All told, Kline et al. (2003) claim that video games are 'ideal commodities' for post-Fordism retains conceptual purchase. The video game industry is still characterised by market segmentation and by stark divisions in manual and knowledge labour. Video games themselves remain 'instantaneous, experiential, fluid, flexible, heterogeneous, customised, portable, and permeated by a fashion with form and style' (Kline et al., 2003, p. 74). With the foregoing analysis in mind, however, so too does this claim now appear incomplete. The question that arises is whether video games might be ideal devices for *neoliberalism* as well. It would seem that Nintendo is at the very least striving to position them as such.

The relationship between neoliberalism and post-Fordism is complex. Say Tickell and Peck (1995) of the American context: 'The process of social regulation under Fordism was anchored in the Keynesian welfare state, under which collective bargaining and monopoly pricing were institutionalised; policy instruments were deployed to maintain and manage aggregate demand; and norms of mass consumption and "American ways of life" were generalised' (p. 370). It is simple enough to presume that neoliberalism, replete as it is with attacks on Keynesian governance, stands as the prevailing mode of social regulation with the ascendance of Fordism's successor, post-Fordism. In Tickell and Peck's (1995) analysis, however, this logic is problematic: with its crisis tendencies, neoliberalism is too volatile to stand as a mode of social regulation; it is more suggestive of the *absence* of a mode of social regulation instead (also see Peck & Tickell, 2012). What is important for these purposes, though, is neoliberalism's ideological force, regardless of its status as a mode of regulation (or not). Specifically, neoliberalism impresses the virtues of deregulation to fuel the global flow of commodities/services on the one hand and the value of consumer solutions to personal and collective problems on the other. As we have seen, this includes the 'problems' of health and ageing. Indeed, health and ageing are concerns par excellence for neoliberal times: they are *perpetual* concerns, and so are perfect constructs upon which to fasten the technology sector's need for perpetual innovation. Just as Helen Mirren desires new forms of (physical) activity – a new 'lover' everyday – so as to feel modern and youthful, so too must the gaming industry constantly devise new products to sustain and fulfil this need.

The most direct implication of Nintendo's integration of health into their product line pertains to the company's broadening of its representational politics. Female and older consumers are now targeted through mainstream advertising campaigns – a trend that is sure to continue in the years ahead. As noted, the perception that gaming is for male youth alone has long been an erroneous one. Apart from past efforts at establishing a girls' games market, a 2013 report from the Entertainment Software Association (2013) showed that 45% of computer and video gamers are female. The figure from their 2006 report – the year of the Wii's release – was a lesser but still robust 38% (Entertainment Software Association, 2006; also see Hayes, 2007). In Europe, 43% of women were found to be video gamers in 2012. The same description applies to more than a quarter of those aged 55–64 (Ipsos MediaCT, 2012). Nonetheless, and as we have seen, male youth have received disproportionate attention from the industry's marketing arm. It is noteworthy that even the statistics noted above reach their ceiling at the 55–64 age demographic, whereas Nintendo spokesperson Helen Mirren is now in her late 60s. If the cultural 'ghettoization' of certain demographics is problematic, as (for example) Gilleard (2005) avers, the arrival of more inclusive marketing campaigns should not be overlooked nor dismissed.

But Nintendo's quest for a new 'blue ocean' has important conceptual implications as well. This is true first in relation to the concept of entertainment. Nintendo President Satoru Iwata effectively imagines an ontological rupture when it comes to entertainment. No longer does it suffice to 'put smiles on faces', entertainment can and should improve one's Quality of Life. In theory, this remedies what has been one of the video game industry's key contradictions: that gaming is pleasurable, and thus desirable, but also unhealthy, and thus problematic. With *Wii Fit Plus*, entertainment is permeated by 'responsible', healthy living. This is guiltless pleasure.

But the corollary to Iwata's claim is that the meaning of *health* is shifting as well. Health becomes a matter of interactive, technology-enhanced, playful and ultimately consumption-based experience. To modify Kline et al. (2003) language, health, and not just video games, is made, 'instantaneous, experiential, fluid, flexible, heterogeneous, customised, portable and permeated by a fashion with form and style' (p. 74). The optimist's view of this approach to health promotion may well be that it can effectively serve as a Trojan horse. Healthy living is 'smuggled in' with entertainment. A more critical view, however, is that this arrangement holds the potential to over-simplify health and to fortify extant social divisions. Indeed, health is in one sense an exceedingly complex construct, determined by social forces that extend far beyond the individual (e.g. see Wilkinson & Marmot, 2003). In another sense, and in keeping with the above-described criticisms of healthism and the 'third age', to entangle health/healthy ageing with consumer choice is to favour those with the capacity to consume. Of course, on this latter point, Nintendo's products are not guaranteed to make one healthier in the end, even if the scientific literature has taken to evaluating the effectiveness of video games as health promotion tools (rather than depicting them as anathema to healthy living – e.g. see Entertainment Software Association, 2014). At the very least, though, the company's recent corporate activity is reflective and productive of the *ideological* salience of neoliberal forms of health promotion at the contemporary moment. Health is a super value, to be addressed assiduously at the marketplace; entertainment products are imagined as friends and not foes in such pursuits. It is indeed instructive that Nintendo has promised to more thoroughly embrace health-entertainment against the backdrop of waning corporate profits.

Conclusion

This paper has examined the entwined cultural and political economies underlying the arrival of health-entertainment in the video game industry. On the one hand, the industry's natural cycle of perpetual innovation was deemed an important pre-condition in Nintendo's adoption of active gaming. The upshot of pulling gamers up off the couch is that it might attract new consumers, and not just the young males that video game companies – at least the most well known among them – have traditionally courted. On the other hand, wider cultural forces were deemed important in the quest among companies like Nintendo to diversify their product catalogues. Never before has there been a more suitable time than the present to proffer consumer solutions to the 'problems' of health and ageing; this is a moment of particular salience for healthist and third age discourses. And so whereas Helen Mirren may not have foreseen the possibility of exercising through a video game console at one point in her life (as she expresses in her *Wii Fit Plus* sales pitch), it is also true that video game consoles have not previously been sold with such fervour to women and consumers aged 65 and over.

What remains to be explored further are the manners in which consumers perceive new technologies like *Wii Fit Plus*, as well as their perceptions and experiences of the general trend towards health-entertainment. The contextual variability of these responses is worthy of consideration as much as anything else. Nintendo spokespeople have understandably construed healthy living as a universal concern. Yet given that health and ageing have been subject to different cultural interpretations over time – perhaps the best case in point is what Kim et al. (2000) term the 'prevailing cultural stereotype' (p. 7) that ageing is revered in Eastern societies, with older persons more likely to be under the care of family members – so too is it possible, even likely, that health-entertainment will be understood in varied ways. For their part, Nintendo is evidently betting that it will be viewed positively irrespective of context. They will only reach their blue ocean if consumers join them along the way.

References

Ashcraft, B. (2012). *The result of Nintendo's investigation into underage Foxconn workers*. Retrieved February 2014, from http://kotaku.com/5954397/the-result-of-nintendos-investigation-into-underage-foxconn-workers

Brookey, R. A. (2010). *Hollywood gamers: Digital convergence in the film and video game industries*. Bloomington: Indiana University Press.

Cassell, J., & Jenkins, H. (1998). Chess for girls? Feminism and computer games. In J. Cassell & H. Jenkins (Eds.), *From Barbie to Mortal Kombat: Gender and computer games* (pp. 4–46). Cambridge: MIT Press.

Chambers, D. (2012). 'Wii play as a family': The rise in family-centred video gaming. *Leisure Studies, 31*, 69–82.

Consalvo, M. (2003). Hot dates and fairy tale romances: Studying sexuality in video games. In M. J. P. Wolf & B. Perron (Eds.), *The video game theory reader* (pp. 171–194). New York, NY: Routledge.

Crawford, R. (1980). Healthism and the medicalization of everyday life. *International Journal of Health Services, 10*, 365–388.

Crawford, R. (2006). Health as a meaningful social practice. *Health, 10*, 401–420.

Dietz, T. (1998). An examination of violence and gender role portrayals in video games: Implications for gender socialization and aggressive behavior. *Sex Roles, 38*, 425–442.

Duhigg, C., & Barboza, B. (2012). *In China, human costs are built into an iPad*. Retrieved from http://www.nytimes.com/2012/01/26/business/ieconomy-apples-ipad-and-the-human costs-for-workers-in-china.html?_r=2&hp

du Gay, P., & Pryke, M. (2002). Cultural economy: An introduction. In P. du Gay & M. Pryke (Eds.), *Cultural economy: Cultural analysis and commercial life* (pp. 1–19). London: Sage.

Dyer-Witheford, N. (2001). Nintendo capitalism: Enclosures and insurgencies, virtual and terrestrial. *Canadian Journal of Development Studies/Revue canadienne d'études du développement, 22*, 965–996.

Dyer-Witheford, N., & de Peuter, G. (2009). *Games of empire: Global capitalism and video games*. Minneapolis, MN: University of Minnesota Press.

Entertainment Software Association. (2006). *Essential facts about the computer and video game industry*. Retrieved May 2014, from http://www.theesa.com/facts/pdfs/esa_ef_2006.pdf

Entertainment Software Association. (2013). *Essential facts about the computer and video game industry*. Retrieved May 2014, from http://www.theesa.com/facts/pdfs/esa_ef_2013.pdf

Entertainment Software Association. (2014). *Games: Improving health*. Retrieved June 2014, from http://www.theesa.com/games-improving-what-matters/health.asp

Gilleard, C. (2005). Cultural approaches to the ageing body. In M. L. Johnson, V. L. Bengtson, P. G. Coleman, & T. B. L. Kirkwood (Eds.), *The Cambridge handbook of age and ageing* (pp. 156–164). Cambridge: Cambridge University Press.

Gilleard, C., & Higgs, P. (2005). *Contexts of ageing. Class cohort and community.* Malden: Polity.
Hardy, J. (2014). *Critical political economy of the media: An introduction.* New York, NY: Routledge.
Harvey, D. (2010). *The enigma of capital and the crises of capitalism.* Oxford: Oxford University Press.
Hayes, E. (2007). Gendered identities at play: Case studies of two women playing Morrowind. *Games and Culture, 2*, 23–48.
Higgs, P., Leontowitsch, M., Stevenson, F., & Jones, I. R. (2009). Not just old and sick – the 'will to health' in later life. *Ageing & Society, 29*, 687–707.
Ipsos MediaCT. (2012). *Videogames in Europe: Consumer study.* Retrieved May 2014, from http://www.isfe.eu/videogames-europe-2012-consumer-study
Jones, S. E., & Thiruvathukal, G. K. (2012). *Codename revolution: The Nintendo Wii platform.* Cambridge: MIT Press.
Katz, S., & Laliberte-Rudman, D. (2004). Exemplars of retirement: Identity and agency between lifestyle and social movement. In E. Tulle (Ed.), *Old age and agency* (pp. 45–65). New York, NY: Nova Science Publishers Inc.
Katz, S., & Marshall, B. (2003). New sex for old: Lifestyle, consumerism, and the ethics of aging well. *Journal of Aging Studies, 17*, 3–16.
Katz, S., & Peters, K. R. (2008). Enhancing the mind? Memory medicine, dementia, and the aging brain. *Journal of Aging Studies, 22*, 348–355.
Kemp, C., & Denton, M. (2003). The allocation of responsibility for later life: Canadian reflections on the roles of individuals, government, employers and families. *Ageing & Society, 23*, 737–760.
Kim, K., Bengston, V. L., Myers, G. C. & Eun, K. (2000). Aging in East and West at the turn of the century. In K. Kim, V. L. Bengston, G. C. Myers, & K. Eun (Eds.), *Aging in East and West: Families, states, and the elderly* (pp. 3–16). New York, NY: Springer.
Kim, W. C., & Mauborgne, R. (2005). *Blue ocean strategy: How to create uncontested market space and make the competition irrelevant.* Boston, MA: Harvard Business Press.
Kline, S., Dyer-Witheford, N., & de Peuter, G. (2003). *Digital play. The interaction of technology, culture, and marketing.* Kingston: McGill-Queen's Press.
Kohler, C. (2011). *Nintendo's game-killing policies alienate biggest fans.* Retrieved June 2014, from http://www.wired.com/2011/06/xenoblade-the-last-story/
Laslett, P. (1989). *A fresh map of life: The emergence of the third age.* London: Weidenfield and Nicholson.
Lee, D. (2013). *E3: Will console-makers alienate hardcore gamers?* Retrieved June 2014, from http://www.bbc.co.uk/news/technology-22885595
Lee, M. J. (1993). *Consumer culture reborn.* London: Routledge.
Lupton, D. (2012). M-health and health promotion: The digital cyborg and surveillance society. *Social Theory & Health, 10*, 229–244.
Lupton, D. (2013). Quantifying the body: Monitoring and measuring health in the age of mHealth technologies. *Critical Public Health, 23*, 393–403.
Marshall, B. L. (2006). The new virility: Viagra, male aging and sexual function. *Sexualities, 9*, 345–362.
Microsoft. (2010). *Kinect ads: 'You are the controller'.* Retrieved April 2014, from http://www.microsoft.com/en-us/news/features/2010/oct10/10-21kinectads.aspx
Microsoft. (2014). *The future of fitness.* Retrieved June 2014, from http://www.xbox.com/en-ca/xbox-360/fitness
Millington, B. (2009). Wii has never been modern: 'Active' video games and the 'conduct of conduct'. *New Media and Society, 11*, 621–640.
Millington, B. (2012). Use it or lose it: Ageing and the political economy of brain training. *Leisure Studies, 31*, 429–446.
Millington, B. (2014). Amusing ourselves to life: Fitness consumerism and the birth of bio-games. *Journal of Sport & Social Issues, 38*, 491–508.
Millington, B. (in press). Smartphone apps and the mobile privatization of health and fitness. *Critical Studies in Media Communication.*
Mosco, V. (2009). *The political economy of communication* (2nd ed.). Thousand Oaks: Sage.

Negishi, M. (2014). *Nintendo's financial difficulties worsen. Operating loss nearly doubles amid lower sales of Japanese videogame maker's 3DS console*. Retrieved August 2014, from http://online.wsj.com/articles/nintendo-swings-to-net-loss-1406706326

Newcott, B. (2014). *Helen Mirren as a sex symbol? You bet*. Retrieved August 2014, from http://www.aarp.org/entertainment/style-trends/info-2014/helen-mirren-career-photo.html#slide1

Nintendo. (2013). *Annual report 2013*. Retrieved May 2014, from http://www.nintendo.co.jp/ir/pdf/2013/annual1303e.pdf

Nintendo. (2014a). *Volume 1: A new creation. 5. Importance of bodily awareness*. Retrieved June 2014, from http://www.nintendo.co.uk/Iwata-Asks/Iwata-Asks-Wii-Fit/Volume-1-A-New-Creation/5-Importance-of-Body-Awareness/5-Importance-of-Body-Awareness-222454.html

Nintendo. (2014b). *Corporate management policy briefing/third quarter financial results briefing*. Retrieved June 2014, from http://www.nintendo.co.jp/ir/en/library/events/140130/index.html

Nintendo. (2014c). *Hardware and software sales units*. Retrieved August 2014, from http://www.nintendo.co.jp/ir/en/sales/hard_soft/index.html

Nintendo. (2014d). *Top selling software sales units*. Retrieved August 2014, from http://www.nintendo.co.jp/ir/en/sales/software/wii.html

Nintendo Wii UK. (2010). *Helen Mirren Wii Fit Plus*. Retrieved April 2014, from http://www.youtube.com/watch?v=koXke2IrRmg

Nooney, L. (2013). A pedestal, a table, a love letter: Archaeologies of gender in videogame history. *Game Studies: The International Journal of Computer Game Research, 13*. Retrieved August 2014, from http://gamestudies.org/1302/articles/nooney

Peck, J., & Tickell, A. (2012). Apparitions of neoliberalism: Resvisiting 'Jungle law breaks out'. *Area, 44*, 245–249.

Public Health Agency of Canada. (2002). *Canadian Paediatric Society, College of Family Physicians and Canadian Teachers' Federation call for urgent action to boost physical activity levels in children and youth*. Retrieved November 2009, from http://www.phac-aspc.gc.ca/pauuap/paguide/child_youth/media/realease.html

Robertson, A. (2010). *Wii are just good enough*. Retrieved January 2014, from http://archive.wired.com/geekdad/2010/01/wii-are-just-good-enough/

Rudman, D. L. (2006). Shaping the active, autonomous and responsible modern retiree: An analysis of discursive technologies and their links with neo-liberal political rationality. *Ageing & Society, 26*, 181–201.

Shapiro, C., & Varian, H. R. (1999). *Information rules: A strategic guide to the network economy*. Boston, MA: Harvard Business School Press.

Sheff, D. (1993). *Game over: How Nintendo zapped an American industry, captured your dollars, and enslaved your children*. New York, NY: Random House.

Taub, E. (2006). *Nintendo at AARP event to court the grayer gamer*. Retrieved August 2014, from http://www.nytimes.com/2006/10/30/technology/30aarp.html?_r=1&

The Escapist. (2010). *Just good enough to play*. Retrieved January 2014, from http://www.escapistmagazine.com/articles/view/video-games/columns/game-people-calling/6982-Just-Good-Enough-to-Play.2

Tickell, A., & Peck, J. A. (1995). Social regulation after Fordism: Regulation theory, neo-liberalism and the global–local nexus. *Economy and Society, 24*, 357–386.

Totilo, S. (2006). *Nintendo's design guru, Shigeru Miyamoto, says Wii can destroy gamer stereotype*. Retrieved June 2014, from http://www.mtv.com/news/1532607/nintendos-design-guru-shigeru-miyamoto-says-wii-can-destroy-gamer-stereotype/

Totilo, S. (2013). *A year in, the Wii U is still not a must-own*. Retrieved May 2014, from http://kotaku.com/a-year-in-the-wii-u-is-still-not-a-must-own-1471395507

Vandewater, E. A., Shim, M., & Caplovitz, A. G. (2004). Linking obesity and activity level with children's television and video game use. *Journal of Adolescence, 27*, 71–85.

Vincent, J. A., Tulle, E., & Bond, J. (2008). The anti-ageing enterprise: Science, knowledge, expertise, rhetoric and values. *Journal of Aging Studies, 22*, 291–294.

Wilkinson, R., & Marmot, M. (Eds.). (2003). *Social determinants of health: The solid facts* (2nd ed.). Copenhagen: World Health Organization.

Williams, R. (1974). *Television*. London: Fontana.

Williams, S. J., Higgs, P., & Katz, S. (2012). Neuroculture, active ageing and the 'older brain': Problems, promises and prospects. *Sociology of Health & Illness, 34*, 64–78.

Williams, D., Martins, N., Consalvo, M., & Ivory, J. D. (2009). The virtual census: Representations of gender, race and age in video games. *New Media & Society, 11*, 815–834.

Wolf, M. J. P. (2008). *The video game explosion: A history from PONG to Playstation and beyond*. Westport: Greenwood Press.

Exploring online fitness culture and young females

Stephanie T. Jong and Murray J. N. Drummond

ABSTRACT

While previous studies have investigated online health communities and health-seeking behaviours, less attention has been directed at the growing impact of the online fitness movement. This paper draws on the concept of biopedagogies to examine the messages transmitted within fitness culture on social networking sites (SNSs), and their role as a channel for health and fitness information. To explore this, a multi-method approach was conducted. The two methods included a netnography (online ethnography) and 22 semi-structured individual interviews with female participants aged 18–24 in Australia. The study suggests that online fitness use is becoming a popular leisure activity and source of health and fitness information. It reveals how SNSs are used as a platform to gather and teach ideas of health and fitness, and the manner in which textual and photographic online communication facilitates the social construction and transmission of this knowledge. Results indicated that although fitness accounts on SNSs offer differing notions to present alternative and competing realities, users predominantly chose to follow the normalised and dominant health discourses. Noteworthy, the onus is firmly placed on the individual within these health and fitness messages to adhere to norms of correct health practices and choices. This has connotations relevant to eHealth literacy.

Introduction

There has been a cultural shift towards the use of the Internet as a mode of seeking information and communicating about health (Berkman, Davis, & McCormack, 2010; Hesse & Shneiderman, 2007). People seek health information to 'reduce uncertainty regarding health status' and to 'construct a social and personal (cognitive) sense of health' (Tardy & Hale, 1998, p. 338). The Internet can help with this by providing the advantages of up-to-date and available information (Feng & Xie, 2015), social interaction (Toseeb & Inkster, 2015), consumer autonomy and anonymity (Dutta-Bergman, 2004) and information tailoring (Cline & Haynes, 2001). Studies have shown that the information found online is highly trusted, with young people modifying their behaviour on the basis of the information gathered (Ettel, Nathanson, Ettel, Wilson, & Meola, 2012). Health information is defined as 'any information which is related to the practice of medicine and healthcare' (Cullen, 2006, p. 1). In the context of this paper, fitness and diet are subsets of health, with studies inextricably linking these notions (Szabo, 2003; Wright & Halse, 2014).

The rapid adoption of social networking sites (SNSs) such as Facebook and Instagram, as a way of communication, has resulted in SNSs becoming a pervasive means of sourcing information about health for young adults (Feng & Xie, 2015; Oh, Lauckner, Boehmer, Fewins-Bliss, & Li, 2013). Vaterlaus, Patten, Roche, and Young (2015) suggest that social media is a relevant factor in influencing a persons' health behaviour. Other research on the influence of using online information from health communities (see Camerini, Diviani, & Tardini, 2010; Welbourne, Blanchard, & Wadsworth, 2013) found that the primary use of these groups was to support people with communicable and non-communicable diseases (Coulson, Buchanan, & Aubeeluck, 2007; Coulson & Knibb, 2007) and people with mental health disorders (Buchanan & Coulson, 2007; Toseeb & Inkster, 2015). Significantly, it is the link between the influence of peers and SNSs' interactive nature that emphasises the impact on health behaviours (McFerran, Dahl, Fitzsimons, & Morales, 2010). While research has indicated that the Internet does not replace the role of trusted health professionals, or peers and adults (Percheski & Hargittai, 2011), the Internet has provided a forum helping to provide and disseminate health information.

Using these SNSs is a popular leisure activity for young Australian people (Australian Bureau of Statistics, 2012; Sensis, 2014). Although a sedentary activity (Kerner, 2005), it also has a bearing on other leisure time activity, for example, physical activity. Previous research about online fitness has looked at fitspiration (an amalgamation of the words fitness and inspiration) images from Instagram (Tiggemann & Zaccardo, 2015), body perceptions in a bodybuilding community (2012) and gender and the body in the 'blogosphere' (Andreasson & Johansson, 2013, 2013b). Despite this, few studies have explored the fitness movement on SNSs, and more specifically, young females' experiences of using it as a means to gather health information.

This paper explores this practice, and how this process has the capacity to teach and inform online users' ideas of health and healthy practices. It presents a new perspective on gathering health information and allows a better understanding of online health information seekers' needs. Furthermore, it highlights vital improvements that can be made to information assessment and quality.

SNSs and online health information

Drawing from the notion of 'User Generated Content' (Kaplan & Haenlein, 2010), SNSs have paved the way for a change in the usual ways of 'production, distribution and consumption' of information (Meyers, 2012, p. 1022). SNSs differ from other media in terms of their immediacy, interactive nature and active participation, providing a valuable insight into the popularity of messages posted. While health messages are circulated by users within the community, users also provide instant feedback through 'likes' (a thumbs up button pressed to express a person's liking of a picture, video or comment), and the transmission of these messages through 'sharing' a post. These developments have enabled rapid engagement and feedback of online health information, influencing leisure activity.

Previous research has examined the issues faced by consumers seeking health information online, with positive and negative implications (Cline & Haynes, 2001; Rice & Katz, 2001). Across the studies, key factors have been noted, including concerns about the evaluation, credibility and accuracy of health information found using the Internet (Gray, Klein, Noyce, Sesselberg, & Cantrill, 2005; Rice, 2006). Additionally, issues have been linked to difficulties comprehending information (Murero, D'Ancona, & Karamanoukian, 2001), trustworthiness (Peterson, Aslani, & Williams, 2003) and the feeling of being overwhelmed by information (Mcmillan & Morrison, 2006; Velardo & Drummond, 2013).

A SNS-based trend known as 'thinspiration' (an amalgamation of the words thin and inspiration) or 'pro-ana' (short for anorexia) showcases idealised images of emaciated people with additional text desired to motivate viewers' weight loss (Borzekowski, Schenk, Wilson, & Peebles, 2010) and an eating disorder lifestyle (Ghaznavi & Taylor, 2015). The experience of using thinspiration SNSs accounts to gather health information has been shown to have negative effects on female users. These effects relate to self-esteem, appearance self-efficacy, body dissatisfaction and increased disordered eating variables (Harper, Sperry, & Thompson, 2008). Additionally, viewers reported a greater likelihood of over exercising and thinking about their weight (Bardone-Cone & Cass, 2007). These negative impacts are similar to that of exposure to unrealistically thin-ideal body types from traditional mass media (Groesz, Levine, & Murnen, 2002; Hargreaves & Tiggemann, 2003). Interestingly, Brotsky and

Giles (2007) debate the idea that pro-ana sites encourage non-eating disordered people to become eating disordered. They found the most potentially problematic aspect of the sites to be the social interactions of the users.

A more recent SNS-based trend, labelled 'fitspiration', is a hashtag consisting of text and images of '... (people, photographs, skinny jeans, etc.) as inspiration to attain a fitness goal' (K-fig, 2011). Boepple and Thompson (2015) suggest a varied definition of fitspiration to include 'objectifying images of thin/muscular women and messages encouraging dieting and exercise for appearance, rather than health, motivated reasons' (p. 2). Recent research has found that although fitspiration images are inspirational in a number of ways, viewing fitspiration images resulted in negative consequences for body image and increased negative mood (Tiggemann & Zaccardo, 2015). Many of the women in the fitspiration images are one particular body shape: toned, but also relatively thin. This promotes a visual health message through the platform of SNSs. The textual messages layered over the images also focus on appearance-related benefits of a 'healthy' lifestyle (Tiggemann & Zaccardo, 2015). This links to research on exercise motivated by appearance rather than health, leisure or enjoyment and is associated with negative body image (Strelan, Mehaffey, & Tiggemann, 2003).

Online fitness culture

The hashtag fitspiration is commonly used within online fitness culture. It is important to understand that the concept of culture is unstable, transformative and fluid 'worlds of meaning' (Kozinets, 2015). Following anthropologically and sociologically contested and shifting notions, culture is understood as a world of meaning, created by interacting individuals, where there is a 'momentary construction of common ground' (Amit & Rapport, 2002, p. 11). Online fitness culture is created by a number of online communities that are focused on health and fitness. For example, these include general health, fitness and bodybuilding communities on various SNSs, and well-being and healthy living blogs. Although their goals may be superficially diverse, the underlying messages circulated are general with a focus on the concepts of health and fitness. Specifically, attention is given to diet and food, inspiration, exercising, the body and weight and representations of fit bodies (Andreasson & Johansson, 2013, 2013b; Smith & Stewart, 2012).

These underlying messages create unique 'practices, attitudes, modes of thought, and values' (Levy, 2001, p. xvi) that are circulated through online communications. This distinctive culture is developed and maintained through these communications (e.g. images, videos and/or comments). These are shared within the community by 'posting', 'liking', 'following' and 'sharing' information involving health and fitness.

Biopedagogies

Online fitness culture provides a platform where certain disciplinary and regulatory strategies (of health and the feminine body) are effectively promoted, an example of Wright's concept of biopedagogy. Wright (2009) conceptualises the term 'biopedagogies' as the 'disciplinary and regulatory strategies that enable the governing of bodies in the name of health and life' (p. 14). Biopedagogies can also be considered as describing the values and practices, disseminated and regulated within formal education (e.g. schools) and information education (e.g. media and the Internet) (Wright & Halse, 2014). These disseminated messages place 'individuals under constant surveillance', inclusive of self-regulation, through 'increasing their *knowledge* around "obesity" related risks and "instructing" them on how to eat healthily, and stay active' (Wright, 2009, p. 1, original emphasis).

As a 'pedagogized society', the online fitness community utilises specific strategies in which knowledge is negotiated, produced and reproduced (Wright, 2009) and methods to evaluate and self-regulate the body are advocated (Iriart, Franco, & Merhy, 2011; Miah & Rich, 2008). In turn, emphasis is placed on individuals to consume the values and practices disseminated in order to understand and change themselves, and others (Wright, 2009). For example, one can reduce risk factors to serious diseases by adhering to appropriate lifestyle behaviours, such as altering one's diet (Miah & Rich, 2008). It is here where the health practices related to the body are an object of intervention (Williamson, 2014). Assessment of bodies that are perceived to be making lifestyle choices that do not adhere to their responsibilities as good citizens reinforce the ideal of thinness and the association between health and thinness (Wright, 2009). This appears to confirm with findings on other visual mechanisms, such as magazines (Schneider & Davis, 2010), that reinforce the socially constructed norms associated with health and the healthy body.

The present study

The present study explores the way in which young females use fitness on SNSs to gather and use health information. We reflect on the emphasis on health as an individual concern through the messages found online, and the notion of 'taking care of oneself' in order to be considered a 'good global citizen' (Edgley & Brissett, 1990). Furthermore, the view of online fitness culture as a platform for strategies of biopedagogy, and the increasing development of online fitness culture as a tool for self-regulation of the body are highlighted. The present study is motivated by the relative lack of research on the relationship between SNSs and health, more specifically as an aid to gather health information by textual and visual means (Goodings, 2012).

Method

The study used a 'blended netnography' (Kozinets, 2010), involving mixing online data collection with offline data collection. The primary researcher conducted a netnography (derived from ethnography, netnography is an online alternative) and individual in-depth interviews. This multi-method technique offers triangulation (Berg, 1989) and increased depth of understanding (Creswell & Plano Clark, 2011).

In exploring SNSs, it is important that users' online behaviours such as textual (e.g. comments and posts) and non-verbal (e.g. photographs or videos) are examined. Several studies have used similar methods to investigate online communities, termed under a plethora of labels: 'virtual ethnography' (Hine, 2008), online ethnography (Crowe & Bradford, 2006; Crowe & Watts, 2014), 'digital ethnography' and 'cyber ethnography' (Grbich, 2007). Netnography (Kozinets, 2010) was selected for use, however, as it provided structured guidelines which follow five steps: research planning, entrée, data collection, interpretation, ensuring ethical standards and research representation. A rich practice of online community research has used netnographic methods (see Bakardjieva, 2003; Fox & Roberts, 1999; Kozinets, 2010; Vrooman, 2001). In line with a social constructionist approach, the netnography shaped the scope of the project and assisted in establishing a boundary of thinking, informing interview protocol. The interviews provided an opportunity to explore how online fitness culture is created and experienced and the role that individuals play in creating this culture (Gaskell, 2007). This qualitative, semi-structured approach granted the research an emic epistemological stance (Kottack, 2009), giving priority to the views of participants in online fitness culture in relation to their health knowledge-gathering practices. The primary data of this paper are from the individual interviews.

Participants

After attaining ethics approval, the primary researcher recruited participants through SNSs. This approach to recruitment follows Lamb's (2011) recommendations from an online research project based in the United Kingdom. The researcher created alias Instagram and Facebook accounts in order to access the SNSs to conduct the netnography without the use of a personal profile, a method suited to netnography (Kozinets, 2010). Through these accounts, the researcher was able to state the aims of the research, provide an information sheet, dates of data collection and contact information. Participants were purposefully sampled in order to select interviewees who met specific criteria related to the use of online fitness. Consistent with the literature reviewed regarding age group and use of SNSs (Sensis, 2014), the characteristics of online health information seekers (Percheski & Hargittai, 2011; Rice, 2006) and body image concerns (Mission, 2011; Tiggemann & Slater, 2013), females aged 18–24 were invited as participants for this study. In line with homogeneous sampling, participants were required to have a Facebook or Instagram account, and consider themselves a part of the online fitness community. However, the particular community was not defined; it was kept open to encourage an array of participation within the study. As noted by Kozinets (2010), membership within a community is diverse along a 'continuum of participation'. All participants were a part of varying online fitness communities; they each self-identified as online fitness users, and they all had repeat contact, reciprocal familiarity with other users and shared knowledge of some rituals and customs.

Many of the interviews were generated through formal requests for interview (email requests) and further interviewees were contacted through their SNS accounts. While leaving the invitation open to any user of the online fitness community, participants from varying levels of participation, e.g. members with a large social network following to members who were more observers in the community, were included. This ensured that a breadth of experiences and perspectives were represented in the data.

Data collection and analysis

Twenty-two interviews were conducted, lasting between 35 min to over 90 min. Interviews took place either in person or via Skype, dependent on geographical location. Each interview was audio-recorded by a voice recorder. The interviews were transcribed verbatim and coded by the first author. Additional member checks were conducted by the co-author to ensure accuracy. The transcripts were then coded to ensure confidentiality. This research utilised a thematic analysis approach following Braun and Clarke's (2006). Each transcript was coded to identify meaningful segments of text and interpreted into broader themes. This process culminated in the identification of six principal themes that emerged across the 22 individual interviews.

Results

Using SNSs can be considered a leisure activity, where one's body is concurrently away from its workday life. However, as Kohn (2007) describes in her experiences, the time that can be classed as 'free time', a person's 'leisure time', is far from free. She explains that there is a strong commitment to work on the body and 'self', challenging popular notions of the definition of 'leisure'. Turner describes leisure as a 'non-work' or an 'anti-work phase' in life, with associated practices absent from leisure practices (1982), although the idea of 'non-work' has been challenged (Kelly, 1972). Research participants, however, described how their online practices permeate their 'real world' work, inform their knowledge and thoughts and form a strong part of their identity.

Online fitness culture as a source for health information

Within online fitness culture, a fit or athletic looking body has become a powerful icon for users involved, and a place where this body is consumed. Participants are directed to achieving this ideal through messages that are portrayed within the culture, and consumed by them. Participants described obtaining information on 'health' or 'fitness', often pertaining to diet and exercise. Isla, a participant who used online fitness on SNSs to document her health journey, found information on 'food and recipes and stuff, and then gym ideas, and how people do weights at the gym'.

The activities promoted through this information were designed for the masses and advocated that exercise could be done alone or in a group or whenever and wherever (in a gym or not). Accounts often showed exercises that were highly effective for weight loss and body modification (e.g. high-intensity interval training), reinforcing the use of exercise in the quest for thinness, and further the association with thinness and healthiness. The information was conveyed through textual and visual materials, which Miah and Rich (2008) refer to as 'performances of health-related information'. This information was gathered by participants viewing different online fitness users' accounts, from eBooks sold through user's accounts, YouTube videos or Instagram videos attached to fitness accounts. Consistent with Vaterlaus et al.'s study (2015), this information was labelled as 'inspirational', and often used as a motivator. It is the immediate, interactive, widespread access to this information and tailored information that separates this media source from traditional forms of media. This was evident as Niamh, a frequent user and poster within online fitness, stated:

> It is all so quick and easy. You can just turn up [to exercise] look at your phone and something is going to be up there [on the SNSs newsfeed] about a workout idea, or you can search through hashtags…back in the day if you wanted a gym program you couldn't just jump online and have a look at people's pages and see what the best thing to do is, you actually had to go and speak to a trainer. Whereas these days you can jump onto any social media and get a whole list of anything you can do.

All participants found online fitness culture an effective way of sourcing health information, promoting engagement in exercise and a healthy diet, and igniting interest in implementing this information. For example, one participant claimed:

> I did one [work out] the other day from Paige Hathaway [popular fitness person in online fitness culture]; she was doing some donkey kick thing. I tried to do it and it's so hard! I tried to copy some healthy recipes when I wasn't on this prep [currently on body building competition preparation], you can get good information.

The health discourse of neoliberal individual responsibility is deeply entrenched with these online health messages. Often, the quotes supporting images online invited individuals to take responsibility for their bodies, working towards the fit or athletic ideal, e.g. 'Make yourself fit'. These messages ask users to invest in the information provided for body maintenance in order to perform self-presentation appropriate to the culture (Sassatelli, 2010). It can be considered a matter of personal choice as to whether or not one succeeds in attaining this healthy lifestyle (Miah & Rich, 2008). This is reflected in an *Instagram* post:

> You, and only you, are responsibility for shaping your health and your body. You decide what your goals are and how hard you fight to stay on track. The decision, the determination and the choice lies within yourself, no one else can do it or want it for you. You create your own destiny. (Posted on Instagram by a 'fitspo' page, seen 19 March 2014)

This focus on individual responsibility extends to the requirement to control body weight and sustain a healthy lifestyle to be considered a good global citizen. The appearance of the body is representative of a morally responsible lifestyle choice, and an individual's lifestyle practices, attitudes, choices and relationship to the good of the rest of society (Wright, 2009). This creates a dichotomy between population groups. For example, with obesity linked to ill health (Crossley, 2004; Julier, 2008), larger body shapes are not widely publicised online and are thus considered an unhealthy population whose health choices link to irresponsible self-management and require governing. Hence, individual responsibility is evident in the presentation of fitness and health issues and the way in which fatness or overweight bodies are shamed in before and after or transformation pictures. In turn, this creates a restricted view of what it means to be healthy, potentially limiting the possibilities for certain body shapes and weights.

Although the study often encountered the message, 'Be your best you', emphasis was placed on attaining a 'healthy body', visually determined by the fitness community. Through textual and visual communication, the online fitness community constructs a health discourse reflective of the association of weight and health and body shape and health, hence with a strong emphasis on appearance orientation. While shifting away from the depiction of thinness may be looked upon in a positive light, physical attractiveness and perfect attributes are still at the centre of the healthy looking ideal. Markula (2001) raises concerns pertaining to this desirable body which potentially commands greater restrictions, for example, toned muscles on slender women. Noteworthy, the practices promoted by the online fitness community assume that a user has the capacity to make these imperative choices and act on them, with no acknowledgement of social and cultural determinants. Issues arise as the accessibility to the promoted resources to attain this desired look is not taken into consideration (Mosleh, 2014). A critical consumer of online health information, Charlotte, reflected on this:

> People who have their MACCA powder smoothie with spirulina and their chia seeds … this is not attainable for a normal person, like when someone is living in poorer community.

Similar messages about diet, exercise and individual responsibility are also evident in the presentation of health in traditional media (Wright, 2009).

Participants' use of SNS practices

Through the use of SNS practices, users of online fitness effectively promote disciplinary and regulatory strategies that advocate certain health behaviours in the name of health and life. Users of online fitness act as consumers of this information helped by regulatory strategies that present information as objective and empowering. Site communications (e.g. 'liking', 'sharing' and interacting online) can be viewed as strategies for promoting particular health and body ideals. It is through these social interactions that health messages are circulated, and where users come to identify and confuse popular messages with what is perceived as seemingly 'correct'. Consistent with previous research (Vaterlaus et al., 2015), participants perceived that viewing some circulated messages led to feelings of motivation, feeling the desire to exercise or feeling hungry. In the current study, one participant described that 'from seeing popular pictures' within online fitness culture, it showed her 'what to eat to get a flat stomach'.

As evidenced, online fitness culture has the capacity to motivate and encourage healthy living, emphasising 'strength and empowerment' (Tiggemann & Zaccardo, 2015) through visual and textual messages. By populating news feeds with images of healthy food, fit bodies and video exercises, accompanied by a proliferation of professional and unprofessional advice, the use of hashtags can be viewed as another strategy for consumption of health messages. For example, through the use of the hashtag 'fitspiration', a biopedagogy is created as the health messages circulated act as 'instructions' which direct users to regulate their body by eating healthily and staying active (Wright & Halse, 2014). These easily accessible messages offer a plethora of information for the consumer to make 'informed' decisions about their health and lifestyle practices, and present repeating messages of responsibility for one's health. While some posts are deliberate attempts to change behaviour or to instruct one about how they should live, such as exercise regimes and diet, others are subtler, for example, before and after transformation pictures.

Health fascism

Another strategy within online fitness culture is the use of popular status. Community participants with stated health knowledge and/or credentials (e.g. personal trainers or athletes) enjoyed a higher value within the community, whereby 'expert knowledge' about health was exchanged for popularity expressed by a large following or 'like' base. For example, popular users drew from apparent educational, professional and other personal life experiences when interacting with followers, most often to help with fitness journeys or alleviate any concerns. On Instagram, these popular users can be referred to as 'Insta-celebrities'. These popular users urge people to 'work' on their bodies, positioning their followers (or audience) as active agents to adhere to the created truths and standards produced around health and the body (Wright, 2009).

Popular users teach followers how to eat healthily, exercise and transmit a number of ideals that frame a particular body shape as superior and certain products as desirable or exercises as necessary. They also utilise a range of approaches to teach followers how to maintain self-discipline and stay motivated, how to complete exercises, how to set goals, etc. Common techniques used to teach followers these practices were: suggesting they follow people on SNSs who embodied their goal, to choose a diet which worked for them, to exercise with others, to purchase eBooks often designed by the popular person, to sign up for exercise events and to remain regularly involved within the fitness family online through posting images and comments. The seemingly always positive responses on SNSs from followers often positioned the advice received as important and useful, thereby encouraging the self-assessment and self-monitoring of bodies and behaviours against 'norms of appearance and body shape and moral imperatives regarding eating and exercise' (Wright, 2009, p. 10). This further reinforced the disciplining of bodies, urging people to work on themselves.

Edgley and Brissett's (1990) idea that health is a moral obligation gives justification to people who wish to intrude into other people's lives who are either 'ignorant', 'unable' or 'unwilling' to act on health (p. 259). This is reflected online with various popular users asserting increasing observation and control over what people do with their bodies and what they put into their bodies with everyone's acts said to 'affect others' (Edgley & Brissett, 1990, p. 260). This public surveillance, monitoring and regulating of the personal habits of people suspected of not following the socially constructed ideals of the health norm (Carlyon, 1984) can be labelled as 'Health Fascism' (Edgley & Brissett, 1990, p. 260). Health Fascism is strongly linked to the quest for a 'perfect body' for all (Edgley & Brissett, 1990). Throughout the past decade, the 'obesity epidemic' has become the most visible target of these Health Fascists or as Edgley and Brissett (1990) term it, 'Health Nazis' (p. 260). Personal characteristics such as laziness, weak will power and defective character are often blamed for the causes of obesity (Gard & Wright, 2005). Hence, it becomes a moral obligation to ensure that the 'problem' (Edgley & Brissett, 1990) is fixed and that people attain the perfect body or healthy ideal as perpetuated within online fitness culture. This occurs through the transmission of ideals in online interactions from popular users. Scarlett, a study participant with many online followers, explained the way in which sharing particular images can articulate to her followers the type of idealised body she desires:

> If I see a really good picture of a girl's body, I'm going to post it. It's only because I personally feel like that's what I want, that's what I like, and I post it because it inspires me. I know it might not inspire everyone, but the only reason I post it is just to show people what I'm trying to aim for.

Therefore, the understanding of health for users within the online fitness movement is impacted upon by the processes of modelling and discussions around health:

> Alexa: Her [popular online fitness female] page is really bright and colourful. You wake up in the morning and you're like, 'Oh, that's really nice. I'm going to get that smoothie that she shared, 'cos it's green and it looks cool'.

> Tess: Look at the example, Adriana and stuff, who are champions and the pros, who are my role models, who I want to be like, they inspire me to work out.

In turn, this shapes the health beliefs, norms and constructions around the body, diet, fitness and health. For example, often, health messages within online fitness perpetuate healthy as linking to biophysical aspects. Reinforcing this, study participant, Ava, stated that 'being skinny and toned is healthy' as seen through fitness posts, coinciding with Tiggemann and Zaccardo's (2015) findings linking to exercise motivated by appearance rather than health, leisure or enjoyment.

The idea of health online is increasingly being governed by a hybrid mix of popular participants and advertising companies with business interests. The messages promoting specific diets and active leisure (such as jogging, aerobics, gym work, sport and other purposefully chosen forms of exercise) can be understood as neoliberal practices implicated in the everyday exercise of power over the self (Markula & Pringle, 2006). Hence, the promotion of individual leisure and health practices through SNS platforms is a means through which neoliberal discourse is exercised over population groups. By endorsing particular truths about health and healthy living, governing power is formed, inherent in the processes of self-regulation and self-care (Fullagar, 2002; Rose, 1999). Noteworthy, the promoted health messages act as a strategy that is directed towards the body as an object for health, and an object of intervention.

Online fitness culture provides the potential for a 'new' lens through which to view health discourses and for the development of alternative discourses of health (Miah & Rich, 2008), as well as opportunities for rebellion and resistance (Wright, 2009). While some body stereotypes are challenged (e.g. female muscularity), the participants do not suggest that dominant discourses are being challenged, irrespective of the potential for these 'safe' spaces and sites to do so (Siibak, 2010). Individuals are encouraged to govern their own healthy lifestyle practices in the name of freedom. This 'freedom' to develop users' own health discourses and identity does not entice them to break the mould as they lapse into dominant health discourses associated with young females. This is echoed by 'healthy ideas' taken as truth. One partitipant, Cienna, stated, 'I have heard that whatever the picture is depicting actually works towards getting a healthy body'.

In this way, we can see how entrenched health discourses are and the way in which they are globally represented and yet narrowly understood and reconfigured. Hence, SNSs act as another media platform to govern health behaviour as a platform for the development of disciplinary and regulatory strategies. These concepts drawn from analysis strongly link to how online fitness communities persuade users, as individuals, to monitor and regulate themselves and others by 'increasing their knowledge around food and health, and by instructing them on how to change their lives by eating healthy and staying active' (Wright & Halse, 2014, p. 839).

Conclusion

This paper examined the way in which health, as an individual responsibility, is perpetuated through key strategies formed within SNSs. To this end, this paper has explored the idea that SNS structures are an emerging form of biopedagogy concerned with governance of the body. These biopedagogies are part of the culture of health fascism and self-management. Qualitative methods were employed to listen to insights from the perspective of young females, given the wealth of data indicating that this population is most susceptible to health issues relating to body aesthetics. Significantly, much of this data has focused on analyses of traditional media and its subsequent effects. While there is an emerging understanding of the need to investigate the implications of SNSs, Goodings (2012), suggests that more attention needs to be paid to research looking at the combination of the textual and visual. Furthermore, Vaterlaus et al. (2015) suggest future research to explore the influence of social media on young adult health behaviours.

Dworkin and Wachs (2009) present the idea that a fit body is synonymous with 'good' health, which is often perpetuated by strategies of biopedagogy within fitness magazines. Through the development of Facebook and Instagram, it is evident that online fitness culture also uses strategies of biopedagogy to express health ideas and ideals. The ideas and ideals reproduced and transmitted by users within the culture act as regulatory strategies, values and practices to govern bodies in the name of health (Wright, 2009). Where fitness magazines are printed monthly, SNSs provide a platform for immediate transmission of constructions of ideals, such as health and healthy bodies.

It is evident that SNSs have the capacity to act as a platform for informal dissemination of health information to a broad audience. Health professionals have been encouraged to use SNSs to share quality information about health topics to the public (Robillard, Johnson, Hennessey, Beattie, & Illes, 2013). Previous evaluations of formal health interventions implemented using SNSs have had slight benefits (Williams, Hamm, Shulhan, Vandermeer, & Hartling, 2014). Significantly, Laranjo et al. (2015) found a positive effect from SNS interventions on health behaviour outcomes, although considerable heterogeneity was noted. However, researchers have raised concerns regarding the integrity of health information presented online (Brodie et al., 2000; Ettel et al., 2012) or misinformation being given and received in a highly unregulated environment (Hallows, 2013; Jordan, Buchbinder, & Osborne, 2010). Users of online fitness notably require further critical analytical skills relevant to eHealth literacy. The online population should be aware of the bias of some online accounts, and the fact that some sources of information spreading are paid by private groups to pursue commercial interests. In practice, users should be able to critically analyse how the information is created, by whom and for what purpose, denoting the interests behind this information. As the onus of good health is placed primarily on the individual, this study raises issues over the ability to achieve eHealth literacy in order to distinguish accurate facts from misleading information, which is at times transmitted by numerous SNSs users. Regulations on SNS content may potentially ensure that the generation and distribution of health information are valid and non-biased. This may allow strength in SNS health interventions and communications. However, we are aware that regulating information is a controversial matter. Further study is warranted to explore how SNSs and other online platforms may provide a venue to disseminate credible health information and promote positive behaviour change.

Noting participants' admittance to passing judgement on other's health status based on aesthetics, the findings from this research suggest that more work may need to be done to promote the idea that healthy can be embodied in diverse shapes and sizes. Adding to this, Bordo (2003) argues that there is an 'institutionalised system of values and practices within which girls and women (and, increasingly, boys and men as well) come to believe they are nothing (and frequently treated as nothing) unless they are trim, tight, lineless, bulgeless, and sagless' (p. 32). This is an area of concern, which can be brought to attention through education around the societal construction of health, and through body image acceptance. Education has the capacity to challenge the messages of biopedagogies either within a formal or informal setting. Education may also address the need for positive health promotion discourses in talking about the use of leisure time and health and critical analytical skills required for SNS practices. This paper adds to the literature about work on the body and work and leisure as a single domain within leisure (Kohn, 2007; Waring, 2008).

(1) All participants have been given pseudonyms.
(2) Trivial words have been omitted from participant quotations

Acknowledgements

Thank you to all of the interviewees who shared their stories and experiences. Without their consent, this research would not have been possible. Thank you to the two anonymous reviewers for their suggestions, comments and insightful feedback. Thank you also to Andrew Craig for providing valuable support during this process.

Disclosure statement

No potential conflict of interest was reported by the authors.

References

Amit, V., & Rapport, N. (2002). *The trouble with community: Anthropological reflections on movement, identity and collectively*. London: Pluto.

Andreasson, J., & Johansson, T. (2013). Female fitness in the blogospere: Gender, health, and the body. *Sage Open*. 1–10. doi:http://dx.doi.org/10.1177/2158244013497728

Andreasson, J., & Johansson, T. (2013b). The health guru: Masculinity and fitness coaching in the blogosphere. *The Journal of Men's Studies, 21*, 277–290.

Australian Bureau of Statistics. (2012). *Children's Participation in Cultural and Leisure Activities* (4901.0). Australian Bureau of Statistics. Retrieved from http://www.abs.gov.au/ausstats/abs@.nsf/Latestproducts/4901.0Main%20Features7Apr%202012?opendocument&tabname=Summary&prodno=4901.0&issue=Apr%202012&num=&view

Bakardjieva, M. (2003). Virtual togetherness: An every-day life perspective. *Media, Culture & Society, 25*, 291–313.

Bardone-Cone, A. M., & Cass, K. M. (2007). What does viewing a pro-anorexia website do? An experimental examination of website exposure and moderating effects. *International Journal of Eating Disorders, 40*, 537–548. doi:http://dx.doi.org/10.1002/eat.20396

Berg, B. L. (2001 [1989]). *Qualitative research methods for the social sciences* (4th ed.), Neeham Heighs, MA: Pearson Education Company.
Berkman, N. D., Davis, T. C., & McCormack, L. (2010). Health literacy: What is it? *Journal of Health Communication, 15*, 9–19. doi:http://dx.doi.org/10.1080/10810730.2010.499985
Boepple, L., & Thompson, J. K. (2015). A content analytic comparison of fitspiration and thinspiration websites. *International Journal of Eating Disorders. 49*, 98–101. doi:http://dx.doi.org/10.1002/eat.22403
Bordo, S. (2003). *Unbearable weight: Feminism, western culture, and the body* (10th Anniversary ed.). London: University of California Press.
Borzekowski, D. L., Schenk, S., Wilson, J. L., & Peebles, R. (2010). e-Ana and e-Mia: A content analysis of pro-eating disorder web sites. *American Journal of Public Health, 100*, 1526–1534. doi:http://dx.doi.org/10.2105/AJPH.2009.172700
Braun, V., & Clarke, V. (2006). Using thematic analysis in psychology. *Qualitative Research in Psychology, 3*, 77–101. doi:http://dx.doi.org/10.1191/1478088706qp063oa
Brodie, M., Flournoy, R. E., Altman, D. E., Blendon, R. J., Benson, J. M., & Rosenbaum, M. D. (2000). Health information, the Internet, and the digital divide. *Health Affairs, 19*, 255–265. doi:http://dx.doi.org/10.1377/hlthaff.19.6.255
Brotsky, S. R., & Giles, D. (2007). Inside the 'pro-ana' community: A covert online participant observation. *Eating Disorders, 15*, 93–109. doi:http://dx.doi.org/10.1080/10640260701190600
Buchanan, H., & Coulson, N. (2007). Accessing dental anxiety online support groups: An exploratory qualitative study of motives and experiences. *Patient Education and Counseling, 66*, 263–269.
Camerini, L., Diviani, N., & Tardini, S. (2010). Health virtual communities: Is the self lost in the net? *Social Semiotics, 20*, 87–102. doi:http://dx.doi.org/10.1080/10350330903507230
Carlyon, W. H. (1984). Disease prevention/health promotion: Briding the gap to wellness. *Health Values: Achieving High Level Wellness, 8*, 27–30.
Cline, R. J. W., & Haynes, K. M. (2001). Consumer health information seeking on the Internet: The state of the art. *Health Education Research, 16*, 671–692.
Coulson, N., Buchanan, H., & Aubeeluck, A. (2007). Social support in cyberspace: A content analysis of communication within a Huntington's disease online support group. *Patient Education and Counseling, 68*, 173–178. doi:http://dx.doi.org/10.1016/j.pec.2007.06.002
Coulson, N., & Knibb, R. (2007). Coping with food allergy: Exploring the role of the online support group. *CyberPsychology and Behavior, 10*, 145–148. doi:http://dx.doi.org/10.1089/cpb.2006.9978
Creswell, J. W., & Plano Clark, V. (2011). *Designing and Conducting Mixed Methods Research (2nd ed.)*. Thousand Oaks, CA: Sage.
Crossley, N. (2004). Fat is a sociological issue: Obesity rates in late modern, 'body-conscious' societies. *Social Theory & Health, 2*, 222–253. doi:http://dx.doi.org/10.1057/palgrave.sth.8700030
Crowe, N., & Bradford, S. (2006). 'Hanging out in runescape': Identity, work and leisure in the virtual playground. *Children's Geographies, 4*, 331–346. doi:http://dx.doi.org/10.1080/14733280601005740
Crowe, N., & Watts, M. (2014). 'We're just like Gok, but in reverse': Ana Girls – Empowerment and resistance in digital communities. *International Journal of Adolescence and Youth*, 1–12. doi:http://dx.doi.org/10.1080/02673843.2013.856802
Cullen, R. (2006). *Health information on the Internet: A study of providers, quality, and users*. Westport: Praeger.
Dutta-Bergman, M. J. (2004). Primary sources of health information: Comparisons in the domain of health attitudes, health cognitions, and health behaviors. *Health Communication, 16*, 273–288. doi:http://dx.doi.org/10.1207/S15327027HC1603_1
Dworkin, S., & Wachs, F. (2009). *Body panic: Gender, health, and the selling of fitness*. New York, NY: New York University Press.
Edgley, C., & Brissett, D. (1990). Health Nazis and the cult of the perfect body: Some polemical observations. *Symbolic Interaction, 13*, 257–279. doi:http://dx.doi.org/10.1525/si.1990.13.2.257
Ettel, G., Nathanson, I., Ettel, D., Wilson, C., & Meola, P. (2012). How do adolescents access health information? And do they ask their physicians? *The Permanente Journal, 16*(1), 35–38.
Feng, Y., & Xie, W. (2015). Digital divide 2.0: The role of social networking sites in seeking health information online from a longitudinal perspective. *Journal of Health Communication, 20*, 60–68. doi:http://dx.doi.org/10.1080/10810730.2014.906522
Fox, N., & Roberts, C. (1999). GPs in cyberspace: The sociology of a 'virtual community'. *Sociological Review, 47*, 643–671.
Fullagar, S. (2002). Governing the healthy body: Discourses of leisure and lifestyle within Australian health policy. *Health: An Interdisciplinary Journal for the Social Study of Health, Illness and Medicine, 6*, 69–84.
Gard, M., & Wright, J. (2005). *The obesity epidemic. Science, morality and ideology*. USA & Canada: Routledge.
Gaskell, G. (2007). Individual and Group Interviewing. In M.W. Bauer & G. Gaskell (Eds.), *Qualitative Researching with text, image and sound*. London EC2A: SAGE Publications Ltd.
Ghaznavi, J., & Taylor, L. D. (2015). Bones, body parts, and sex appeal: An analysis of #thinspiration images on popular social media. *Body Image, 14*, 54–61. doi:http://dx.doi.org/10.1016/j.bodyim.2015.03.006
Goodings, L. (2012). Understanding social network sites: Lessons from MySpace. *Visual Communication, 11*, 485–510. doi:http://dx.doi.org/10.1177/1470357212454098

Gray, N. J., Klein, J. D., Noyce, P. R., Sesselberg, T. S., & Cantrill, J. A. (2005). Health information-seeking behaviour in adolescence: The place of the internet. *Social Science & Medicine, 60*, 1467–1478. doi:http://dx.doi.org/10.1016/j.socscimed.2004.08.010

Grbich, C. (2007). *Qualitative data analysis. An introduction*. London: Sage.

Groesz, L. M., Levine, M. P., & Murnen, S. K. (2002). The effect of experimental presentation of thin media images on body satisfaction: A meta-analytic review. *International Journal of Eating Disorders, 31*(1), 1–16. doi:http://dx.doi.org/10.1002/eat.10005

Hallows, K. M. (2013). Health information literacy and the elderly: Has the Internet had an impact? *The Serials Librarian, 65*, 39–55. doi:http://dx.doi.org/10.1080/0361526x.2013.781978

Hargreaves, D., & Tiggemann, M. (2003). The effect of 'thin ideal' television commercials on body dissatisfaction and schema activation during early adolescence. *Journal of Youth and Adolescence, 32*, 367–373. doi:http://dx.doi.org/0047-2891/03/1000-0367/0

Harper, K., Sperry, S., & Thompson, J. K. (2008). Viewership of pro-eating disorder websites: Association with body image and eating disturbances. *International Journal of Eating Disorders, 41*, 92–95. doi:http://dx.doi.org/10.1002/eat.20408

Hesse, B. W., & Shneiderman, B. (2007). eHealth research from the user's perspective. *American Journal of Preventive Medicine, 32*, S97–S103. doi:http://dx.doi.org/10.1016/j.amepre.2007.01.019

Hine, C. (2008). The Internet and research methods. In N. Gilbert (Ed.), *Researching social life* (3rd ed., pp. 304–320). London: Sage.

Iriart, C., Franco, T., & Merhy, E. E. (2011). The creation of the health consumer: Challenges on health sector regulation after managed care era. *Globalization and Health, 7*, 1–12. doi:http://dx.doi.org/10.1186/1744-8603-7-2

Jordan, J. E., Buchbinder, R., & Osborne, R. H. (2010). Conceptualising health literacy from the patient perspective. *Patient Education and Counseling, 79*, 36–42. doi:http://dx.doi.org/10.1016/j.pec.2009.10.001

Julier, A. (2008). The political economy of obesity: The fat pay all. In C. Counihan & P. V. Esterik (Eds.), *Food and culture: A reader* (pp. 484–499). New York, NY: Routledge.

Kaplan, A. M., & Haenlein, M. (2010). Users of the world, unite! The challenges and opportunities of Social Media. *Business Horizons, 53*, 59–68. doi:http://dx.doi.org/10.1016/j.bushor.2009.09.003

Kelly, J. R. (1972). Work and leisure: A simplified paradigm. *Journal of Leisure Research, 4*, 50–62.

Kerner, M. S. (2005). Leisure-time physical activity, sedentary behavior, and physical fitness among adolescents. *Journal of Physical Education, Recreation & Dance, 76*, 26–30. doi:http://dx.doi.org/10.1080/07303084.2005.10608294

K-fig. (2011). *Fitspiration*. Retrieved from http://www.urbandictionary.com/define.php?term=fitspiration

Kohn, T. (2007). Bowing onto the mat: Discourses of change through martial arts practice. In S. Coleman & T. Kohn (Eds.), *The discipline of leisure: Embodying cultures of 'recreation'* (pp. 171–186). United States: Berghahn Books.

Kottack, P. C. (2009). *Mirror for humanity. A concise introduction to cultural anthropology* (7th ed.). New York, NY: McGraw-Hill.

Kozinets, R. (2010). *Netnography. Doing ethnographic research online*. London: Sage.

Kozinets, R. (2015). *The international encyclopedia of digital communication and society* (2nd ed.). London: Sage.

Lamb, R. (2011). Facebook recruitment. *Research Ethics, 7*, 72–73. doi:http://dx.doi.org/10.1177/174701611100700208

Laranjo, L., Arguel, A., Neves, A. L., Gallagher, A. M., Kaplan, R., Mortimer, N., ... Lau, A. Y. (2015). The influence of social networking sites on health behavior change: A systematic review and meta-analysis. *Journal of American Medical Informatics Association, 22*, 243–256. doi:http://dx.doi.org/10.1136/amiajnl-2014-002841

Levy, P. (2001). *Cyberculture (t. b. R* (Bononno ed.). Minneapolis: University of Minnesota Press.

Markula, P. (2001). Firm but shapely, fit but sexy, strong but thin: The postmodern aerobicizing female bodies. In J. R. Johnston (Ed.), *The American body in context. An anthology* (pp. 273–309). USA: Scholarly Resources.

Markula, P., & Pringle, R. (2006). *Foucault, sport and exercise. Power, knowledge and transforming the self*. London: Routledge.

McFerran, B., Dahl, D. W., Fitzsimons, G. J., & Morales, A. C. (2010). I'll have what she's having: Effects of social influence and body type on the food choices of others. *Journal of Consumer Research, 36*, 915–929.

Mcmillan, S. J., & Morrison, M. (2006). Coming of age with the internet: A qualitative exploration of how the internet has become an integral part of young people's lives. *New Media and Society., 8*, 73–95. doi:http://dx.doi.org/10.1177/1461444806059871

Meyers, E. A. (2012). 'Blogs give regular people the chance to talk back': Rethinking 'professional' media hierarchies in new media. *New Media & Society, 14*, 1022–1038. doi:http://dx.doi.org/10.1177/1461444812439052

Miah, A., & Rich, E. (2008). *The medicalization of cyberspace*. Oxon, MD: Routledge.

Mission, A. (2011). *National survey of young Australians 2011. Key and emerging issues: Young people*. Australia.

Mosleh, D. (2014). *The biomedical and holistic practices of the continuum of healthism* (Major Research Papers, 2).

Murero, M., D'Ancona, G., & Karamanoukian, H. (2001). Use of the Internet by patients before and after cardiac surgery: An interdisciplinary telephone survey. *Journal of Medical Internet Research, 3*, e27.

Oh, H. J., Lauckner, C., Boehmer, J., Fewins-Bliss, R., & Li, K. (2013). Facebooking for health: An examination into the solicitation and effects of health-related social support on social networking sites. *Computers in Human Behavior, 29*, 2072–2080. doi:http://dx.doi.org/10.1016/j.chb.2013.04.017

Percheski, C., & Hargittai, E. (2011). Health information-seeking in the digital age. *Journal of American College Health, 59*, 379–386. doi:http://dx.doi.org/10.1080/07448481.2010.513406

Peterson, G., Aslani, P., & Williams, K. A. (2003). How do consumers search for and appraise information on medicines on the Internet? A qualitative study using focus groups. *Journal of Medical Internet Research, 5*, e33. doi:http://dx.doi.org/10.2196/jmir.5.4.e33

Rice, R. E. (2006). Influences, usage, and outcomes of Internet health information searching: Multivariate results from the Pew surveys. *International Journal of Medical Informatics, 75*, 8–28. doi:http://dx.doi.org/10.1016/j.ijmedinf.2005.07.032

Rice, R. E., & Katz, J. E. (Eds.). (2001). *The Internet and health communication*. Thousand Oaks, CA: Sage.

Robillard, J. M., Johnson, T. W., Hennessey, C., Beattie, B. L., & Illes, J. (2013). Aging 2.0: Health information about dementia on Twitter. *PLoS One, 8*, e69861. doi:http://dx.doi.org/10.1371/journal.pone.0069861

Rose, N. (1999). *Powers of freedom*. Cambridge: Cambridge University Press.

Sassatelli, R. (2010). *Fitness culture. Gyms and the commercialisation of discipline and fun*. ebook. Basingstoke: Palgrave Macmillan.

Schneider, T., & Davis, T. (2010). Fostering a hunger for health: Food and the self in 'The Australian Women's Weekly'. *Health Sociology Review, 19*, 285–303.

Sensis. (2014). *Yellow social media report 2014. What Australian people and businesses are doing with social media*. Australia: Yellow.

Siibak, A. (2010). Constructing masculinity on a social networking site: The case-study of visual self-presentations of young men on the profile images of SNS Rate. *Young, 18*, 403–425. doi:http://dx.doi.org/10.1177/110330881001800403

Smith, A. C. T., & Stewart, B. (2012). Body perceptions and health behaviors in an online bodybuilding community. *Qualitative Health Research, 22*, 971–985. doi:http://dx.doi.org/10.1177/1049732312443425

Strelan, P., Mehaffey, S. J., & Tiggemann, M. (2003). Self-objectification and esteem in young women: The mediating role of reasons for exercise. *Sex Roles, 48*, 89–95.

Szabo, A. (2003). The acute effects of humor and exercise on mood and anxiety. *Journal of Leisure Research, 35*, 152–162.

Tardy, R. W., & Hale, C. L. (1998). Getting 'plugged in': A network analysis of health-information seeking among 'stay-at-home moms'. *Communication Monographs, 65*, 336–357. doi:http://dx.doi.org/10.1080/03637759809376457

Tiggemann, M., & Slater, A. (2013). NetGirls: The Internet, Facebook, and body image concern in adolescent girls. *International Journal of Eating Disorders, 46*, 630–633. doi:http://dx.doi.org/10.1002/eat.22141

Tiggemann, M., & Zaccardo, M. (2015). 'Exercise to be fit, not skinny': The effect of fitspiration imagery on women's body image. *Body Image, 15*, 61–67. doi:http://dx.doi.org/10.1016/j.bodyim.2015.06.003

Toseeb, U., & Inkster, B. (2015). Online social networking sites and mental health research. *Front Psychiatry, 6*, 1–4. doi:http://dx.doi.org/10.3389/fpsyt.2015.00036

Turner, J. (1982). Towards a cognitive redefinition of the social group. In H. Tajfel (Ed.), *Social identity and inter-group relations* (pp. 15–40). London: Academic Press.

Vaterlaus, J. M., Patten, E. V., Roche, C., & Young, J. A. (2015). #Gettinghealthy: The perceived influence of social media on young adult health behaviors. *Computers in Human Behavior, 45*, 151–157. doi:http://dx.doi.org/10.1016/j.chb.2014.12.013

Velardo, S., & Drummond, M. J. N. (2013). Understanding parental health literacy and food related parenting practices. *Health Sociology Review, 22*, 137–150.

Vrooman, S. S. (2001). Flamethrowers, slashers, and witches: Gendered communication in a virtual community. *Qualitative Research Reports in Communication, 2*, 33–41.

Waring, A. (2008). Health club use and 'lifestyle': Exploring the boundaries between work and leisure. *Leisure Studies, 27*, 295–309. doi:http://dx.doi.org/10.1080/02614360802048845

Welbourne, J. L., Blanchard, A. L., & Wadsworth, M. B. (2013). Motivations in virtual health communities and their relationship to community, connectedness and stress. *Computers in Human Behavior, 29*, 129–139. doi:http://dx.doi.org/10.1016/j.chb.2012.07.024

Williams, G., Hamm, M. P., Shulhan, J., Vandermeer, B., & Hartling, L. (2014). Social media interventions for diet and exercise behaviours: A sustematic review and meta-analysis of randomised controlled trials. *BMJ Open, 4*(e003926), 1–16. doi:http://dx.doi.org/10.1136/bmjopen-2013003926

Williamson, B. (2014). Algorithmic skin: Health-tracking technologies, personal analytics and the biopedagogies of digitized health and physical education. *Sport, Education and Society, 20*, 133–151. doi:http://dx.doi.org/10.1080/13573322.2014.962494

Wright, J. (2009). Biopower, Biopedagogies and the obesity epidemic. In J. Wright & V. Harwood (Eds.), *Biopolitics and the 'obesity epidemic': Governing bodies* (pp. 1–14). New York, NY: Routledge.

Wright, J., & Halse, C. (2014). The healthy child citizen: Biopedagogies and web-based health promotion. *British Journal of Sociology of Education, 35*, 837–855.

Be who you are and be proud: Brittney Griner, intersectional invisibility and digital possibilities for lesbian sporting celebrity

Megan Chawansky

ABSTRACT

This article examines current professional basketball player, Brittney Griner, and the ways in which her personal and athletic lives are represented on social media. In particular, her visibility and posts on her public Instagram account allow for a consideration of the digital possibilities for social change by lesbian sporting celebrities. This analysis interrogates these possibilities through a close reading of several Instagram posts regarding Griner's romantic relationship with fellow basketball star, Glory Johnson. This article ultimately argues that Griner's Instagram profile helps challenge the intersectional invisibility of Black lesbian sporting celebrities and discusses the implications of this visibility for similarly positioned LGB youth.

> When I knew I had a chunk of time to myself, I would go to the living room and hop on the computer … I would load the yahoo search page, type in the words gay and lesbian, or some combination of the two, then read articles and watch documentaries for hours … I knew, from the first afternoon I spent reading about the LGBT community, I was reading about myself, that there were many other people out there like me. I was not alone, and the knowledge of that soothed some of my pain. (Griner, 2014, pp. 39–40)

The above excerpt is taken from Brittney Griner's 2014 memoir, In My Skin, which chronicles the 24-year-old Women's National Basketball Association (WNBA) star's journey, with a particular emphasis on the challenges she faced as a young Black lesbian. Griner's (2014) description of her middle and high school years presents a familiar 'narrative of gay youth in crisis' as she discusses bullying classmates, an over-protective father who actively denied and discouraged her sexual identity and the coping mechanisms she adopted to get through school (Denizet-Lewis, 2009). Her accomplishments as a high school basketball player and especially the presence of other young lesbians on her team brought some support. She also found some relief – as noted above – from discovering more about who she was and could be as a Black lesbian through information she located online. Griner's turn to the digital world is similar to many other lesbian, gay and bisexual (LGB) youth whose 'negative experiences of their immediate physical world and the lack of [physical] places in which they can explore and practise same-sex attraction' necessitates exploration into digital spaces for solace and support (Hillier & Harrison, 2007, p.84).

While existing studies document that LGB youth use the Internet and various mobile platforms to explore, navigate and practice their same-sex attractions, we know little about the specific kind of digital content that might be seen as productive and useful in formulating a positive sense of LGB identity (Craig

& McInroy, 2014). In an article on the experiences of young Black lesbians at a US HBCU (Historically Black Colleges and Universities), it is suggested that 'Internet access serves to augment or expand a community of support' and that 'young people have more options to imagine themselves than they did a mere generation ago' in the light of digital cultures (Patton & Simmons, 2008, p. 210). Some of these imagined options come in the form of celebrity culture and research by Gomillion and Giuliano (2011) who found that support, inspiration and comfort for LGB-identified people (not only youth) may come from parasocial relationships with mediated and 'out' celebrities. In this article, then, I argue that Griner's use of a public Instagram profile (@brittneygriner) to visually document and discuss her lesbian identity and her intimate relationship with fellow WNBA player, Glory Johnson, could be considered an example of the type of digital content that can support, inspire and comfort LGB youth.[1] It does this insofar as it offers a challenge to the invisibility of Black women (Sesko & Biernat, 2010) and Black lesbian athletes, in particular, as it presents images of lesbian desire and romance.

In this instance, I suggest that as an image-based mobile social network (IB-MSN) (Olszanowski, 2014), Instagram allows for a unique form of digital activism that challenges the intersectional invisibility (Purdie-Vaughns & Eibach, 2008) of Black lesbian sporting celebrities (King, 2009). This is done through Griner and Johnson's active self-production of imagery of lesbian romance, intimacy and physicality, both on and off the basketball court.[2] The context of US professional women's basketball proves especially important in the light of the league's aversion and indifference to lesbian athletes and fans as noted by other scholars (e.g. Banet-Weiser, 1999; King, 2009; McDonald, 2002, 2008, 2012; Myrdahl, 2009). Furthermore, although there are digital spaces wherein LGB youth in sport can turn for support (for example, the Go Athletes! Facebook page or Outsports.com), I suggest that this imagery might prove especially significant for LGB youth involved in sport, considering the low number of publicly 'out' professional athletes who might serve as role models in navigating a sport context (Stoelting, 2011).

By suggesting that Griner's Instagram posts can be read as a form of digital activism, I am accessing the feminist mantra that the personal is political and proffer that Griner's frequently articulated desires to be seen as a role model to youth extend to her (re-) presentation of self on Instagram (ESPN.com, 2015). Instead of 'slacktivism' – the dismissive term often given to examples of online activism which include things such as signing an online petition or joining a Facebook group (Christensen, 2011) – this article suggests that an Instagram post can be both 'personal, yet socially impactful through its ability to influence the existing ways of looking', seeing and being seen (Tiidenberg & Cruz, 2015; p. 9). This is especially important for Black lesbians in the public sphere and in research, for as Bowleg et al. (2008) note: Black lesbian and bisexual women (LBW) are 'a population and topic that remains virtually invisible in social science research' (p. 162). There is still much to be understood about the experiences of young Black lesbians, and this paper makes a modest contribution to the conversation by examining Griner's complicated relationship with digital cultures.

To begin this analysis, I introduce Griner as an important contemporary LGB cultural icon and classify her as a 'lesbian sporting celebrity' (Chawansky & Francombe, 2011, 2013). In utilising the term, lesbian sporting celebrity, I access Gever's (2003) concept of the lesbian celebrity to refer to 'instances where a celebrity is known to be and does not deny being a lesbian' and wherein her 'stardom … is achieved and authorised within the institutions of popular culture and [is] endorsed by the mainstream media' (p. 6). This is the case for Griner, whose lesbian subjectivity is regularly acknowledged by media outlets and who was the first 'openly gay athlete' to be endorsed by Nike. Nike now sells a rainbow-themed #BETRUE line of apparel, 'inspired by the LGBT community' (Nike #BETRUE Collection, 2014). These external endorsements – the financial ones and the mediated ones – and her subsequent visibility bring both opportunities and constraints, which Griner actively and currently navigates. As her relationship narrative with Johnson follows a fairly homonormative trajectory, many might be inclined to argue that her socially sanctioned visibility is not surprising and therefore must also be critically interrogated (King, 2008). I would concur and wish to note here that while the documentation and celebration of Black lesbian celebrity are fundamental to this article, it seeks to remain cognizant of the concern of simply equating increased visibility with political power and social change.

Locating @brittneygriner

> Lesbian and Proud! Be who you are and be beautiful! Do what makes you happy no matter what the world say is right! [sic] – @brittneygriner, 2014a [her biographical description on her Instagram page]

Brittney Griner is best known as a US women's basketball player, who played collegiately at Baylor University from 2009 to 2013 and who currently plays professionally in the WNBA for the Phoenix Mercury and in China for the Zhejiang Golden Bulls of the Women's Chinese Basketball Association (Fagan, 2014). Her dominance in basketball relies largely on her physicality; she is 6′8″ tall and has an 86-inch wingspan (Fedotin, 2009). She regularly dunks in games and possesses agility unseen by previous players of her size. Her ability to 'dunk while female' made her a YouTube sensation (Glass, 2013), with over six million views recorded on a clip of her dunking effortlessly during a high school practice session (CutCreator, 2007). While her size proves an asset on the court, it often proved to be a source of tension for Griner outside of basketball. Her height, deep voice and angular physique inspired bullying by classmates and online trolls[3] when she was younger and which still persists. As a presumed lesbian who adopts a stud[4] aesthetic, Griner faces/d criticism and attacks via a variety of social media formats, with trolls using various digital formats to – among other things – question her 'true' sex, view the punch she threw at opponent Jordan Barncastle in 2010, and comment on the article entitled, 'Brittney Griner discusses being gay' wherein she was said to publicly come out as gay (ESPN.com, 2013).

The (limited) academic and popular writing about Griner tends to present her as the recipient of sexist media coverage (Lavelle, 2014) and as a victim of persistent online abuse (e.g. Bruce & Hardin, 2014; Dixon, 2012; Fagan, 2013). For instance, noted gender and sport expert, Cahn (2011) briefly explored the treatment of Griner (then an athlete at Baylor University) on the Internet when she wrote:

> This December Baylor University fans broke a school attendance record for men's or women's basketball when they packed the stands for the Baylor–Tennessee game. As thousands cheered 6′8″ center, Brittney Griner, on I was aware of a nastier internet buzz about Griner, an African American with a slender frame and low voice. I tried a simple exercise, typing in 'is Brittney Griner …' as a Google search. Immediately, my browser completed the search with the most frequently asked questions: Is Brittney Griner a man, gay, a hermaphrodite, a boy, a girl, a woman, and 'a girl or a boy?' (p. 42)

The persistent online attacks of Griner even inspired her college coach, Kim Mulkey, to address the abuse during a 2012 press conference:

> This [Griner] is a human being. She didn't wake up and say make me look like this, make me 6-foot-8 and have the ability to dunk. This child is as precious as they come. … The stuff she's had to read about, the stuff she's had to hear, the stuff people say about her, the stuff people write about her, it's got to stop. That stuff's got to stop. (Associated Press (AP), 2012)

While most coverage of Griner does make some reference to the online abuse she continues to face, Griner (2014) notes that she has a 'love-hate relationship with social media' (p. 10). For as much as she experiences the wrath of trolls, especially after 'publicly' coming out[5] in 2013, she has also found support and a sense of place and connection in the digital world. In the article mentioned above, Griner noted that she does read some of the negative things that people write about her on Twitter, but that it does not bother her (Associated Press (AP), 2012). She is quoted as saying that she prefers to keep a low-key online profile, uses an alias on Twitter, noting that she only has about 200 followers (ibid.).

However, a different version of her limited engagement with social media while in college emerged after she finished her basketball career at Baylor. In her autobiography, Griner (2014) suggests that her decision to adopt a limited presence online related primarily to the monitoring of her digital profile by Baylor University (athletic) compliance officers. As Griner (2014) recounts:

> The first 'incident' was at the beginning of my sophomore year, during preseason training, before we officially started on-court basketball practice. I sent out a tweet to my girlfriend in Atlanta, something sweet, saying I missed her. That same night, I retweeted a post from an LGBT group that I followed. They had sent out a message – something along the lines of 'No More Hate' or 'Love One Another for Who You Are' – and I sent it to my followers as well. I didn't give it much thought at the time, because it wasn't anything out of the ordinary on Twitter, but Kim [the Baylor coach] called me into her office the next day. (p. 108)

Griner reported that her coach told her that she would need to take down her posts, and that they could not 'have that stuff out there' (ibid.). Griner grasped the message that she needed to keep quiet about her lesbian sexuality so as to not impact the team's image or its ability to recruit future players into the Baylor basketball programme (ESPN.com, 2013). This stance aligns with the documented homophobia and heterosexism within women's college and professional sport by scholars such as Griffin (1998), Plymire and Forman (2001) and Lenskyj (2003). Furthermore, it reflects Baylor University's – a private, Baptist university – ban on homosexual acts by students within its sexual misconduct policy (Atteberry, 2013).

The low profile she maintained during her years at Baylor University serves as a marked change from how Griner currently represents herself online. In addition to feeling more freedom after leaving Baylor, she 'realised there was no point in policing her own digital space when so many people could say whatever they wanted to say on social media' (Fagan, 2013). Currently, Griner has her own website (brittneygriner.com), is crowdsourcing funds for her anti-bullying app (called BG:BU) and boasts 210,000 'likes' on her Facebook page, 67,000 followers on Twitter (@brittneygriner) and 151,000 followers on Instagram (as of 13 May 2015). She is frequently asked to comment on LGB issues, and Griner consistently refers to her desire to be a role model and to be visible to youth who are like her, which is something she feels that she lacked while growing up. She invoked the potential role of social media in this process during her 2013 acceptance speech at the GLAAD[6] awards, wherein she was given the organisation's Visibility Award:

> I just want to say [that] growing up, I always knew that I wanted to do something big in the world, and have, you know, a place. And, I never knew that sports was gonna be my outlet, but with sports, I have a lot of media attention, and a lot of spotlight on me, and I'm able to use that for something that is close to my heart. That's close to me. And, just recently, I came out to the public. I've been out since about the ninth grade … Not everybody has that smooth coming out, but you know, once you do it, it's like, a light came on. On me. In the inside, around me, everything. I felt like I was Brittney Griner. Like, I was who I am now. I wasn't hiding anymore. I encourage all youth, [pause] elder. It doesn't matter what age group you fall in. It's never too late. It's never too early. If you know, then you know. Come out. Don't hide it. Don't try to be like anybody else. Be who you are. Be comfortable in your own skin. [Audience applauds and Griner laughs.] And, that's my message to everybody, especially the youth. And if there is ever a problem, I always want to say: Find somebody. Find anybody. Find me on Twitter. DM [direct message] me. At [@] me. We will find help. We will help everything out. It will be okay. (my italics, GLAAD, 2013)

The potential role of digital media as a tool of support for LGB youth is underscored in Griner's comments, as is the significance of role modelling/mentoring, an issue that Hillier and Harrison (2007) suggest is currently under-valued and under-developed within the LGB community. They suggest that the limited outreach to LGB youth by LGB-identified adults may be part of the reason that youth turn to the Internet for information and a sense of community (Hillier & Harrison, 2007). In the next section, I summarise the key literature that examines the function of digital media in the lives of LGB youth. In doing this, I seek to set up my argument on the importance of Griner's direct challenge to Black lesbian invisibility via her Instagram account in the light of what is known from studies with LGB youth.

LGB youth and digital culture: a brief overview

Broad discussion about youth, sexuality and digital cultures frequently positions them as naïve victims or potential prey for an increasingly sexualised digital world. This hyper-sexualised digital world includes perceived risks such as sexting or the sending/receiving of sexually explicit imagery, online paedophiles, exposure to online pornography and cyber-sex. While it is not my intent to minimise the potential negative consequences of some of these experiences for youth, I do wish to highlight that the overarching narrative of sexualised risk on the Internet often supersedes the potential 'sex positive' perspectives on a digital world that curates and presents a multitude of sexual subjectivities and practices. This can potentiality be an asset for LGB youth who may not encounter these ideas or subjectivities elsewhere. For example, Hillier and Harrison (2007, p. 88) demonstrate that many 'same-sex attracted young Australians' used the Internet for testing out the following experiences as a way to anticipate and prepare for their 'physical' world equivalents. These included: 'practicing sexual identity on the net' (for instance, performing homosexuality or heterosexuality in chat rooms), 'practicing same-sex friendships on the net' (e.g. meeting other LGB young people with similar experiences), 'practicing disclosure on the net' (coming out online as LGB), 'practicing same-sex intimacy', 'practicing homosex' (finding out via online searches what LGB sex looks like/is/can be) and 'finding out about and practicing living as part of gay community' (pp. 89–94).

DeHaan et al. (2013) advance the above research and attempt to ascertain how LGBT youth connect their online and offline behaviours as previous (limited) research suggests that an overreliance on online support systems can limit 'offline' engagement. They interviewed 32 youth (aged 16–24) from a large, US city and found that although participants used online tools for a variety of reasons, 43% did so 'to make meaning of their same-sex attractions or to gain information, confidence, and support after having already established their identities ... [and] to increase their general self-esteem and learn to accept their sexual identities' (p. 426). This intrapersonal use of the Internet parlayed into positive offline experiences for these particular youth. In a related study with 19 LGBTQ youth (aged 18–22) from Toronto, Craig and McInroy (2014) found that participants became more comfortable with their own

> identities by watching the journeys of other LGBTQ youth online, through video blogs, textual blogs or forums where LGBTQ people shared their experiences with peers. While not all participants shared their stories online themselves, many consumed the stories shared by others. (p. 102)

This particular finding of Craig and McInroy's (2014) research signifies the importance of the present analysis, which seeks to better articulate how Instagram photographs that document Griner's relationship and 'journey' with Johnson could be read as offering an opportunity for LGB youth to 'find likeness' online (p. 102). The ability to find positive and affirming representations of LGB sexual expression online is one way to counter the experiences of negative offline encounters that many of the participants of the above studies noted.

Method

This analysis of Griner's Instagram images uses Azzarito's (2010) insights on visual methodologies in physical culture to guide its considerations. As Azzarito (2010) suggests, 'cultural images of the body, as they are delivered through visual culture ... inform the subjective experiences of young people, and their choices to 'act' ... in crafting their bodies' (p. 157). Similar, then, to what has been found in the previous section, Azzarito (2010) re-establishes the importance of taking seriously what is seen and in particular how the lesbian body is seen when considering the identity and interpersonal development of LGB youth. In choosing to analyse Griner's self-presentations of romance, intimacy and physicality on Instagram – a decidedly visually focussed IB-MSN – this research examines the Black lesbian sporting celebrity body within a professional sporting context that might prefer it (still) remain invisible (King, 2009; McDonald, 2002, 2008, 2012).

I perform a 'critical reading of visual body texts' (Azzarito, 2010 p. 160) in order to contextualise Griner within larger discussions of intersectional invisibility, heteronormative sporting contexts and homonormative narratives of LGB relationships. To do this, I examine Griner's publicly visible Instagram page (@brittneygriner) with a focus on the visual posts that document her romantic relationship with Johnson, who it should be noted, is a highly successful professional basketball player in her own right. She played collegiately at the University of Tennessee and currently plays for the WNBA's Tulsa Shock. She was the fourth (overall) pick in the 2012 WNBA draft, and has been selected as a WNBA All-Star twice in 2013 and in 2014.

This analysis of Griner and Johnson's relationship begins when Johnson first appears (visually) on Griner's Instagram page on 23 June 2014 to the time of writing (13 May 2015). In total, 336 Instagram posts appear during this time, though not all of these images include Johnson or tag her on Instagram

(@missvol25). It also considers the captions supplied by Griner and notes (when appropriate) some of the responses provided by Griner's Instagram followers. This analysis is less concerned with the quantity of posts and images, and more interested in the qualitative interpretation of a purposefully selected group of images.

The use of Instagram proves an especially important dimension of this study for although research which explores the use of social media (e.g. Twitter and Facebook) by athletes is rapidly accumulating, there has been limited engagement with athletes' uses of Instagram. The notable exception is Geurin-Eagleman and Burch (2015) who examined the Instagram accounts of eight athletes with a focus on branding and management themes. The limited academic engagement with Instagram is somewhat surprising as it now boasts more active users than Twitter. However, one challenge may be in how to actually conduct research using Instagram. (See Farman (2015) and Highfield and Leaver (2015) for more on methodological considerations when studying Instagram.) For example, though the appeal and allure for many users is the visual representation and not the conversation/text format of other apps or tools, Geurin-Eagleman and Burch (2015) used a decidedly text-focussed coding system for their content analysis of Instagram posts as they noted the following variables:

> coder ID, athlete's name, date the photo was taken, number of likes, number of comments, photo caption, number of user tags (@), number of hashtags (#), the main content of the photo, and whether or not the athlete was in the photo. (p. 5)

While their analysis was primarily concerned with the implications of an athlete's representation for brand management and promotion, they did consider the differences in self-representation based on gender. Interestingly, they use this portion of the analysis in part to consider the notion of the 'sex sells' thesis that is often invoked when considering representations of female athletes and the promotion of women's sports. Unfortunately, their analysis did not consider the representations of LGB athletes nor did they actively engage with the construct of racial differences or detail how the 'sex sells' thesis might work differently for LGB audiences and athletes (Fink, 2012). As such, while their study does offer some insights for this analysis, a more useful model is by Olszanowski (2014) who examines three feminist artists and their attempts to circumvent Instagram's censorship policies. Olszanowski (2014) examines the ways in which the self-images of these artists raise important questions about what types of representations of women's bodies are able to freely circulate, both on Instagram and in the broader public. In a similar way, I identify three prototypical images from Griner's account to 'flesh out' the broader implications of each type of image, and in my conclusion, suggest how and why these images may have positive implications for LGB youth.

Intersectional Invisibility meets #noselfiecontrol

In this section, I work towards contextualising three Instagram posts on Griner's account within larger understandings of intersectional invisibility and also within what some might consider a 'selfie obsessed' cultural moment. The tension between critiques over making oneself (excessively) visible through the production of a selfie – which is a photograph of yourself taken with the intention of sharing it with others through social media – and the notable invisibility of certain bodies (Black lesbian bodies) is evident throughout this analysis. In articulating their notion of intersectional invisibility, Purdie-Vaughns and Eibach (2008) suggest that when individuals with 'subordinate identities do not fit the prototypes of their constituent subordinate group … they are relegate[d] to a position of acute social invisibility' (p. 381). The understanding of how and why certain groups become more/less visible argues that 'the influence of ethnocentrism (i.e. white as prototypical) and androcentrism (i.e. men as prototypical) will cause the prototypical gay person to be defined as a white man' and subsequently this leads to invisibility for those who do not fit the prototype (ibid., p. 381). Interestingly, they highlight that this social invisibility brings both advantages and disadvantages. The primary perceived advantage is that active forms of discrimination might be temporarily avoided. The disadvantages of invisibility are multiple and complex, but in this case, can be said to lead to a distortion or erasure of the experiences of specific groups or of individuals within those groups. The particular ways in which the racialisation of homophobia produces this invisibility have been explored by King (2009) and her insights on Sheryl Swoopes resonate with the case of Griner. As a star athlete, Griner cannot be said to be invisible to the wider public, and it is indeed the implications of her representations of the intersectionally invisible Black lesbian athlete that is of interest here.

With this last sentence, I am essentially contending that Griner's Instagram self-representations are simultaneously about her and not about her at all; they can be classified as a form of the 'ironic selfie' discussed by Collings (2014). In her analysis of the rapper, Cazwell's song/video/promotion entitled, 'No Selfie Control', Collings (2014) provides critical commentary on the prevalence of selfies and the tensions within the form. Of relevance to this analysis is the interpretation of the ways in which debates surrounding authentic and inauthentic representations of the self manifest in the form of the ironic (celebrity) selfie. Collings (2014) argues that through his trans-media product, 'No Selfie Control', Cazwell plays with the selfie and as such,

> highlights an irony around the content and function of such pictures that is applicable to the phenomenon of celebrity selfies in general: while these photographs typically present themselves as providing a privileged glimpse of the backstage/private celebrity self, making this seem authentic often means drawing upon aspects of the frontstage/public persona – catering to viewer expectations, in effect. This, in turn, shows how arguments surrounding authenticity in celebrity self-presentation become far more complex when inauthenticity can be argued to have an authenticity of its own. (p. 513)

This tension reveals itself in the images posted by Griner, and as such, I am less concerned with debates about the filtering of images or the (in-)authenticity of her imagery. I am interested in highlighting the dominant narratives that can be read by viewers and the 'take away' messages that invariably integrate Griner's public and private lives. To this effect, I comment on three representative images below that relate to (1) the courting phase or 'build up' of the Griner–Johnson relationship, (2) their 'on court' relationship, which helps challenge a heteronormative sporting space and (3) an image of them 'post court' from the day of their wedding.

Courting

The trajectory and history of Griner and Johnson's relationship is concisely summarised by Reinhart (2015) in a short article that followed their wedding on 8 May 2015. It is also illustrated on Griner's Instagram account via the increasingly romantic and physical imagery that appears from June 2014 to the time of writing. For example, an image of the two posted on 11 September 2014 shows the couple early on in their relationship, and presumably in the locker room at the 2014 WNBA All-Star game (@brittneygriner, 2014b). Both were selected as league all-stars and played for the Western Conference team. In the black and white selfie from the day in July 2014 (but posted in September), the women tilt their heads in towards the centre of the image, and their heads touch at the top. Johnson smiles broadly, whereas Griner offers a half-smile, appearing happy and relaxed, with her eyes slightly shut. They are both wearing matching Adidas t-shirts with the word, 'West' across the top. In the background, one can see the familiar signs of a locker/changing room, with additional sports gear, hangers and cubicles visible.

The image itself shows two women who can be read as close friends or teammates and is not necessarily signifying a romantic relationship. It was taken in July 2014 (during the All-Star game) only one month after the two began dating, photographing and sharing images of themselves as a couple online. As such, it is the accompanying caption that proves significant in the designation of this as an image that represents their romantic relationship. It tags Johnson (@missvol25) and reads: 'Hey my little sugar pie honey bun!!! My little All-Star #WCW !!! love you baby! @missvol25' (@brittneygriner, 2014a). In this caption, Griner references Johnson as her 'Woman Crush Wednesday (#WCW)', a hashtag used to indicate that someone has affection for a woman (whether it is a celebrity or someone that is only known to that person) and also as her 'baby'. The two frequently used the #WCW to refer to one another early on in their relationship, especially while they were slowly revealing themselves as a couple to fans and followers. The comments from followers are mainly positive, with many celebrating the couple in various ways, though a few do use religious references to criticise Griner for being gay. Overall, 7520 followers 'liked' the image by choosing the ♥ option available to intimate approval of an image, which is in line with many other posts featuring Johnson and Griner. Photos of them together tend to elicit more likes that other 'backstage' photos of Griner engaged in other non-basketball-related activities.

On court

In addition to having basketball-related (albeit, off court) images, Griner's Instagram page features a number of images which highlight the two women playing against each other on the court. Johnson and Griner competed against each other as college athletes and currently do so as members of opposing teams in the WNBA, and in one particular image from 21 February 2015, Griner has a created a humorous meme that acknowledges their shared excellence in basketball and also invariably 'queers' the basketball court (@brittneygriner, 2015a). The image is a professional photograph (not a selfie) of the two women competing against each other in the WNBA (Griner for the Phoenix Mercury and Johnson for the Tulsa Shock). The photo features Griner blocking a shot attempt by Johnson by pinning it against the backboard, an action that is not common in women's basketball. Griner's hand is seemingly only a few inches below the rim, and her face looks intense as she stretches to block the shot. The tattoos on her arms are readily visible and her dreadlocked hair is contained in a hair tie at the base of her neck. Though it is an intense action shot, Johnson appears slightly vulnerable as her head is extended back in the course of her shot attempt. Her long ponytail is splayed to the left of her head and her red-painted fingernails are discernible as her arms stretch up to shoot the ball. Though presumably dictating action as the offensive player who is positioned close to the basket, Johnson's body seems to be off-kilter.

While the image is impressive in and of itself as a photo of two highly skilled basketball players, it is the addition of text that helps to further demonstrate the many layers to this photo. Griner has added the text 'When You Get Denied By Bae' into the lower left-hand corner of the image. To be 'denied' in basketball means that you have your shot attempt blocked by another person and is usually more than a mere block, but represents an active and impressive 'rejection' of a shot. More importantly in this image, Griner (as the shot blocker) refers to herself as 'bae' which is a slang term for baby or sweetie. By incorporating this text onto the photo itself to create a version of a meme, Griner refuses to let this image be read simply as an impressive sport photograph. It is very much an image wherein the multiple facets of their subjectivities – as competitors and as partners in a lesbian relationship – refuse to be separated. This refusal to be silenced on the court appears in other images as well, wherein Griner plays with and queers the norms of basketball to make Black lesbian desire and relationships visible and apparent on the court. This refusal represents a direct challenge to practices employed to sanitise and de-sexualise sporting spaces for lesbians.

Post-court

Much of the imagery and posts on both Griner and Johnson's Instagram accounts invariably deals with their basketball experiences, celebrity and lives. They actively chronicle their relationship ups and downs (mostly ups) via Instagram, and this included the times when they were in disparate locations playing basketball in their WNBA off-seasons (Griner in China and Johnson in Russia) as well as when they were together with family and friends. Their relationship follows a homonormative narrative; their initial courting was followed by an engagement (announced via Instagram), wedding planning and then a wedding in Phoenix on 8 May 2015 (Reinhart, 2015). This narrative, however, was abruptly disturbed on 22 April 2015, when both women were arrested and charged with assault and disorderly conduct in what has been described as a domestic dispute between the two (ESPN.com, 2015). Both women suffered minor injuries including a bite mark on Griner's finger (ibid.) and, it was later revealed, a concussion for Johnson. Both undertook counselling, were sanctioned by the WNBA and suspended for seven games without pay (WNBA, 2015).

Both Instagram accounts were relatively silent after the incident; Griner posted a veiled message to a family member (but not a new image) on 22 April and then not again until 10 May 2015, when she posted a picture of the two women on their wedding day (@brittneygriner, 2015b). In the image, the two face one another and are dressed in their wedding attire – Johnson in a strapless white dress and Griner in a suit. Their eyes are closed and both are smiling. Johnson's head is tilted back and she nuzzles/bites Griner's chin with her smiling mouth. This playful bite resembles an image posted on Johnson's page shortly after their arrest, wherein Johnson posted a selfie of her playfully biting Griner's cheek with the following message to their followers:

> WE'RE OK! @brittneygriner and I are home, injury-free, and still wedding planning! We know we must set better examples, even during the most trying times, and we are EXTREMELY sorry for all the negative attention we brought to ourselves, our family, and the league. We are actively seeking help in order to do BETTER. Thanks for all the Love, Support, and Prayers that were sent our way. #LoveLife #StillBlessed #WorkInProgress #NobodysPerfect. (@missvol25, 2015)

This incident, image and the accompanying message come at a time when US professional sport leagues are being asked to seriously consider the issue of domestic violence as perpetuated by their sport stars. This particular incident sparked calls for the WNBA to address the issue and punish the players for the involvement. They responded with the issuance of suspensions and a commitment to educate other players in the league about the topic. However, if their wedding and wedding imagery are any indication, Griner and Johnson seemingly moved on quickly by posting 'humorous' images and references. In addition to the text above, Griner released a public statement through her attorney, David Michael Cantor, which proved to be a bit more serious and reinforced her status as a role model for others:

> It is never OK for an argument to turn physical. This will never happen again, and I take my relationship and my responsibility as a role model seriously. I am committed to making positive changes and I plan to use what I have learned to set a good example and help make a difference in the world around me. (qtd. in ESPN.com, 2015)

As the incident and subsequent responses are still relatively current, the full implications and consequences of the transgression remain to be seen.

In/conclusion

> We as the readers must continually ask ourselves not simply what we are looking at but what are we looking for. What are the deepest desires of the self that one might expect from a certain text and what happens when those desires or expectations are unmet? Is this the fault of the creator or the reader for projecting? We want to be shown so vividly and accurately the truth of our lives and of ourselves, but that story is not always triumphant. (Green, 2013, p. 292)

In addition to providing imagery which challenges the invisibility of Black lesbian desire, romance and physicality, Griner and Johnson will also inevitably open up discussions about the invisibility about discussions of domestic abuse within LGB relationships. Judging by their followers' responses, it appears that both challenges to these invisibilities might be equally necessary and productive. The aforementioned wedding picture of Griner and Johnson garnered 10,700 likes (followers choosing the ♥ option alongside the image) which is higher than any other post on Griner's page. Many of the followers' comments proved congratulatory in nature and encouraged the couple to move forward with their relationship. While this could be an indication that domestic violence is not taken seriously, I would also like to suggest that it emphasises the need for a 'happy ending' and 'positive' visibility for a Black couple in a lesbian relationship. However, I am cognizant that my limited engagement with audience responses to Griner's posts is a significant limitation of this paper. Future research should consider the viability of this paper's suggestion of digital activism by Griner through interviews and analysis with followers who consume and engage with these images.

Furthermore, my reading of several visual representations of their relationship as positive is open to critique, especially in the light of concerns related to their domestic violence incident, their support of the 'mainstreaming of LGB activism' and the performance of homonormativity within their relationship (Leimbach, 2011). Nevertheless, I contend that their reach via Instagram in the light of their status as celebrity athletes allows them to potentially support, inspire and comfort a variety of young followers who now have an additional way to consider, imagine and understand Black lesbian relationships, desire and romance, even when they are not triumphant (Green, 2013). This proves especially important to LGB youth who invoke digital cultures as they come to understand and experience their sexual lives, bodies, subjectivities and possibilities.

Notes

1. Since the first draft of this manuscript was submitted for review (16 May 2015), the romantic relationship between Griner and Johnson has ended. The two were married in Arizona on 8 May 2015, and their wedding was featured in a New York Times article shortly thereafter (see Reinhart, 2015). Reinhart (2015) chronicles their relationship, discusses their recent arrests for domestic violence and includes references to their future aspirations, which involved having children. On 5 June 2015, Johnson took to Instagram to announce that she was pregnant and supplied the tag: #WelcomeToTheJohnsonGrinerFamily, effectively implying that this news would be greeted positively by Griner and Johnson. On 6 June 2015, it was reported that Griner had filed for an annulment of their marriage, effectively seeking to document their marriage as null and void. This annulment request was denied, and the case is proceeding as a 'dissolution of the marriage with minor children' with the next court date set for 23 September 2015 (Voepel, 2015). The break-up of the Johnson–Griner marriage invariably led to the erasure (from their personal accounts) of many Instagram photos featuring the two women together as a couple. Nevertheless, screenshots of many images of the two still exist online and can be accessed through a basic search on google of 'Griner and Johnson images'. I suggest that the current status of their relationship invariably impacts, but it does not negate, the central argument of this paper which is that this imagery can be read as a form of digital activism in that it challenges the invisibility of Black lesbian athletes.
2. The use of the term 'lesbian' within this article is contentious insofar as Johnson has stated that she is not a lesbian (Reinhart, 2015). Therefore, I avoid using this term when referring to Johnson, but I do refer to her relationship with Griner as being a lesbian relationship. In using this term, I mean to suggest that they are two women involved in an intimate relationship. While this tension around identification and categories is worthy of further analysis, and does reference questions about lesbian identify for Black women in particular, a thorough discussion of the politics and tensions of LGB identification and terminology is beyond the scope of this essay. See Bowleg et al., 2004, 2008 .
3. I use the term troll to refer to someone who seeks to instigate conflict on social media platforms. This is sometimes equated with online harassment or abuse.
4. A term adopted by some Black lesbians who embrace a more masculine or gender-neutral aesthetic. I have used this term and did not locate it among the terminology utilised by Griner to define herself. See Lane-Steele (2011) for more on black female lesbian masculinity and Moore (2006) for discussions of gender expression in Black lesbian communities.
5. I put 'publicly' in quotations to indicate the tensions around the publication declaration assigned to Griner. Griner asserted that she did not feel a formal announcement about her sexuality was warranted as she has been open about her lesbian sexuality. However, SI.com released a video wherein Griner speaks of coming out, and this generated a separate news story. For more analysis of this, see Fagan (2013).
6. GLAAD is a US NGO that works on issues related to LGBT rights, mainly as they relate to media. Originally, GLAAD was an acronym that stood for 'Gay and Lesbian Alliance against Defamation', though now, the organisation seeks to be more inclusive in its work.

Acknowledgements

The author would like to thank Olu Jenzen, Lakesia Johnson, Anne Michelle Mitchell and the two anonymous reviewers for important feedback and support on the preparation of this manuscript. Any errors are my own.

Disclosure statement

No potential conflict of interest was reported by the author.

References

@brittneygriner. (2014a). Retrieved May 15, 2015, from https://instagram.com/brittneygriner/

@brittneygriner. (2014b, September 11). Retrieved May 15, 2015, from https://instagram.com/p/syf2pJTBR6/?taken-by=brittneygriner

@brittneygriner. (2015a, February 21). Retrieved May 15, 2015, from https://instagram.com/p/zW3MJBTBQJ/?taken-by=brittneygriner

@brittneygriner. (2015b, May 10). Retrieved May 15, 2015, from https://instagram.com/p/2ggdaOzBXW/?taken-by=brittneygriner

@missvol25. (2015, April 25). Retrieved May 15, 2015, from https://instagram.com/p/14hPyJywm4/?taken-by=missvol25

Associated Press (AP). (2012, April 3). Kim Mulkey bothered by taunts. Retrieved May 15, 2015, from http://espn.go.com/womens-college-basketball/tournament/2012/story/_/id/7767542/kim-mulkey-irked-social-media-taunts-brittney-griner

Atteberry, E. (2013, December 5). Baylor students seek to remove gay ban from student code. Retrieved May 15, 2015, from http://www.usatoday.com/story/news/nation/2013/10/30/baylor-student-gov-removes-gay-ban/3295217/

Azzarito, L. (2010). Ways of seeing the body in kinesiology: A case for visual methodologies. *Quest, 62*, 155–170.

Banet-Weiser, S. (1999). Hoop dreams: Professional basketball and the politics of race and gender. *Journal of Sport and Social Issues, 23*, 403–420.

Bowleg, L., Burkholder, G., Teti, M., & Craig, M. L. (2008). The complexities of outness: Psychosocial predictors of coming out to others among Black lesbian and bisexual women. *Journal of LGBT Health Research, 4*, 153–166.

Bowleg, L., Craig, M. L., & Burkholder, G. J. (2004). Rising and surviving: A conceptual model of active coping among Black lesbians. *Cultural Diversity and Ethnic Minority Psychology, 10*, 229–240.

Bruce, T., & Hardin, M. (2014). Reclaiming our voices: Sportswomen and social media. In A. C. Billings & M. Hardin (Eds.), *Routledge handbook of sport and new media* (pp. 311–319). London: Routledge.

Cahn, S. (2011). Testing sex attributing gender: What Caster Semenya means to women's sports. *Journal of Intercollegiate Sport, 4*, 38–48.

Chawansky, M., & Francombe, J. (2011). Cruising for Olivia: Lesbian Celebrity and the cultural politics of coming out in sport. *Sociology of Sport Journal, 28*, 461–477.

Chawansky, M., & Francombe, J. (2013). Wanting to be Anna: Examining lesbian sporting celebrity on The L word. *Journal of Lesbian Studies, 17*, 134–149.

Christensen, H. (2011). Political activities on the Internet: Slacktivism or political participation by other means? *First Monday, 16*(2). doi:10.5210/fm.v16i2.3336

Collings, B. (2014). #selfiecontrol: @CAZWELLnyc and the role of the ironic selfie in transmedia celebrity self-promotion. *Celebrity Studies, 5*, 511–513. doi:10.1080/19392397.2014.980652

Craig, S. L., & McInroy, L. (2014). You can form a part of yourself online: The influence of new media on identity development and coming out for LGBTQ youth. *Journal of Gay & Lesbian Mental Health, 18*, 95–109. doi:10.1080/19359705.2013.777007

CutCreator. (2007). Britney Griner: High school girl dunker. Retrieved May 1, 2015, from https://www.youtube.com/watch?v=tuDfRzY2Vqw (YouTube)

DeHaan, S., Kuper, L. E., Magee, J. C., Bigelow, L., & Mustanski, B. S. (2013). The interplay between online and offline explorations of identity, relationships, and sex: A mixed-methods study with LGBT youth. *The Journal of Sex Research, 50*, 421–434.

Denizet-Lewis, B. (2009, September 27). Coming out in middle school. *The New York Times Magazine*, 36–44.

Dixon, R. (2012, April 5). Brittney Griner called a man because she is athletic. Retrieved May 1, 2015, from http://www.clutchmagonline.com/2012/04/brittney-griner-called-a-man-because-she-is-athletic/

ESPN.com. (2013). Brittney Griner discusses being gay. Retrieved May 1, 2015, from http://espn.go.com/wnba/story/_/id/9185633/brittney-griner-comes-says-just-are

ESPN.com. (2015). Brittney Griner enters diversion programme, must complete counselling. Retrieved May 1, 2015, from http://abcnews.go.com/Sports/brittney-griner-enters-diversion-program-complete-counseling/story?id=30657785

Fagan, K. (2013, May 29). Owning the middle. Retrieved May 1, 2015, from http://espn.go.com/espn/feature/story/_/id/9316697/owning-middle

Fagan, K. (2014, October 15) Held up in customs. Retrieved from http://espn.go.com/womens-college-basketball/story/_/id/10787294/wnba-star-brittney-griner-adjusts-life-china-espn-magazine

Farman, J. (2015). Stories, spaces, and bodies: The production of embodied space through mobile media storytelling. *Communication Research and Practice, 1*, 101–116. doi:10.1080/22041451.2015.1047941

Fedotin, J. (2009, February 26). Griner named nation's no. 1 player, Yahoo Sports. Retrieved April 19, 2015, from https://www.rivals.com/content.asp?CID=916007

Fink, J. S. (2012). Homophobia and the marketing of female athletes and women's sport. Homophobia and the marketing of female athletes and women's sport. In G. B. Cunningham (Ed.), *Sexual orientation and gender identity in sport* (pp. 49–60). College Station, TX: Center for Sport Management Research and Education.

Geurin-Eagleman, A. N., & Burch, L. M. (2015). Communicating via photographs: A gendered analysis of Olympic athletes' visual self-presentation on Instagram. *Sport Management Review*. doi:10.1016/j.smr.2015.03.002

Gever, M. (2003). *Entertaining lesbians: Celebrity, sexuality, and self-invention.* New York, NY: Routledge.

GLAAD. (2013, May 11). Awards 24th Annual GLAAD Media Awards 2013. Retrieved May 1, 2015, from https://www.youtube.com/watch?v=IJZddnpzUB4 (YouTube)

Glass, A. (2013, April 16). It's Official, Brittney Griner will be dunking in the WNBA. Retrieved May 1, 2015, from http://www.forbes.com/sites/alanaglass/2013/04/16/its-official-brittney-griner-will-be-dunking-in-the-wnba/

Gomillion, S., & Giuliano, T. (2011). The influence of media role models on gay, lesbian, and bisexual identity. *Journal of Homosexuality, 58*, 330–354. doi:10.1080/00918369.2011.546729

Green, K. (2013). "What the eyes did Not wish to behold": Lessons from Ann Allen Shockley's Say Jesus and come to me. *South Atlantic Quarterly, 112*, 285–302.

Griffin, P. (1998). *Strong women, deep closets: Lesbians and homophobia in sport.* Champaign, IL: Human Kinetics.

Griner, B. (2014). *In my skin: My life on and off the basketball court.* New York, NY: It Books.

Highfield, T., & Leaver, T. (2015). A methodology for mapping Instagram hashtags. *First Monday, 20*, 1–5. Retrieved from http://firstmonday.org/ojs/index.php/fm/article/view/5563/4195. doi:http://dx.doi.org/10.5210/fm.v20i1.5563

Hillier, L., & Harrison, L. (2007). Building realities less limited than their own: Young people practising same-sex attraction on the internet. *Sexualities, 10*, 82–100.

King, S. (2008). What's queer about (queer) sport sociology now? *A review essay, Sociology of Sport Journal, 25*, 419–442.

King, S. (2009). Homonormativity and the politics of race: Reading Sheryl Swoopes. *Journal of Lesbian Studies, 13*, 272–290.

Lane-Steele, L. (2011). Studs and protest-hypermasculinity: The tomboyism within Black lesbian female masculinity. *Journal of Lesbian Studies, 15*, 480–492.

Lavelle, K. (2014). "Plays like a Guy": A Rhetorical Analysis of Brittney Griner in Sports Media. *Journal of Sports Media, 9*, 115–131.

Leimbach, J. (2011). Strengthening as they undermine: Rachel Maddow and Suze Orman's homonormative lesbian identities. In S. Holmes & D. Negra (Eds.), *In the Limelight and under the Microscope: Forms and functions of female celebrity* (pp. 242–260). New York, NY: Continuum International Publishing Group.

Lenskyj, H. J. (2003). *Out on the Field: Gender, Sport, and Sexualities.* Toronto, ON: Women's Press.

McDonald, M. (2002). Queering whiteness: The particular case of the women's national basketball association. *Sociological Perspectives, 45*, 379–396.

McDonald, M. (2008). Rethinking resistance: The queer play of the women's national basketball association, visibility politics and late capitalism. *Leisure Studies, 27*, 77–93.

McDonald, M. (2012). Out-of-bounds plays: The women's national basketball association and the neoliberal imaginings of sexuality (211–224) In D. L. Andrews & M. Silk (Eds.), *Sport and Neoliberalism*, 211–224. Philadelphia, PA: Temple University Press.

Moore, M. R. (2006). Lipstick or timberlands? Meanings of gender presentation in Black lesbian communities. *Signs: Journal of Women in Culture and Society, 32*, 113–139.

Myrdahl, T. K. M. (2009). "Family-friendly" without the double entendre: A spatial analysis of normative game spaces and lesbian fans. *Journal of Lesbian Studies, 13*, 291–305.

Nike #BETRUE Collection. (2014). Retrieved May 15, 2015, from http://www.nike.com/us/en_us/c/launch/2014-06/nike-betrue-collection

Olszanowski, M. (2014). Feminist self-imaging and instagram: Tactics of circumventing sensorship. *Visual Communication Quarterly, 21*, 83–95. doi:10.1080/15551393.2014.928154

Patton, L. D., & Simmons, S. (2008). Exploring complexities of multiple identities of lesbians in a black college environment. *Negro Educational Review, 59*, 197–215.

Plymire, D. C., & Forman, P. J. (2001). Speaking of Cheryl Miller: Interrogating the lesbian taboo on a women's basketball newsgroup. *NWSA Journal, 13*(1), 1–21.

Purdie-Vaughns, V., & Eibach, R. P. (2008). Intersectional invisibility: The distinctive advantages and disadvantages of multiple subordinate-group identities. *Sex Roles, 59*, 377–391.

Reinhart, M. K. (2015, May 11). For Brittney Griner and Glory Johnson, A Complicated match made on the hardwood. *New York Times*, Retrieved May 15, 2015, from http://www.nytimes.com/2015/05/11/fashion/weddings/photographs-from-brittney-griner-and-glory-johnsons-wedding.html?_r=0

Sesko, A. K., & Biernat, M. (2010). Prototypes of race and gender: The invisibility of Black women. *Journal of Experimental Social Psychology, 46*, 356–360.

Stoelting, S. (2011). Disclosure as an Interaction: Why lesbian athletes disclose their sexual identities in intercollegiate sport. *Journal of Homosexuality, 58*, 1187–1210.

Tiidenberg, K., & Cruz, E. G. (2015). Selfies, images and the re-making of the body, *Body & Society, 21*, 77–102. doi:10.1177/1357034X15592465

Voepel, M. (2015, August 18). Brittney Griner, Glory Johnson make court appearance in divorce proceeding. Retrieved September 8, 2015, from http://espn.go.com/wnba/story/_/id/13459982/brittney-griner-glory-johnson-make-court-appearance-divorce-proceeding

WNBA. (2015, May 15). WNBA President Laurel J. Richie statement regarding Brittney Griner and Glory Johnson incident. Retrieved May 15, 2015, from http://www.wnba.com/news/statement_on_griner_johnson_2015_05_15.html

Towards typologies of virtual maltreatment: sport, digital cultures & dark leisure

Emma Kavanagh, Ian Jones and Lucy Sheppard-Marks

ABSTRACT

A changing technological context, specifically that of the growth of social media, is transforming aspects of leisure behaviour, especially in terms of negative interactions between followers of sport and athletes. There is a growing body of research into the maltreatment of adult athletes, exploring issues such as abusive acts or behaviours against the individual, including acts of physical and/or psychological violence to the person. Existing research, however, focuses upon face-to-face behaviours, and to date the nature of abuse in online spaces has been overlooked. It is becoming ever more apparent that virtual environments create optimal climates for abuse to occur due to the ability for individuals to communicate in an instantaneous, uncontrolled and often anonymous manner in virtual worlds. Using a netnographic approach, an analysis of a popular social media platform (Twitter) was conducted to examine the types of abuse present in online environments. This paper presents a conceptual typology, identifying four broad types of abuse in this setting; physical, sexual, emotional and discriminatory; examples of each form are presented. Findings highlight how online environments can pose a significant risk to individual emotional and psychological safety.

Introduction

As Deborah Lupton cogently argues, 'we now live in a digital society' (2015, p. 2), with social institutions – such as sport and leisure – now being not just underpinned by, but rather intertwined with digital technology. As such, our relationships and interactions with others have altered, with changing patterns of participation and power evident within the virtual environment. Such changes had a significant impact on the ways that we interact with others. In this paper, we explore a particular type of deviant interaction, that of abuse within digital environments, with a specific focus upon sport. Sport provides an environment within which the exploitation of power and authority may lead to the abuse of performers, and it is now accepted that athletes can be exposed to, or directly experience abuse within the sporting environment. Much of the work on abuse in sport has, to date, focused upon behaviour experienced during face-to-face interactions (Fasting, Brackenridge, & Kjølberg, 2013; Rhind, McDermott, Lambert, & Koleva, 2014) and has therefore failed to acknowledge the Internet as a space in which individuals can be subjected to, and experience abuse. This paper explores the types of abuse present in virtual spaces using sport as a vehicle to examine one of the darker dimensions of online behaviour and interaction.

The mass publication of vitriol online is becoming increasingly significant as a social problem. Virtual environments provide an outlet for a variety of types of hate to occur and in many ways 'enable' abuse rather than act to prevent or control it (Kavanagh & Jones, in press), yet to date such spaces have received limited scholarly attention. More importantly these spaces are recognised as an increasingly important site of contemporary leisure activity. The rise of anti-social or morally questionable behaviour in such spaces pose wider questions concerning the acceptance of abuse and what this means for declining or changing societal values, and acceptable leisure behaviour. The ability to appropriately define and classify abuse types is essential for conceptual clarity among researchers, as well as to inform safeguarding initiatives, however, relatively little is known about the types of abuse that occur in online spaces. The abuse of elite athletes in sport has been used here as a platform to commence critical discourse surrounding deviant behaviour in online spaces. Therefore, the primary aim of this study was to investigate the types of abuse that are present, and subsequently to offer a conceptual typology of abuse in order to increase understanding of this phenomenon and guide future research in the area.

Virtual worlds and the changing face of leisure

The technological revolution has reshaped notions of reality and behaviour. At the centre of such a revolution has been the advent of online spaces and virtual environments. Barlow (1990) created the term cyberspace to refer to the present day nexus of computer and information technology networks to create a non-physical terrain created by computer systems. Such space can be used to simply describe the World Wide Web, the Internet as a whole and also to include all global media and communication channels (Blakemore, 2012). In June 2014, it was recorded that there are over three billion Internet users currently active (Interlive Stats, 2015) and the number of Internet users worldwide is estimated to have grown by more than 74% since the turn of the century. The Internet is recognised as the essential communication and information medium within our society (Castells, 2010) and around 40% of the world population has an Internet connection (Hutchins & Rowe, 2013).

In technologically advanced societies, people use technology in a habitual, almost automated manner (Chan, 2014). We barely pay attention to the ways in which it has infiltrated our lives, this is especially true for young people (Guan & Subrahmanyam, 2009). Chan contends that people are living in cyberspace but are not consciously aware of it because material and virtual space have become intertwined and embedded in everyday life, merging the two 'realities' the virtual and real, disrupting the conceptual and empirical stability of the public/private divide (Berriman & Thomson, 2015). Technology is therefore no longer considered separate but embodied. In many ways, it is impossible to separate the person from technology; personal computers or smart phones have become an extension of the self and seamlessly entangled in everyday realities and existence. Digital technologies have refashioned the ways in which people communicate and interact and have a significant influence on every aspect of people's lives; social networking websites and technology remain continually accessible through access to smartphones and personal computers. The Internet provides a new and parallel universe, where virtual reality allows entirely new forms of social interaction (Matijasevic, 2014), where it is easier to reach out to others, to exchange information, to learn, to conduct business, to strengthen social relationships and activities, and form whole new personalities and identities (Matijasevic, 2014; Vakhitova & Reynald, 2014). The immense benefits and opportunities afforded by this continually evolving environment are seemingly endless (Hunton, 2012).

One area that has been significantly impacted by the advent of digital technologies is that of the leisure experience, making it more complex and thus changing the boundaries of leisure space (López Sintas, Rojas de Francisco, & Garcia Álvarez, 2015). Virtual worlds are increasingly providing novel arenas for experiencing, producing and consuming leisure (Arora, 2011). In contemporary society, traditional leisure activities and spaces (television, cinema, socialising and sports) exist alongside those that are technological, in many ways these experiences may be augmented through the use of digital technologies (Bryce, 2001). Traditional notions of leisure can also be reproduced technologically in virtual space; we shop online, communicate and socialise with others, update our knowledge, plan travel, consume and play sport. The Internet has infiltrated our lives and the digital revolution permeates everyday leisure experiences, so much that we cannot ignore the significant impact of these spaces on leisure behaviour. As a pervasive site of leisure activity, it offers a variety of opportunities for both social and antisocial leisure behaviours. The Internet is a heterotopic (Foucault, 1998) liminal (Turner, 1992) space, a space of otherness; attractive due to the sense of anonymity and ambiguity it offers (Bryce, 2001; Rojek, 1995; Suler, 2004). Freedom to move and communicate in these spaces may increase the lure of virtual worlds, but can also be the reason why this can be the site of darker, deviant leisure activities (Rojek, 1995; Spracklen, 2013), where norms and values related to leisure behaviour may differ from the 'real' world. As James and James (2008) suggest, this has led to a realignment of broader agendas of young people, specifically in terms of their being in need of protection *from* risk or as naïve victims or potential prey (Chawansky, 2016) towards a greater acknowledgement of protecting young people from being a risk *to* others. This paper examines one type of deviant deregulated online behaviour, which has become apparent since the advent of social media by examining the idea of virtual maltreatment in online sport spaces. Importantly, the paper explores how deviant leisure activities – in the form of invective digital discourses – can contribute to our understandings of contemporary gendered, racialised and sexual politics and difference. Prior to examining abuse and fan behaviour, it is important to understand social media and its use in modern sport.

Social media and sport

Social media is a term used to group Internet-based applications that allow the creation and exchange of User Generated Content (Hanna, Rohm, & Crittenden, 2011), with an emphasis upon prosumption rather than consumption (Zajc, 2015). Social networking opportunities are vast and ever changing; they help us communicate, share information, learn and access news. These sites include applications that enable users to connect by creating personal information profiles, inviting friends, colleagues and unknown individuals to have access to those profiles. People correspond through these mediums by sending emails, posting written or video content and sending instant messages between each other. Currently, there are hundreds of social media platforms available online including social networking sites (Twitter, Facebook and Pinterest, for example), text messaging, podcasts, wikis, blogs, online forums and discussion groups (Ferrara, 2015; Kaplan & Haenlein, 2009). Over three quarters of adults in Great Britain use the Internet everyday (76%) and social networking remains one of the primary uses (Office for National Statistics, 2015). One area in which social media has had a significant impact is the way in which individuals consume and experience sport. Most professional sports organisations utilise social media platforms (primarily Facebook and Twitter) to keep fans abreast of news (Sanderson, 2011). Professional sports teams, athletes, journalists and sport media outlets connect with audiences creating a social media experience (Sanderson, 2011; Sanderson & Kassing, 2011). Sport is therefore connected, and fans take part in both physical and virtual experience, watching games, communicating with other fans and providing a virtual commentary as if in the stands of any major event. Real-time interaction occurs across sports and fans do not need to attend events to experience connection to a sport.

Although the rapid advancement of computer technology has allowed multiple social networks to proliferate (Hambrick, Simmons, Greenhalgh, & Greenwell, 2010), Twitter appears to be the dominant social media platform adopted by sports organisations and athletes alike (Sanderson & Kassing, 2011). Despite the increasing pervasiveness of social media, however, 'the literature is sparse, inside and outside of sport, that deals with Twitter' (Clavio & Kian, 2010, p. 486), especially in terms of its role in leisure behaviour, and to date, much of the research has focused on the tweeting behaviour of the athlete (e.g. Clavio & Kian, 2010; Hambrick et al., 2010; Pegararo, 2010) or social media use by sport managers and organisers (Hambrick, 2012). An area that has yet to be systematically explored is the growing interaction between fans and athletes (Sanderson, 2016). Twitter allows followers to communicate either directly with, or about high profile athletes, communication can be instantaneous, uncontrolled and often anonymous (Price, Farrington, & Hall, 2013, p. 452) in an environment where, according to Hansen, Shneiderman, and Smith (2011) the norms and values related to the ways in which people interact with one another within their social worlds have changed significantly. Crucially, and unlike other forms of mass media such as television (Boehmer, 2015), the nature of Twitter also allows fans the opportunity for parasocial interaction, or the illusion of an actual interpersonal relationship with an athlete, especially where the disclosure of personal information from an athlete (for example, regarding their home or family life) may create a sense of artificial intimacy with the follower (Marwick & Boyd, 2011). Although parasocial interactions are – in many cases – positive, the nature of social media also makes it a rich environment for less desirable parasocial interaction. It is to this concept, that of 'maladaptive parasocial interaction' (Sanderson & Truax, 2014, p. 337) that we turn, specifically through the idea of virtual maltreatment.

Abuse on social media

Virtual maltreatment in sport is becoming increasingly significant as a social problem (Kavanagh & Jones, in press). The Internet has created an environment where a whole different set of behaviours is possible, where 'old school hate is having a renaissance' (Chen, 2015, p. 52). An illustration of this can be seen in Twitter reactions to the 2013 Wimbledon tennis tournament. The male winner, Andy Murray, received overwhelmingly supportive and congratulatory tweets (Twitter, 2013), yet the female champion, Marion Bartoli, was the subject of a barrage of hostile and abusive messages, demonstrating a clear example of maltreatment through social media. The International Rugby Union Referee Nigel Owens was subjected to homophobic abuse following the 2015 England–France International (Owens, 2015), and Aston Villa Footballer Jack Grealish received threats following his decision to turn down an international call to the Irish squad (Bezants, 2015). Unfortunately, instances such as these are becoming more common. In the daily social commentary surrounding major sporting events, we are continually witnessing significant negative online interaction and in many cases, such abusive and or/threatening discourse.

In line with recommendations from the World Health Organisation, Stirling (2009) uses the term maltreatment more broadly to account for a variety of abusive or violent behaviours that can be witnessed or experienced in the sporting environment including physical or psychological acts that occur within the context of a power differential. Maltreatment can therefore incorporate acts of physical, sexual and emotional abuse as well as bullying and neglect of individuals and accounts for the variety of behaviours that can occur independently or co-occur in sport (Kavanagh, 2014). Recent research in sport indicates that athletes are not immune to experiences of physical (Kerr, 2010; Stafford, Alexander, & Fry, 2013), sexual (Fasting, Chroni, Hervik, & Knorre, 2011; Hartill, 2009; Parent, 2011) and emotional abuse (Stirling, 2013; Stirling & Kerr, 2013, 2009), along with other forms of maltreatment including neglect (Kavanagh, 2014). Stirling (2009, p. 1091) suggests, 'coaches, parents, administrators and athletes all represent both potential victims and perpetrators of maltreatment'. We would go further and suggest that fans and followers of sport should also be added to this list, and that their role as potential perpetrators through the use of online environments should not be understated. Knowledge and understanding of this form of abuse, however, is lacking, and has yet to be subject to any systematic examination.

Research into the nature and prevalence of virtual maltreatment, commonly referred to as 'cyberbullying', is relatively recent (Kowalski & Limber, 2013), and focuses largely upon abuse by and against young people. There is, however, a growing body of literature that explores the nature of online abuse against adults. The literature is somewhat clouded by the variety of terms used to describe such acts. Jane (2014), for example, notes that researchers have used descriptions such as 'hateplay', 'rapeglish', 'signviolence', 'flaming' and 'trolling' to explore the phenomenon. In examining the use of online communication to silence women involved in public discourse, Jane further uses the term 'e-bile' to describe 'the extravagant invective, the sexualized threats of violence, and the recreational nastiness that have come to constitute a dominant tenor of Internet discourse' (p. 532). Willard (2007) sought to provide more clarity to the area through the development of a typology for understanding negative online interaction that includes seven types of behaviours that are witnessed online.

(1) Flaming: sending angry, rude or vulgar messages directed at a person or to an online group.
(2) Harassment: repeatedly sending a person offensive messages.
(3) Denigration: posting rumours, harmful or untrue information about a person.
(4) Cyber stalking: harassment that includes threats of harm.
(5) Impersonation or pretending to be another person.
(6) Outing or trickery: tricking a person into sending information such as secrets or embarrassing information that can be used to send to others.
(7) Exclusion: excluding someone purposefully from an online group.

Willard's classification is useful when examining abuse experienced by athletes and other celebrities within online environments as it helps increase understanding of the spectrum of behaviours that can be experienced, yet it doesn't allow understanding of the content or types of abuse experienced. Thus, there is a clear lack of definitional clarity over the relevant terms. We suggest that, as an umbrella term, 'maltreatment' offers an appropriate starting point with which to examine the types of online abuse seen within the follower–athlete relationship.

A recent study by anti-racism in football group 'Kick it Out' examined social media abuse of English Premier League players and revealed that there had been approximately 130,000 discriminatory posts between August 2014 and March 2015. This equates to an average of approximately 17,000 abusive posts per month (Kick It Out, 2015). Parry, Kavanagh, and Jones (2015) have identified that virtual maltreatment has a number of negative consequences for the victims including psychological, behavioural and performance impacts. These can range from negative impacts on an athlete's self-esteem and/or confidence to sleep disturbances and reduced performance on the field of play. Such behaviour can have a significant effect on all aspects of the victim's life, not just their athletic performance.

The existence of virtual maltreatment and its potential to cause harm, is irrefutable, however, the variety of types of behaviour that constitute such abuse have yet to be systematically explored. Literature examining abuse in other setting relies on the ability to appropriately identify and classify abuse in order to promote detection, prevention and safeguarding. Thus, the paper will now outline a conceptual typology of the different types of maltreatment that can be experienced as part of the virtual athlete/fan relationship.

Methodology

The research design adopted was that of online ethnography, also referred to as 'netnography' involving participant observational research based on online fieldwork (Kozinets, 2010). Due to high growth in Internet forums and the ease of access to rich data-sets within online environments, this form of data collection is widely accepted and used in many fields (Janta, Lugosi, & Brown, 2014). The study focused on the collection of archival, rather than elicited or field note data (Kozinets, 2010) as it used existing tweets, rather than having any researcher involvement or interaction with the online community. The data screening process took place over a two-year period, whereby content from the social media platform Twitter was collected. Two methods were adopted for the collection of data. Brand watch analytics was adopted as a means to screen large data-sets. This commercial software package was designed to identify Twitter posts using keywords based on discriminatory and abusive terms. Searches were run through screening both hashtags and variants of spelling to identify as many instances of virtual maltreatment as possible. An illustrative example could be 'Serena Williams OR Bartoli AND man OR ugly OR lesbian'. In addition to computer-aided data collection, Twitter was observed by the research team and abusive tweets were stored within an excel spreadsheet along with the date of the tweet, the time and the target of the comment and their sport. The research team became 'lurkers' within online environments and did not interact within or manipulate the online space.

Thousands of posts were read and sifted in the development of the conceptual typology. Typologies – defined as organised systems of types – make crucial contributions to the social sciences and enable the forming and refining concepts, drawing out underlying dimensions, creating categories for classification and measurement and sorting cases (Collier, LaPorte, & Seawright, 2012). Descriptive names were assigned to tweets, attached to particular behaviours and grouped in relation to descriptive abuse types in order to create the broad classifications presented. Tweets were grouped based on similar attributes in order to keep types within a classification as close as possible in order to create discrete dimensions of the typology. The process of qualitative description (Sandelowski, 2000) adopted provided a mechanism through which to analyse and subsequently group tweets based on abuse types.

Presenting a typology of virtual maltreatment

It is suggested here that there is a need for context-specific typologies; that is for the typology to both accurately reflect the nature of the phenomenon, and also be useful as a tool with which to analyse such behaviour. The use of typologies has been subject to criticism in sport, for example Green and Jones (2006) have noted that it is rare for activities to fall into the ideal-types that are proposed by typologies, they may over-simplify human behaviour, and that such approaches tend not to acknowledge the dynamic nature of activity, instead presenting a static picture of involvement at a particular time. Finally, typologies may be limited in that they can demonstrate a tendency to examine the activity itself, rather than the meanings, norms and values of the individual undertaking the activity. These are all valid criticisms; however, it is clear that further research in this area is essential. With any emerging area, there is a need for conceptual clarity and consistency in how the area is explored. Consistency of terminology with regard to online abuse in sport is important to allow the transferability of data both between studies and over time (Stirling, 2009), and it is with this purpose that the typology is presented. Based on this, we propose a working definition of virtual maltreatment and a conceptual framework for classifying abuse online within sport building upon existing typologies, but adapted in terms of, and informed by the qualitatively different (Slonje & Smith, 2008) nature of online abuse.

The proposed typology is presented in Figure 1. We use the term virtual maltreatment to encompass the variety of cyber-enabled abuses that can manifest in virtual environments and define it as:

> Direct or non-direct online communication that is stated in an aggressive, exploitative, manipulating, threatening or lewd manner and is designed to elicit fear, emotional and psychological upset, distress, alarm or feelings of inferiority.

Maltreatment online is likely to occur within virtual relationships and is enabled by the instantaneous access and global reach that the Internet affords the perpetrator. Virtual relationships include the follower-to-athlete (coach or official) or athlete-to-athlete relationship, and abuse can be experienced directly or indirectly within such relationships (Kavanagh & Jones, in press). Direct refers to incidents that directly target a recipient, through, for example, the use of the '@' symbol to send a message to a specific user or includes a hashtag # as an identifier or link to the subject of the abuse. Non-direct refer to cases, whereby a message is posted about, rather than directly to an individual. It is also possible for individuals to be alerted to non-direct messages, through 'retweeting', and thus non-direct can also become direct.

Four types of abuse can be experienced either directly or indirectly within virtual relationships (see Figure 1). These are physical, sexual, emotional and discriminatory, of which the final type can be further categorised into discrimination based upon gender, race, sexual orientation, religion and/or disability. An overview of each virtual maltreatment type is presented below.

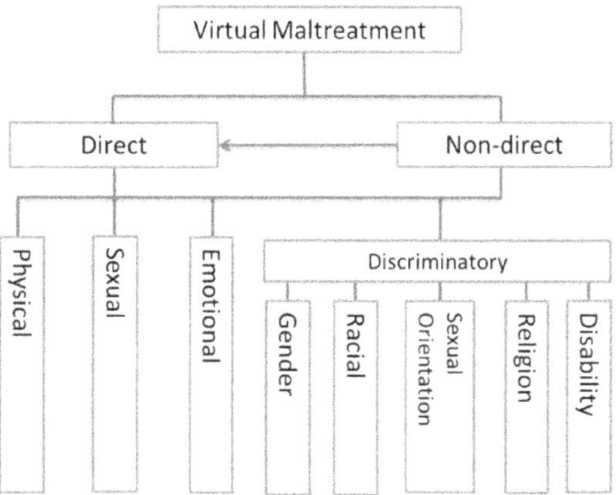

Figure 1. Categorisation of virtual maltreatment in sport.

Virtual physical maltreatment

Virtual physical maltreatment can include threats of physical violence and/or focus towards an individual's physical attributes. Comments can be stated in an aggressive, exploitative, manipulative or threatening manner and can be designed to elicit fear, emotional or psychological upset and distress, alarm and/or inferiority. As Jane (2014) notes, such aggression sometimes manifests as a direct threat, but most commonly appears in the form of hostile wishful thinking. Examples of direct and indirect physical maltreatment can be seen with messages to the Premiership footballer Wayne Rooney, Olympic gymnast Beth Tweddle and tennis player Andy Murray:

> @WayneRooney cheers Wayne you fat ugly wanker
>
> @SkySportsNews #Sportswomen Beth Tweddle on a scale of 1/10 how pig ugly would you class yourself?
>
> I hope Andy Murray loses, breaks an arm and never plays tennis again, cunt.

The examples show a continuum between abuse concerning physical appearance (for example, towards Wayne Rooney) and more serious threats of actual harm (targeted and Andy Murray). New York Jets quarterback Mark Sanchez, for example, received a number of direct physical threats from a fan:

> @mark_sanchez kill yo self tonight! or imma do it for you Wednesday at practice

Indirect physical maltreatment also demonstrated a continuum from 'the relatively trivial, although still unacceptable tweets about athlete appearance:

> Test Serena Williams. No way is she clean. Looks way too much like a man

To more threatening behaviour, such indirect physical abuse focused on the 2013 Wimbledon champion Marion Bartoli was evident: a typical comment was:

> If Bartoli fist pumps one more time I'm gonna knock her out the slag

Thus, it is clear that despite the 'unreal' nature of online interaction, virtual physical maltreatment still exists, albeit in the form of focusing on physical attributes or through threat of physical violence.

Virtual sexual maltreatment

Virtual sexual maltreatment can include threats of rape and sexual assault or sexual acts to which the adult would not consent or comments regarding sexual behaviour with or of an individual. Comments can be stated in an aggressive, exploitative, manipulative, threatening or lewd manner and can be designed to elicit fear, emotional or psychological upset, distress and alarm. Contrasting tweets regarding the two 2013 Wimbledon women finalists, Marion Bartoli and Sabine Lisicki demonstrate the presence of this behaviour:

> Bartoli wouldn't get raped let alone fucked #wimbledon

> Sabine Lisicki – I'd definitely let her sit on my face. Not a great face but those legs are amaze, body ain't too shabby either #wimbledon

It is important to note the use of a 'hashtag' (#wimbledon) within these messages. A hashtag allows messages to be grouped together, and subsequently searched for by other users. Thus, those interested in the Wimbledon tournament can follow tweets using the relevant hashtag, further spreading the message.

Although men are disproportionately the perpetrators and women disproportionately the victims of online sexual hostility (Herring, Job-Sluder, Scheckler, & Barab, 2002), sexual maltreatment is also evident for male athletes. The diver Tom Daley was the subject of the following tweet:

> Tom Daley has a face that's all like: I wanna hug you, but then has a body like: I wanna fuck you #true

As with virtual physical maltreatment, it is again through the focus on physical attributes or the use of threats that creates the key issue here rather than actual physical or face-to-face behaviours.

Virtual emotional maltreatment

Virtual emotional maltreatment includes comments designed to elicit a negative emotional and or psychological reaction and can include rumour spreading, ridiculing, terrorising, humiliating, isolating, belittling and scapegoating. Comments can be stated in an aggressive, exploitative, manipulative or threatening manner and can be designed to elicit fear, emotional or psychological upset, distress and alarm. At a basic level, tweets may simply be designed to humiliate and belittle athletes, for example:

> Fuck u @shelveyJ. Do us LFC supporters a favour and just leave LFC. Or do everyone a favour and just stop playing football.

> Raheem Stirling is a cunt and a waste of space @MCFC enjoy and good riddance

An example of a tweet designed to elicit emotional distress was that sent to Tom Daley after a disappointing Olympic performance:

> @TomDaley1994 you let your dad down I hope you know that

This referred to Daley's father, who had died of cancer before the Games. This type of tweet was echoed by a message regarding football referee Mark Halsey, who had previously suffered from cancer:

> I hope Mark Halsey gets cancer again and dies

> Mark Halsey should've died of cancer

This was an example of a non-direct tweet being received by the recipient, leading to Halsey actually making a complaint to the police about the tweet (BBC Sport, 2012). The level of abuse directed at Halsey and his family was so severe that his wife and daughter were forced to relocate after threats were made on his young daughter's life. This illustrates that tweets about, rather than to an individual still have the potential to cause harm, fear or distress, and should thus be seen as maltreatment.

Virtual discriminatory maltreatment

Virtual discriminatory maltreatment can include comments that negatively refer to an individual's membership of a particular social group based on gender, race, religion, nationality, disability and/or sexual orientation. Comments can be stated in an aggressive, exploitative, manipulative, threatening or lewd manner and can be designed to elicit fear, emotional or psychological upset, distress and alarm. Gender discrimination was illustrated by a direct tweet to the female American racing driver *Danica* Patrick:

@DanicaPatrick you will never win a race they only got you in the sport because you look good now go back to the kitchen

Similar sentiments were seen towards the England Womens' football coach, Hope Powell and Australian Cricketer Ellyse Perry:

Women coaches can't work in mens football just wouldn't work for me imagine Hope Powell managing Utd #neverever

She must have a really long chain to reach a cricket pitch, still don't understand why she is out of the kitchen

Two highly publicised tweets, reported widely in the press demonstrated blatant racial discrimination, both directly sent to the recipient:

@anton_ferdinand RT this you fucking black cunt

@louissaha08 go back to France ya fuckin nigger

Discrimination based on sexual orientation is evident in terms of male and female sexuality. Marion Bartoli received a number of high-profile tweets about her sexuality that were reported in the national press, such as:

I hate Bartoli already fucking dyke come on Lisicki u sexy thing

The former athlete and athletics presenter on the BBC, Colin Jackson, was subject to a variety of messages regarding his sexual orientation:

2 gays involved in tonight's Olympic coverage … Justin Gay … and Colin Jackson #100mfinal

It is clear that a variety of discriminatory behaviours thus take place within the virtual environment.

Understanding virtual maltreatment

The conceptual typology of virtual maltreatment is presented as a starting point for critical dialogue concerning abuse in online environments and can be used to understand the nature of such behaviour in these spaces. This paper, as a position piece, has attempted to provide a framework to guide future research into what may well be one of the most important leisure phenomena to emerge in recent years.

Digitising people, relationships and groups has stretched the boundaries of how and when humans interact, creating a space where darker behaviours can manifest and individuals can feel protected by the sense of anonymity the Internet affords. Virtual spaces create an optimal environment for both illegal and harmful activity. The term trolling has been adopted by the media to broadly account for any harassment, via communications systems. Trolling has been collectively referred to as the 'sending of provocative messages via a communications platform for the entertainment of oneself, others or both' (Bishop, 2013, p. 302). Bishop (2013) differentiates between types of trolling behaviours that occur online and believes that while some 'troll' to harm others or cause discomfort (flame trolls), others are more interested in the entertainment that comes from trolling and gaining gratification from their actions (kudos trolls). As Bishop (2013) notes, trolls show a darker, sinister and perhaps more transgressive side of cyberspace in the form of abuse and vitriol (p. 7), yet not all abuse is carried out by trolls and not all transgressive behaviour could constitute trolling. This media fuelled moral panic concerning the presence of 'dangerous Internet trolls' leads us to miss an important fact; we all have the potential to be abused or become the perpetrators of maltreatment in online environments, it is not just the 'trolls' who chose to harm or attack others in cyberspace; as demonstrated through negative fan interaction.

Certainly, virtual maltreatment can span one off hateful comments within the running commentary of sports consumption to far more targeted, systematic and pervasive examples of abuse. Virtual maltreatment can sit anywhere on a spectrum from statements thought to be idol 'banter' or said in jest to those that include threats of physical violence, racist and/or sexually degrading and demeaning content. Threats target the individual or extend to people close to them including family members, teammates and friends and content spans the very minor to the extremely violent, lewd or abusive, making this a diverse problem to classify and subsequently police. It is therefore important to understand the nature of cyberspace to provide an explanation for the negative behaviour present within it if we are to better safeguard individuals in these spaces. The conceptual typology presented in this paper represents a useful and important starting point in this process.

Some of the characteristics that make online spaces most attractive such as the freedom of expression, perceived or actual anonymity, reduction of inhibition and expression of thought also make this environment difficult to regulate and police (Awan & Brakemore, 2011; Farrington, Hall, Kilvington, Price, & Saeed, 2015). As Suler (2004, p. 321) identifies, 'people say and do things in cyberspace that they wouldn't normally say and do in face-to-face interaction', explaining that much of this behaviour, which he describes as 'toxic disinhibition' directly affects the way in which we behave and interact in these environments. The anonymity or even perception of anonymity can make people more likely to disclose information and enact different moral codes in online environments (Hollenbaugh & Everett, 2013).

The concept of Dissociative Anonymity (the protection afforded by the anonymity of online identities enabling individuals to separate the real and the virtual self) is particularly interesting, leading to a state of 'virtual deindividuation' whereby the personal identity of the perpetrator becomes lost, not within a physical crowd as proposed by traditional notions of deindividuation, but within an environment of safety and anonymity that leads to the social self dominating the personal self. This is augmented by notions of Invisibility (the inability to be seen, or to see others' responses) and Dissociative Imagination (the idea that online interaction is somehow 'separate' from 'real life'). Social media therefore has the potential to become a safe space for would be offenders:

> People don't have to worry about how they look or sound when they type a message. They don't have to worry about how others look or sound in response to what they say. Seeing a frown, a shaking head, a sigh, a bored expression, and many other subtle or not so subtle signs of disapproval or indifference can inhibit what people are willing to express. (Suler, 2004, p. 322)

Online behaviour lacks essential cues in human interaction and virtual spaces act as a cloak of invisibility: 'text communication offers a built in opportunity to keep one's eyes averted' (ibid). As the individual's physical and virtual worlds become intimately entangled, the online persona can become an extension of the individual's mind and personality creating, embodied, temporal and spatial experiences (Suler, 2005). In addition to the perception of cyberspace as a physical space, it can also be regarded as a 'transitional space' – an extension of one's conscious and unconscious mind. It is a space that one may personalise and interact in such a way that it becomes a part of them (ibid), whereby individuals can create hybrid personas. As such, online behaviours have the potential to be significantly different to, and often more extreme and divergent from expected norms of face-to-face behaviour, especially given the broader lack of control of online interaction. Suler refers to these factors as some of the unique psychological features of the Internet that make it most attractive and alarming as a heterotopic space. As a consequence, the virtual environment is a particularly dangerous one in terms of its potential for maltreatment to occur.

Importantly, virtual worlds have shaped modern leisure time; new technologies present endless opportunities for performing leisure, and social media has become a common site of leisure activity for many people. As Rojek (2000) notes, the organisation of leisure has often been driven by technology, and given that we are currently in the period of the greatest technological change ever seen, it is logical to argue that leisure organisation and behaviour will reflect this. Some years ago, Bryce (2001, p. 7) suggested that 'One area that has not been sufficiently considered in the literature is the influence of technology on the organisation and experience of leisure', and to some extent this is an argument that remains valid today.

The sheer nature of cyberspace, together with the formation of ideographic online communities, provides an opportunity for deviant leisure activity. As this discussion demonstrates cyberspace is a deregulated space and can therefore play host a variety of activities varying from legal to illegal providing opportunity for the pursuit of invasive and mephitic leisure (Rojek, 2000). As Bryce (2001, pp. 12, 13) suggested:

> The wild zones of the Internet with their relative freedom from regulation and censorship are able to support deviant leisure ideologies … Legitimization and support of such ideologies in cyberspace may increase deviant behaviour in society as a whole. This suggests that utopian claims concerning empowerment and freedom in cyberspace must be tempered by the acceptance of the use of the medium for deviance, and an examination of mechanisms of regulation to protect the rights of individuals using the Internet for leisure.

It is clear that the Internet and social media in particular provide an environment where people are afforded the power and opportunity to enact 'dark leisure' through abusive behaviours towards other, often high-profile and high-status individuals.

Suler and Phillips (1998) believe that two factors help shape deviance demonstrated in online environments, one technical (people will negotiate technical features to exploit environments) and one social (people will follow the sub-cultures of an environment or act against them). The social element is perhaps most interesting in terms of leisure behaviour spending time abusing others. It could be argued that online environments have a greater acceptance of abusive language and thus this desensitises individuals to the negative nature of such content. Conversely, this activity is carried out as a transgressive act, masked by the cover the virtual world affords allowing individuals a space through which they can break normative face-to-face rules and subvert norms. As Suler and Phillips (1998, p. 276) stated:

> The community and all that is happening there is entertainment in the form of recapitulation of the real world.

The significance of social media as a leisure activity now means that scholars can no longer afford to ignore this aspect of leisure behaviour. The sheer pervasiveness of social media as a leisure activity, when taken alongside the changing power and opportunity provided to young people especially, suggests that this is a growing area of significance within contemporary society. Deviant behaviour such as virtual maltreatment may be upsetting or abusive for some, yet for others it is all a part of the leisure experience and a draw to engage in these social worlds. What is clear from the typology, and data presented here, is that the issue of virtual maltreatment is a serious one and will – in all likelihood – remain so. Further examination is needed to explore online environments as contemporary sites of leisure activity, but more importantly places where deviant or morally questionable leisure pursuits are enacted. As well as understanding such behaviours from the perspective of the individual, the phenomenon of virtual maltreatment allows us to examine a changing landscape in terms of broader deviant leisure practices. As we noted earlier, virtual worlds are providing new arenas for the production and consumption of leisure. Within such arenas, online, less-inhibited interaction may lead to a change in 'traditional' power relations, whereby power increasingly lies with the (often younger) perpetrator, protected from the norms and values associated with face-to-face interaction. Thus, such deviant leisure behaviour becomes, in many ways, easier to enact. From a pragmatic perspective, it becomes easier to target those who are 'different', and from a psychological perspective it becomes safer to do so. Hence, as a leisure activity, online interaction of this nature provides a microcosm within which we can observe the enactment of gendered, racialiced and sexualised politics, often at an extreme level, allowing a potentially illuminating insight into these issues, providing a rich environment with which to further our understanding of such politics, as well as the broader social landscape itself.

Disclosure statement

No potential conflict of interest was reported by the authors.

References

Arora, P. (2011). Online social sites as virtual parks: An investigation into leisure online and offline. *The Information Society, 27*, 113–120.
Awan, I., & Brakemore, B. (2011). *Policing cyber hate, cyber threats and cyber terrorism*. Farnham: Ashgate. ebook.
Barlow, J. P. (1990). Crime and puzzlement: In advance of the law on the electronic frontier. *Whole Earth Review* [online]. Retrieved January 2015, from https://w2.eff.org/Misc/Publications/John_Perry_Barlow/HTML/crime_and_puzzlement_1.html
BBC Sport. (2012). Mark Halsey complains to police after Twitter abuse. *BBC Sport* [online]. September 24. Retrieved September 2014, from http://www.bbc.co.uk/sport/football/19703504
Berriman, L., & Thomson, R. (2015). Spectacles of intimacy? Mapping the moral landscape of teenage social media. *Journal of Youth Studies, 18*, 583–597.
Bezants, J. (2015). AstonVilla midfielder Jack Grealish receives vile Twitter abuse after choosing to play for England over Ireland. *The Daily Mail* [online]. September 28. Retrieved September 2015, from http://www.dailymail.co.uk/sport/football/article-3252028/Aston-Villa-midfielder-Jack-Grealish-chooses-represent-England-Ireland-international-level.html
Bishop, J. (2013). The art of trolling law enforcement: A review and model for implementing 'flame trolling' legislation enacted in Great Britain (1981–2012). *International Review of Law, Computers & Technolohy, 27*, 301–318.
Blakemore, B. (2012). Cyberspace, cyber crime and cyber terrorism. In B. Blakemore & A. Imran (Eds.), *Policing cyber hate, cyber threats and cyber terrorism* (pp. 5–20). London: Ashgate.
Bryce, J. (2001). The technological transformation of leisure. *Social Science Computer Review, 79*, 1–16.
Boehmer, J. (2015) Does the game really change? How students consume mediated sports in the age of social media. *Communication & Sport*. Published online before print. doi: 10.1177/2167479515595500
Castells, M. (2010). *The rise of the network society*. Chichester: Wiley-Blackwell.
Chan, M. (2014). *Virtual reality representations in contemporary media*. London: Bloomsbury.
Chawansky, M. (2016). Be who you are and be proud: Brittney Griner, intersectional invisibility and digital possibilities for lesbian sporting celebrity. *Leisure Studies* [online]. doi: 10.1080/02614367.2015.1128476
Chen, A. (2015). The troll hunters. *Technology Review, 118*, 51–57. Add.
Clavio, G., & Kian, T. (2010). Uses and gratifications of a retired female athlete's Twitter followers. *International Journal of Sport Communication, 3*, 485–500.
Collier, D., LaPorte, J., & Seawright, J. (2012). Putting typologies to work: Concept, formation, measurement and analytic rigour. *Political Research Quarterly, 65*, 217–232.
Farrington, N., Hall, L., Kilvington, D., Price, J., & Saeed, A. (2015). *Sport, racism and social media*. London: Routledge.
Fasting, K., Brackenridge, C., & Kjølberg, G. (2013). Using court reports to enhance knowledge of sexual abuse in sport. *Scandinavian Sports Studies Forum, 4*, 49–67.
Fasting, K., Chroni, S., Hervik, S. E., & Knorre, N. (2011). Sexual harassment in sport towards females in three European countries. *International Review for the Sociology of Sport, 46*, 76–89.
Ferrara, E. (2015). Manipulation and abuse on social media. *Computer Science Social and Information Networks Position Paper* [online]. May 11, 2015. Retrieved from http://arxiv.org/abs/1503.03752
Foucault, M. (1998). Different spaces. In J. Faubion (Ed.), *Aesthetics: The essential works, 2* (pp. 175–185). London: Allen Lane.
Guan, S. A., & Subrahmanyam, K. (2009). Youth Internet use: Risks and opportunities. *Current Opinion in Psychiatry, 22*, 351–356.
Hambrick, M. (2012). Six degrees of information: Using social network analysis to explore the spread of information within sport social networks. *International Journal of Sport Communication, 5*, 16–34.
Hambrick, M., Simmons, J., Greenhalgh, G., & Greenwell, C. (2010). Understanding professional athletes' use of Twitter: A content analysis of athlete tweets. *International Journal of Sport Communication, 3*, 454–471.
Hanna, R., Rohm, A., & Crittenden, V. (2011). We're all connected: The power of social media ecosystems. *Business Horizons, 54*, 265–273
Hansen, D., Shneiderman, B., & Smith, M. (2011). *Analyzing social media networks with NodeXL: Insights from a connected world*. Boston, MA: Elsevier.
Hartill, M. (2009). The sexual abuse of boys in organized male sports. *Men and Masculinities, 12*, 225–249.

Herring, S. C., Job-Sluder, K., Scheckler, R., & Barab, S. (2002). Searching for safety online: Managing 'Trolling' in a feminist forum. *The Information Society, 18*, 371–383.
Hollenbaugh, E. E., & Everett, M. K. (2013). The effects of anonymity on self-disclosure in blogs: An application of the online disinhibition effect. *Journal of Computer- Mediated Communication, 18*, 283–302.
Hunton, P. (2012). Data attack of the cybercriminal: Investigating the digital currency of cybercrime. *Computer Law & Security Review, 28*, 201–207.
Hutchins, B., & Rowe, D. (2013). *Digital media sport*. London: Routledge.
Interlive Stats. (2015). *Internet users in the world*. Retrived November 21, from http://www.internetlivestats.com
James, A., & James A. L. (2008). Changing childhood in the UK: Reconstructing discourses of 'risk' and 'protection'. In A. James & A. L. James (Eds.), *European childhoods: Cultures, politics and childhoods in Europe* (pp. 105–128). New York, NY: Palgrave.
Jane, E. (2014). You're a ugly, whorish, slut. *Feminist Media Studies, 14*, 531–546.
Janta, H., Lugosi, P., & Brown, L. (2014). Coping with loneliness: A netnographic study of doctoral students. *Journal of Further and Higher Education, 38*, 553–571.
Kaplan, A. M., & Haenlein, M. (2009). The fairyland of second Life: Virtual social worlds and how to use them. *Business Horizons, 52*, 563–572.
Kavanagh, E. J. (2014). *The dark side of sport: Athlete narratives of maltreatment in high performance environments* (Thesis unpublished PhD). Bournemouth University, UK.
Kavanagh, E. J., & Jones, I. (in press). Understanding cyber-enabled abuse in sport. In D. McGillvray, G. McPherson, & S. Carnicelli (Eds.), *Digital leisure cultures: Critical perspectives*. London: Routledge.
Kerr, G. (2010). Physical and emotional abuse of elite child athletes: The case of forced physical exertion. In C. Brackenridge & D. Rhind (Eds.), *Elite child athlete welfare: International perspectives* (pp. 41–50). London: Brunel University Press.
Kick It Out. (2015). Kick it out unveils findings of research into football-related hate crime on social media. *Kick it Out* [online]. April 16, 2015. Retrieved April 2015, from http://www.kickitout.org/news/kick-it-out-unveils-findings-of-research-into-football-related-hate-crime-on-social-media/#.VxkpRIQUZ0u
Kowalski, R., & Limber, S. (2013). Psychological, physical, and academic correlates of cyberbullying and traditional bullying. *Journal of Adolescent Health, 53* (supplement), S13–S20.
Kozinets, R. (2010). *Netnography, doing ethnographic research online*. London: Sage.
López Sintas, J., Rojas de Francisco, L., & Garcia Álvarez, E. (2015). The nature of leisure revisited: An interpretation of digital leisure. *Journal of Leisure Research, 47*, 79–101.
Lupton, D. (2015). *Digital Sociology*. London: Routledge.
Marwick, A., & Boyd, D. (2011). To see and be seen: Celebrity practice on Twitter. *The International Journal of Research into New Media Technologies, 17*, 139–158.
Matijasevic, J. (2014). The significance and modalities of internet abuse as the primary global communication computer networks in cyberspace. *Megatrend Review, 11*, 279–298.
Office for National Statistics. (2015) Internet users 2015. *ONS* [online]. May 22, 2015. Retrieved July 28, 2015, from http://www.ons.gov.uk/ons/rel/rdit2/internet-access–households-and-individuals/2014/stb-ia-2014.html
Owens, N. (2015). Being a gay referee has been tough, but coming out was like being born again. *The Independent* [online]. March 30, 2015. Retrieved July 28, 2015, from http://www.independent.co.uk/voices/comment/referee-nigel-owens-on-coming-out-and-homophobic-twitter-abuse-im-gay-in-a-macho-world-but-i-wont-10144815.html
Parent, S. (2011). Disclosure of sexual abuse in sport organizations: A case study. *Journal of Child Sexual Abuse, 20*, 322–337.
Parry, K. D., Kavanagh, E., & Jones, I. (2015) Adoration and abuse: The impact of virtual maltreatment on athletes. *The Conversation* [online]. December 14, 2015. Retrived from www.theconversation.com
Pegararo, A. (2010). Look who's talking? – Athletes on Twitter: A case study. *International Journal of Sport Communication, 3*, 501–515.
Price, J., Farrington, N., & Hall, L. (2013). Changing the game? The impact of Twitter on relationships between football clubs, supporters and the sports media. *Soccer & Society, 14*, 446–461.
Rhind, D., McDermott, J., Lambert, E., & Koleva, I. (2014). A review of safeguarding cases in sport. *Child Abuse Review, 6*, 418–426.
Rojek, C. (1995). *Decentring leisure*. London: Sage.
Rojek, C. (2000). *Leisure and culture*. London: Macmillan.
Sandelowski, M. (2000). Whatever happened to qualitative description? *Research in Nursing & Health, 23*, 334–340.
Sanderson, J. (2011). To tweet or not to tweet: Exploring division 1 athletic departments' social-media policies. *International Journal of Sport Communication, 4*, 492–513.
Sanderson, J. (2016). Its all your fault: Identity and fan messaging at the intersection of fantasy sport and social media. In N. Bowman, J. Spinda, & J. Sandserson (Eds.), *Fantasy sports and the changing sports media industry: Media, players, and society* (pp. 197–214). Lanham, MD: Lexington.

Sanderson, J., & Kassing, J. W. (2011) Tweets and blogs: Transformative, adversarial, and integrative developments in sports media. In A. C. Billings (Ed.), *Sports media: Transformation, integration, consumption* (pp. 114–127). New York, NY: Idea Group Global.
Sanderson, J., & Truax, C. (2014). "I hate you man!": Exploring maladaptive parasocial interaction expressions to college athletes via Twitter. *Journal of Issue in Intercollegiate Athletics, 7*, 333–351.
Slonje, R., & Smith, P. (2008). Cyberbullying: Another main type of bullying? *Scandinavian Journal of Psychology, 49*, 147–154.
Spracklen, K. (2013). *Leisure, sport and society*. London: Palgrave Macmillan.
Stafford, A., Alexander, K., & Fry, D. (2013). Playing through pain: Children and young people's experiences of physical aggression and violence in sport. *Child Abuse Review, 22*, 287–299.
Stirling, A. E. (2009). Definitions and constituents of maltreatment in sport: Establishing a conceptual framework for research practitioners. *British Journal of Sports Medicine, 43*, 1091–1099.
Stirling, A., & Kerr, G. (2009). Abused athletes' perceptions of the coach athlete relationship. *Sport in Society, 12*, 227–239.
Stirling, A. E. (2013). Understanding the use of emotionally abusive coaching practices. *International Journal of Sports Science and Coaching, 8*, 625–640.
Stirling, A. E., & Kerr, G. A. (2013). The perceived effects of elite athletes' experiences of emotional abuse in the coach-athlete relationship. *International Journal of Sport and Exercise Psychology, 11*, 87–100.
Suler, J. (2004). The online disinhibition effect. *Cyber Psychology & Behaviour, 7*, 321–326.
Suler, J. (2005). *The basic psychological features of cyberspace. Elements of a cyber-psychology model.* The Psychology of Cyberspace [online]. Retrieved January 14, 2016, from http://users.rider.edu/~suler/psycyber/overview.html
Suler, J., & Phillips, W. (1998). The bad boys of cyberspace: Deviant behavior in a multimedia chat community. *CyberPsychology & Behavior, 1*, 275–294.
Turner, V. (1992). *Blazing the trail*. Tucson, AZ: University of Arizona Press.
Twitter. (2013). Murray wins Wimbledon. *Twitter.com* [online]. Retrieved August 20, 2013, from http://blog.uk.twitter.com/2013/07/murray-wins-wimbledon.html
Vakhitova, Z. I., & Reynald, D. M. (2014). Australian Internet users and guardianship against cyber abuse: An empirical analysis. *International Journal of Cyber Criminology, 8*, 156–171.
Willard, N. (2007). *Cybersafe kids, cyber-savvy kids: Helping young people learn to use the internet safely and responsibly*. San Francisco, CA: Jossey-Bass.
Zajc, M. (2015). Social media, prosumption, and dispositives: New mechanisms of the construction of subjectivity. *Journal of Consumer Culture, 15*, 28–47.

(Re)constructing the tourist experience? Editing experience and mediating memories of learning to dive

Stephanie Merchant

ABSTRACT

Through an analysis of the mediative techniques involved in the production of videographic tourist memorabilia (specifically souvenir DVDs of learning to SCUBA dive), in this paper I seek to render visible the often unconsidered aspects of visual media production that result in not only visual images themselves, but also by extension, the construction of alternate realities of leisure space and tourist performance. A connectionist approach to the study of memory is advocated highlighting that mediatory technologies, whilst acting as stimulants for recollection, actually inform and construct memories rather than transmitting realistic snippets of past experience. In the paper, it is questioned whether 'authenticity' is a relevant frame of reference bearing in mind that the 'post-tourist' is often perfectly aware of the lack of authenticity in many tourist activities and happy to go along with a pretence. With this in mind, the paper concludes by stating that 'reality' is arguably being edited out of memories concerning tourism's places and practices through the production of commercially driven and produced 'souvenirs'. For the most part, the paper focuses on the experiences of young tourists between the ages of 18–25, the key demographic attracted to the field site in question.

Introduction

> I've been travelling for 9 months now and have collected 11 souvenir DVDs. From America, Mexico, Peru, South Africa, Cuba, Honduras, New Zealand … of all sorts of activities like bungee jumping, snorkelling, shark diving, hand gliding, rafting … one a of a trek … all the theme parks in the US do them.
>
> Emma

At a time when audio-visual technologies significantly infiltrate young (and indeed older) people's practices and experiences, the structure and content of personal and collective memory is becoming evermore mediated and transmogrified (Bolter & Grusin, 1999; Jansson, 2007; Tussyadiah & Fesenmaier, 2009). As such, future understandings of self and place are entering a slippery realm where reality and imagination combine in the construction of virtual histories, ever in process yet never fully loyal to the original instance of experience. This digitisation of the young person's gaze has resulted in increased attention being given to technological mediators such as digital cameras and camcorders by scholars (Tussyadiah & Fesenmaier, 2009), particularly at a time when the use of such imagery on social media platforms becomes so integral to the portrayal of the self, the construction of the generic gap year experience and the ongoing development (or *becoming*) of each young person's identity. As Lupton (2014, p. 164) argues, 'it is not only the data or images produced via digital technologies that are important to research and theorise, but also how the objects themselves [...] are used in practice'. This paper explores such debates in a leisure tourism context, one which, not exclusively but predominantly, caters for young people between the ages of 18–25 (henceforth referred to as 'young tourists'.

The Island of Koh Tao has an established reputation as one of Asia's most popular party and learn-to-dive centres. As part of such learn-to-dive experiences, it is becoming common practice for trainees to be filmed during the final stages of their open water training. As the above quote illustrates, this practice is not limited to the SCUBA scene, but rather is widespread within the tourism sector, but particularly routine within the Adventure Tourism/Sport Tourism industries. Tourists who engage in such activities are commonly given the opportunity to buy a souvenir DVD featuring their skilled selves in the thick of the action, which they can then take home to show their families and friends or to upload on to social networking sites such as Facebook, Instagram and Twitter. It is argued that people have a vested interest in such 'objects' as 'they come to serve as material triggers of personal memories' (van Dijck, 2007, p. xii). The mediated memories triggered by souvenir DVDs though are not mere extensions of the brain, rather they are the products of a 'complex interaction between brain, material objects and the cultural matrix from which they arise' (van Dijck, 2007, p. xii). Thus, using the SCUBA context and training DVD as a case study, in this paper I explore how video technologies can alter young tourists' understandings of underwater space and the memories they develop of embodied actions and experiences.

Firstly, I provide an overview of existing research which has taken the role of photography and videography seriously in relation to tourist activities. Secondly, I go on to outline the history of where philosophers from Descartes (Sutton, 1998) to Bergson (2004) and Deleuze (2003), believe memory to be located, moving chronologically from a 'static, files in the mind' theorisation to an approach that emphasises the ongoing process of becoming *in conjunction with* stimuli from cultural artefacts, such as DVDs (Marks, 2000), and the present. By acknowledging that matter 'informs' recollection, the paper will be set up to consider what entwining these elements means for memory, when their materiality (screen, DVD etc.) is not only an instigator for remembering but also transformative in itself (Damasio, 1999).

Thirdly, I consider the precise ways young tourists' original experiences are altered in the production process. Including an outline of the technological means by which images are 'improved' to become visually more stunning and vivid than the often dark and almost monochrome blue scenes that are seen *in situ*. Finally, the paper will consider the mediation process from the perspective of the young people who took part in the study. Following Barthes (1981), I will consider the various means by which young tourists perform and present themselves whilst being filmed, in order to illustrate that they want to see themselves, and be seen by others, at a later date, in a certain light (for example as adventurous, skilled, happy, etc.).

Having covered these themes, the paper will conclude by asking what these mediatory acts and processes mean for young tourists' individual and shared constructions of space and young tourists' identity. I will argue that the souvenir DVDs encourage the creation of a 'virtual consciousness', where memories are informed by technologies that picture a place that never looked so polished and of a person who (at times at least) was acting for the camera.

Image capturing and tourist practices

For the most part, it is photography that has received considerable attention within touristic studies of identity and place rather than videography. This is predominantly due to the relatively recent accessibility of cheap and compact filmic equipment and production facilities, to the general population. However, the increase in purchases of video cameras led Tagg (1982) and Stallabrass (1996) to declare that videography has followed photography, 'on the one hand democratizing aesthetic production and, on the other, colonizing an ever-expanding range of spaces and experiences' (Crang, M., 1997, p. 363). Additionally though, the advantage of videography is that it also allows what Crang, P. (1997) describes as 'levity and enjoyment' to be captured (as well as sound, motion and a sense of chronology), whilst also adhering to Sontag's utilitarian notion of imagery existing as proof that 'the trip was made, the project was carried out, the fun was had' (Sontag 1977, p. 8).

Dating further back, the picturing practices of photography have been argued to be inextricably linked with tourist activities since the first Grand Tour (Albers & James, 1988; Cohen, Nir, & Almagor, 1992; Crang, M., 1997; Feighey, 2003; Garlick, 2002; Griffin, 1988; Markwell, 1997). Indeed, Belk and Hsiu-yen Yeh (2010) argue that photography and tourism owe the success of each to the other. Heidegger goes so far as to say that the enframing powers of technology were the key characteristic in the turn to modernity, 'the conquest of the world as picture' (1977, p. 134), a way of 'revealing the world in which everything within it comes to be seen as, 'standing-reserve', that is, as something that 'stands by', as a resource, rationally ordered and ready to be exploited' (Garlick, 2002, p. 293). Thus, resources can become knowable and systematised, as Sontag states 'through being photographed, something becomes part of a system of information, fitted into schemes of classification and storage' (1977, p. 156). This way of thinking about visual imagery perpetuated the myth that photography is a realist medium, a representative of truth and science (Slater, 1995). By extension then, photographic practices positioned tourists as disconnected and disengaged from the people and landscapes which they came across, with the camera epitomising the occularcentic and objective nature of their travel experience (Adler, 1989; Craik, 1997; Urry, 1992).

Whilst the study of photography and tourism has been prolific and sustained, actual studies that analyse tourist-produced imagery until late have been rare. As Garrod (2009) has explained, studies of images tended to concentrate on those produced by professional photographers which appear in brochures, posters, postcards etc. (e.g. Dann, 1988; Edelheim, 2007; Hunter, 2008; Pike, 2002; Scarles, 2004). In recent years, studies concerning the specificities of tourist produced imagery have opened up theorisations of how and why tourists engage with the practice of photography and/or videography. Indeed research has begun to explore the ways in which tourists produce and consume touristically through the medium of photography (Caton & Santos, 2008; Haldrup & Larsen, 2004; Larsen, 2006; Scarles, 2009). This paper sits somewhere in between both such approaches, as on the one hand, the analysis focuses on professionally produced imagery that is burned onto a DVD, but on the other, this footage is of the young tourists themselves as they learn to negotiate the underwater world as part of the PADI, Open Water, SCUBA dive training. Consequently, the paper cross cuts the aims of previous research, attempting to deconstruct the image-making processes which contribute to the production of the underwater souvenir DVD (processes which are common within broader tourism film productions such as adverts, documentaries and interactive entertainment stations), whilst also taking into account the potential for memory manipulation such media may have on tourist divers. This, I would argue, could be synonymous with the even more contemporary 'selfie'/'head-cam' productions people create for themselves. In line with this, within a tourism context, Larsen has argued that 'instead of understanding photographs as reflections or distortions of a pre-existing world, photography can be understood as a technology of worldmaking' (2006, p. 78)

Considering why people choose to capture their experiences and extending the argument above – that visual practices allow for an ordering of understandings of place and people – Garlick (2002) has noted that, whilst picturing practices dislocate visual stimuli from the sites in which they were first conceived, they become re-ordered into sites of self-representation, contributing to the construction of memory and self identity. Thus, Garlick (2002) links photography to the Foucauldian concept of one's 'life as a work of art'. Pictures, and more recently footage of holiday activities can be captured and brought back for a number of reasons, but existing research has pinpointed two in particular, which I later argue are not mutually exclusive, yet result in a tension over meaning construction in the production process. On the one hand then, images are taken, uploaded to social media *in situ* and/or brought home for public viewing. This fits with Garrod's (2009, p. 347) contention that photos (and by extension film) become part of a hermeneutic cycle of 'tourism (re)production, in which tourists seek to acquire photographic images of the place they are visiting so that they can prove to others that they have been there'. On the other hand though, this objective collation of time and place has been deconstructed of late, with tourists themselves being written back into the story as embodied active agents within the context of image production (Haldrup & Larsen, 2004). As such, the agency of the tourist is implicated into the 'narrative construction', consequently feeding back into Foucault's idea of 'life as a work of art'.

In Foucault's words, 'arts of existence' are 'those reflective and voluntary practices by which men [*sic*] not only set themselves rules of conduct, but seek to transform themselves, to change themselves in their singular being, and to make their life into an oeuvre that carries certain aesthetic values and certain stylistic criteria' (Foucault, 1992, pp. 10–11). In other words, not only is an idealised self-image constructed and manipulated to present to others, but also for the self. Keepsakes or souvenirs become the instigators of memory work concerning past activities, and on one's gap year these may allow for a certain 're-configuring' of the self, due to increased freedom and an escape from the lifestyle constraints of the home (Urry, 1992). A prefigured scene can be transformed into a souvenir for times to come (Crang, M., 1997). Even with a postmodern resurgence in 'retro' photo/video-graphic artefacts such as Polaroid Prints, Photo-Booth Strips and Hi-8 tapes, such vintage-esque imagery serves as a marker of devotion to the disjointed styling practices of the time. This then is not just retrospective use of imagery, but it informs the imagery's very construction. Memories and their 'tone' are not merely *captured* in the process of taking a photo or video but are often *created* in the very act. However, whilst this may change the way we think about tourist performance and imagery, it does not necessarily reflect insincerity in the image production process. What it does do though, is further infiltrate the practice of image capture within the tourist practice and performance, rendering the various stages of capture and production as impossible to think about in isolation. This highlights that photo- (or video-) graphy is a social performance in itself, not simply a way of transparently capturing the tourist performances taking place *beyond* the viewfinder (Crang, M., 1997; Crang, P., 1997; Edensor, 2001; Haldrup & Larsen, 2004; MacCannel, 1979).

Before turning to the precise ways in which the alterations and mediations noted above are made, I first move on to provide a background to theoretical understandings of memory.

Situated memory?

In John Sutton's (1998) book *Philosophy and memory: Descartes to Connectionism*, the author outlines a timeline of conflicting theorisations of memory's location. It is argued that throughout the nineteenth century, the locus of memory was for the most part believed to rest solely within the mind, stored in a manner similar to the files in a filing cabinet, ready to be retrieved upon being stimulated by an object or image, or more simply, upon the request of the thinker. These stored memories were considered to be hermetically sealed from the changing world in which the perceiver was living – stable in the face of time and unchanging with context. However, in the twentieth century, conceptualisations began to shift, and in so doing, highlighted the interconnectedness that exists between time, context and memory. Bergson's work in this domain was particularly important in changing previous ways of thinking about memory. In *Matter and Memory* (2004), Bergson explains that in perceiving matter we do not simply perceive an object in its present state. By contrast, we mix in with our real-time perception the myriad recollections that we have gained previously, making our understandings complicated deeply by the temporal – 'enriching' perception of the present yet making it vastly subjective. Thus, memory is seen to be an ever evolving, inter-subjective thread which confirms and simultaneously troubles our understanding of the past, at once alluding to encounters which took place but conflating the details of this particular past with those of subsequent pasts, as well as the present. Drawing on Bergson, van Dijck (2007) explains this more clearly, stating that 'the present dictates memories of the past [...] the brain does not store memories but recreates the past each time it is invoked [so that] the memory of the past serves as a base'. Incorporating and building upon Bergson's work, Deleuze (2003) tells a similar story of the intersubjective nature of perception and memory, although he relates this specifically to the receipt and visualisation of cinematic images. Deleuze argues that,

> Instead of a continued memory, as function of the past which reports a story, we witness the birth of memory, as function of the future which retains what happens in order to make it the object to come of the other memory ... [M]emory could never evoke and report the past if it had not already been constituted at the moment when past was still present, hence in an aim to come. It is in fact for this reason that it is behaviour: it is in the present that we make memory, in order to make use of it in the future when the present will be past.
>
> 2005, p. 334

Therefore, we have moved from thinking about memory as being firm and steady, to instead as fractured; 'from a history sought in the continuity of memory to a memory cast in the discontinuity of history' (Hoskins, 2001, p. 334). This troubles our conceptualisations of 'what has been, can, and should be remembered' (Hoskins, 2001, p. 334).

In this paper, I want to think of memories in this way. Not as a collection of static, files in the mind, but rather I want to think about a re-collection as something which is 'rewritten each time' it is intentionally sought, or brought to the fore subconsciously (van Dijck, 2007, p. 32). However, whilst this 'rewriting' may enrich our understanding of the way we perceive the *present*, at the same time it troubles the extent to which we can rely on personal memory to gain realistic accounts of the past. If we intersect here a further mediating player, that of visual media (in this case souvenir DVDs of learning to dive), the blurring of memory, reality and digitally altered imagery would make for a recollection which is even further removed from the original experience, as the merging of 'external' and 'internal' images converge into experience (van Dijck, 2007, p. 125).

The fluid and fluctuating nature of memory is something which psychologists have devoted considerable time and effort to comprehend (Johnson, Oltmanns, & Maher, 1988). Whilst a number of scholars, including myself, have highlighted the benefits of using visual imagery to bring to cognition elements of 'genuine' experience which previously eluded research participants (Merchant, 2011; Pink, 2006; Scarles, 2004; Spinney, 2006), of more relevance to this paper is the work emanating from psychology which explicitly troubles the role visual media plays in contributing to significant memory *alterations* over time. Such work builds on earlier studies that built into their methodology exposure to narratives of plausible events rather than visual images in their research design (Hyman & Billings, 1998; Hyman & Loftus, 1998; Neisser et al., 2000; Weiser, 1990; Williams & Banyard, 1998). Irrespective of the method though, psychologists have gone so far as to demonstrate that not only are research participants capable of recollecting 'aspects' of previous experience that are incorrect or fabricated, but with the aid of visual images, the participants can even fabricate complete events or believe themselves to have attended events fabricated by the researcher (Loftus & Pickrell, 1995; Wade et al., 2002). In fact, it has been argued that memory performance, upon receipt of misleading information can cause between a thirty and forty per cent deficit in accuracy (Loftus & Pickrell, 1995). This type of memory alteration has been labelled 'retroactive interference', the act of altering memory formation after the event (as opposed to 'proactive interference' in which memory is disrupted by events that occurred previous to experience) (Loftus & Pickrell, 1995).

It is argued that people 'tend to think of photographs as frozen moments in time, place faith in them and see them as reliable representations of the past' (Wade et al., 2002, p. 597). Over the last 20 years in particular, witnessing and producing visual images has become particularly commonplace, at times even overwhelming, within our daily encounters. Since the 'digital turn', this has been intensified further still (Laurier, Strebel, & Brown, 2008). Outside of the touristic literature reviewed above, Hoskins similarly (2001) explains that the desire to capture and store memories electronically, in order to compliment our own memory capabilities, whilst not always necessarily the main reason for engaging in photographic and videographic activities, is a process that has increased in demand, particularly over the last 15 years. In conjunction with this, is the increased availability of relatively cheap and accessible image manipulation and film-editing software that further disrupts our understandings of the real and the altered.

It is argued that photographs require less 'constructive processing than do narratives to cultivate a false memory' (Wade et al., 2002, p. 602). If this is true, and research findings seem to corroborate with this theory, then surely, by extension, watching a film of a tourist experience in which the consumer features would prove an even more trustworthy medium of representing past experiences of space and self. As Loftus and Pickrell (1995, p. 725) state;

> After receipt of new information that is misleading in some way, people make errors when they report what they [originally] saw [...] the new, post-event information often becomes incorporated into recollection, supplementing or altering it sometimes in dramatic ways. New information invades us, like a Trojan horse, precisely because we do not detect its influence.

Whilst the souvenir DVDs that form the subject of this paper were not of a fabricated event, they were filmed to certain aesthetic trends of the time. Films were heavily edited and visually modified to produce a product that emphasises the 'positive' aspects of learning to dive, whilst downplaying the 'negative' aspects of learning to dive.

Methodological context

The illustrative quotes and descriptions in this paper emanate from just over a month of ethnographic fieldwork of training and working as an underwater videographer in the popular gap year destination of Koh Tao, Thailand. As part of this role, learner divers would be filmed typically during the last two dives of the PADI Open Water course and consisted of scenes of skills training (mask removal and clearing, compass navigation, regulator retrieval and buoyancy control), with the remainder of each dive being free for 'exploration' under the supervision of the instructor.

As the videographer, I aimed to film the learner divers individually and as groups. I tried to film them looking, moving and interacting as well as the environment and wildlife with which they were interacting. As detailed in the latter sections of this paper, the footage would then be edited and screened to the learner divers after which they were given the opportunity to purchase their souvenir DVD.

Image production

Having contextualised the role of image-making practices in tourist activity, and having considered the mediative capacities of visual imagery to pro- and retro-actively influence memory (and by extension understanding of place and self), this section articulates the specific ways in which meditative practices infiltrate a dive industry that predominantly caters for young tourists. Whilst learning to become an underwater videographer I was instructed to shoot, edit and represent the tourists and the underwater world in a relatively contrived manner. Each aspect of the process is repeatedly rehearsed. The structure of each film is virtually identical yet for the young tourists, each DVD seems personally tailored. Producing films in this manner meets the standards and expectations of underwater videography employers and professional underwater videographer training certification agencies who have developed an efficient, engaging and aesthetically pleasing format of production (typically enabling one film of around 20 min to be shot, edited, produced and screened within a 24 h period).

The cinematographic codes imbued in this format are the culturally constructed ideals of the wider tourist and (the prevalent Gap Year) context. However, they are essentially a compromise between the videographer's capability, creativity, time constraints, the sophistication of the camera equipment and editing suite, the 'performance' of the wildlife, weather conditions and the tourists themselves, as well as the structure of the PADI Open Water course.

Within the broader film framework, certain stylistic techniques are encouraged. A variety of shot types and lengths featuring a mixture of diver action, wildlife and camaraderie are balanced. Thus, contrary to filming in a fluid and continuous way that is more akin to human perception, the film is made to look more interesting, by leaving out the in-between (so called 'boring') moments of perception. The film still alludes to the sequence of events which lead up to the climax of each major wildlife encounter, but the time invested in the search for something 'interesting' to see is portrayed proportionally condensed. Eye-level and low-level angles are deemed more aesthetically pleasing underwater, as they set coral and divers against the blue of the sea and can silhouette divers against a backdrop of solar rays. Adding the occasional Dutch tilt[1] can give a film a more contemporary feel and when combined into a tracking or flyover shot can break up the monotony of continually shooting movement horizontally. These techniques allude to the freedom of movement offered by the viscosity of the water, as to pull them off successfully and smoothly the videographer must roll, stretch and tilt their body with advanced buoyancy skill. Similarly though, picturing the ocean from such 'artistic' angles is not reflective of the views witnessed by the learners who move clumsily and disjointedly above the coral. 'Bookending' the underwater footage of each film are commonly contextual shots of people and places. Jaunty angles of learners 'gearing up', individual zoom-ins, close-ups of boat and school names, company logos, staff banter, staged waving, engineered group shots, with sunset backdrops highlighting the light-hearted and collegial atmosphere in tropical paradise.

Such tactics, tried and tested, evoked the following type of response from the young tourists 'Aaaaahhh, I'll miss you guys!' (Sarah) and 'oh, that's it! I don't want to go home now' (Andrea). However, the tension between the structured and predetermined stylisation of the footage seems almost at odds with the notion of nostalgia. Defined as a subjective sentimental longing to a past event or place, it is surprising that watching an almost generically arranged film has the potential to induce such feelings. Yet the young tourists seem unaware of the routinised nature and construction of not only their DVD but indeed their entire learning to dive experience (or if they are aware of this then they actively go along with the act). This may raise issues surrounding the extent to which relations with videographers, other divers and dive staff are genuine and whether the selective attitude towards what is captured is representative of tourist experience or rather becomes a work of aesthetic appreciation in which tourists feature.

In addition to adhering to certain 'ways of shooting', manipulation of the sequence and aesthetics of the day's diving would continue in the editing stage of production. Editing is an artistic and technical process that requires manipulating shots into an order that enhances the quality of the visual output. Shots may be deleted, added, rearranged. For example, if a number of scenery shots have been filmed on the boat in a row, they might be used to separate the sequences of each diver 'gearing up'. Similarly, if footage of an underwater creature is too dark or out of focus to be digitally improved, older footage of the same species might be integrated into the sequence so as not to disappoint the learners who would often express excitement at the prospect of being able to re-witness certain creatures. For example, Alex commented upon re-surfacing after his second dive; 'did you get the ray? You got so close, I'd like to see it close up, I was too scared of its tail though'. This is perhaps the most ethically dubious element of the film-making process[2] as scenes that were never seen are integrated seamlessly amongst those that were significantly challenging the perceptive skills of the viewers during the screening. The ease with which the divers bought into such alterations either demonstrates their desire to believe in the supposed 'quality' of their experience and/or the trick of 'blind' trust they hold in the videographer. Here then not only is the temporal aspect of the footage re-arranged, but the images are also colour corrected. An underwater camera is fitted with a red filter that maintains the variety of colours that people are used to seeing in underwater documentaries and films. However, as the depth of the filmed dives varies, this can lead to variations in colour intensity throughout the captured footage. To a certain extent, colours can be put back in to the images or taken away to maintain a 'realistic' looking white balance, and so the levels of the footage are played with to achieve this.

The human eye though, is neither equipped with a red filter, nor capable of these sophisticated alterations. Thus, the images that are witnessed post this stage of editing were rarely originally perceived to be so colourful in real-time experience. By contrast, the deeper one dives, the more blue the scenery becomes, as the other colours of the spectrum are gradually filtered out. Divers would rarely comment on this (apparently not so) striking alteration to visual perception. This could be a consequence of the proactive interference that watching underwater films and documentaries has on the divers as well as the retroactive interference caused to their memory by watching their souvenir

DVD. In other words, 'the here and now' is considered to play as much a part in future recollections as the 'there and then' (Barthes, 1981; Hoskins, 2001, p. 335).

In addition to these alterations, further inputs supplement the visual images. Transitions, which seamlessly blur one underwater encounter into the next, allow sudden changes of scenery and activity to wash over the viewer, disguising the extent to which real-time experience has been cropped. Textual headings of dive site locations, fish names, dates etc. are added to remind the learners, when in some distant time in the future they will no longer be able to pinpoint the specific details of the course. And a further yet significant contextualising element is the sound track to the film. Faster paced songs are used for the land/boat sequences to gee up the audience and end on a high, with relaxed and calming songs being used for the underwater scenes. Like the footage the soundtrack is also edited, 4–5 songs cut and arranged to make the film seem longer (and hence better value for money), but equally they change up the pace to maintain the attention of the viewer/listener.

Performing the learner-diver-tourist

As I detailed above in relation to Foucault's notion of the 'self as a work of art' (1991), it is not just the prerogative of the videographer to try and polish the film to the highest possible aesthetic standards. The learner divers themselves, aware of the gazing eye of the camera, contribute to this process quite openly. In *Camera Lucida*, Barthes (1981) analyses the difficulty people have in converging a variety of self images into a single 'image' or representation. The moment a person feels the camera focusing upon them, there is a conflicting desire to acquire a representation that at once captures an essence of reality, but this should also capture the subject in a favourable light so as to ensure that the resultant memory objects will invoke positive recollections and be seen by friends and family favourably. Thus, the aim is to merge one's 'idealized self-image' with one's 'public self image'. In order to carry this out, the young tourists would act for the camera when they realised they were being filmed. Smoothing down hair, hiding and 'not now' gestures would indicate a state of unreadiness to be filmed, whereas 'thumbs up' gestures, performing summersaults, blowing bubble rings or shark impersonations were examples illustrative of a desire to be filmed as the central figure of a shot. Barthes (1981, p. 10) explains his own experiences of being pictured in a similar fashion, 'once I feel myself observed by the lens, everything changes: I constitute myself in the process of "posing", I instantaneously make another body for myself, I transform myself in advance into an image'. Barthes (1981) continues, 'I lend myself to the social game, I pose, I know I am posing, I want you to know that I am posing, but (to square the circle) this additional message must in no way alter the precious essence of my individuality'.

van Dijck (2007, p. 101) referring to the process of photography comments, 'when a picture is taken, we want those photographs to match our idealized self-image- flattering, without pimples, happy, attractive- so we attempt to influence the process by posing, smiling or giving instructions to the photographer'. Thus, the camera's presence not only alters future memories through its mediatory technological apparatus, but it also encourages the young tourists to alter their real-time behaviour, *in order to* make the future memories more pleasurable and exciting. This is further intensified by the commonplace usage of visual productions as media of communication. Indeed sometimes, this is the primary role of the DVDs, as opposed to digital re-memory/embodying aids, their use is solely to portray the 'pleasurable' and 'exotic' experience of learning to dive to friends and family. Thus, 'hyper-mediation creates a new vulnerability [...] a haunting anxiety for missing the 'right' opportunity for communication, and simultaneously the touristic experience itself' (Jansson, 2007, p. 16). The very act of having a camera present shapes the tourist performance into acts of self-presentation; the camera constructs the arena for acting and observing, 'sacrificing the immediacy of experience and orienting activities to (future, distant) viewers' (Crang, M., 1997, p. 365). Consequently, future memory can be determined as much by the divers' imaginative capacities for action as the videographer's 'tools for reconstruction' (van Dijck, 2007, p. 123).

Discussion

In response to Jansson's (2007) call for further research on the nexus between tourism, media, communication and geography, here I have tried to render visible the often unconsidered aspects of visual media production that result in, not only visual images themselves, but also by extension, the construction of alternate realities of place, performance and identity by young tourists and the leisure tourist industry itself. The connectionist approach to the study of memory advocated throughout this paper refutes the notion that 'memories are images of lived experiences stored in the brain that can be recalled without affecting their content' (van Dijck, 2007, p. 41). Furthermore, it highlights that mediatory technologies whilst acting as stimulants for recollection actually inform and construct memories rather than transmitting realistic snippets of past experience. That is not to say that all recollection instigated by film is false or of fictitious events, nor that film is incapable of allowing for an embodying of the sights, sounds and actions presented on the screen. Rather, it is to say that the slippery nature of memory is formed in conjunction with the retroactive influence of the film, which when shot for a particular purpose (to be sold to a particular demographic) is accompanied with a set of experience and place enhancing techniques. From brighter, more colourful images, to seamlessly integrated never-before-seen creatures, footage is cropped, warped in time and made to shine. As Loftus and Pickrell (1995, p. 725) have argued, 'nearly two decades of research on memory distortion leaves no doubt that memory can be altered via suggestion [...] people can be led to remember their past in different ways', and indeed these acts of remembrance will be contingent upon the contexts in which they are taking place.

Thus, there is a tension here surrounding the discontinuity between the DVD as *souvenir* and the DVD as an economically driven, artistic production. The term 'souvenir' literally refers to the act of remembering. The OED (2011) refers to a souvenir 'as something (usually a small article of some value bestowed as a gift) which reminds one of some person, place, or event'. In other words, the purpose of a souvenir is to bring back to consciousness the details relating to a particular experience. Those purchasing a 'dive encounter' souvenir DVD do so to be reminded of the scenery, the people, the animals, the culture and the forms of embodiment which they were exposed to throughout their PADI Open Water course and their time on the island of Koh Tao. Thus, it would follow that they would desire visual imagery that is 'as close' to their real-time encounter as possible. Or do they? It has been argued that the 'post-tourist' is often perfectly aware of the lack of authenticity in many tourist activities and happy to go along with the pretence (Urry, 1992, Wang, 1999). So if the adventure tourist experience 'charade' is entertaining in itself and replete with desirable outcomes, then is *authenticity* even a relevant frame of reference? (Hughes, 1995).

Whilst authenticity is not at odds with the intentions of those producing the DVDs, it is equally not in sync either. As Laurier et al. (2008, p. 9) argue, 'the concerns film editors are orienting to as they assess footage, set edit points and so on are of a filmic order rather than an epistemic one'. The film-makers know that young people don't want to be reminded of negative experiences, and they will only buy DVDs that show the above elements of experience in a favourable manner. Thus, it is in the interest of the film-maker to rely on artistic style, the digital techniques of footage alteration and the manipulability of memory to his/her advantage. This is further complicated by the fact that for the young tourists the DVDs have two roles; the first as memory aids and the second being communication aids; to share the experience with others not present at the time. In this case, the aim of the videographer fits well with the desires of the diver, who is less concerned with accuracy than with perpetuating an idealised representation of place, atmosphere and bodily skill. This may be particularly true due to the demographic and activity being analysed in this paper.

As already noted, the 'idealised self image' comes in to play at this point as divers consciously manipulate their behaviour and attitude when in front of the camera. As van Dijck (2007, p. 127) argues 'the act of memory [...] is already anticipated at the moment of shooting' and consequently filmed dives always involve 'remembrance, fabrication and projection' (p. 123). However, the argument here is that even if the divers recognise the mediatory influence the videographer has had on the production process of film, and similarly recall the way in which they acted up for the camera, for the first two to three times they watch their souvenir DVD, the active practice of forgetting the additional (personal) information, eventually serves to confound the mediated re-presentation with personal recollection. Thus, self-editing out 'reality' whilst becoming increasingly vested in the 'produced'. Comparative future research could explore whether the 'selfie/headcam' prosumption movement yields lesser mediated memories/image products, particularly as the affordability, quality and ownership of associated technologies intensifies further (e.g. through Go Pro, mobile phone, wearable tech). This is particularly poignant in a context predominated by young people whose digital literacy may arguably be developing at a pace that renders the role of professional videographers and photographers somewhat obsolete (or at least reserved for more affluent members of society). This would further question the value of a 'DVD-as-product' i.e. as a material souvenir, as the materialities associated with image production become increasingly superfluous in an age of streaming, cloud storage and online sharing (although as stated the postmodern contradiction in this regard is that young people increasingly seek 'retro' material artefacts to enrich what Benjamin has termed the (1999) 'aura' associated with such purchases.

In addition, whilst for the divers themselves there is the problem of the relatively fast deterioration of personal memory (in contrast to the mediated memories), for those who witness Koh Tao's dive sites for the first time on screen (family, friends, social network users), awareness of the extent to which the images are altered from reality is even more uncertain *from the initial observation*. Thus, as Hoskins (2001) argues, the medium actually becomes the memory as such viewers were not privy to the 'intrinsic dynamic that exists … at the instantaneity of' the live encounter (Hoskins, 2001, p. 342). Ultimately then, neither featured nor unfeatured spectators will be capable of retrieving the 'fullness' of the moment. Jansson (2007) argues that visual media such as these DVDs then, digitally altered and rearranged, become 'scripting devices' which are based on an 'idealized framework for a touristic memoryscape' which are subsequently consumed by the public.

Thus, souvenir DVDs trouble the relationship that the individual young tourist has with the underwater seascape, but they equally construct Koh Tao into a magical tourist destination for those yet to visit. For the divers, previous experience becomes selectively remembered so that the seascape itself is recalled imaginatively as a tropical wonderland, saturated with colour, packed with activity and wildlife. Everyone is happy, everything goes according to plan and everyone gets along in an overtly enthusiastic and outgoing manner. Discoveries are made one after another, new skills are always successfully demonstrated, qualifications are always achieved and at the end of the day the sun always sets majestically into the ocean's horizon. Thus, as van Dijck (2007) argues, moving images, edited, re-arranged, clipped, saturated and framed in a certain style can become contradictory and inconsistent signifiers of a relation *to* and a version *of* tourist space, that was never realised yet is processually remembered and shared with others. Whilst the example of souvenir DVDs of learning to dive are very specific artefacts of digitised and mediated versions of experience within a niche adventure tourism context, I argue that this paper additively contributes to a grander, overarching, contemporary academic focus on the pervasive influence of media technologies on the everyday lives of young people, and in particular on their role in the construction of both personal and spatial identities.

Notes

1. A shot which is framed at a slight angle.
2. However, such occasions did seem rare and were largely due to the failure of an intern to capture good-quality shots in the first place, rather than representing the general ethos of the company.

Disclosure statement

No potential conflict of interest was reported by the author.

References

Adler, J. (1989). Travel as performed art. *American Journal of Sociology, 94*, 1366–1391.
Albers, P. C., & James, W. R. (1988). Travel photography – A methodological approach. *Annals of Tourism Research, 15*, 134–158.
Barthes, R. (1981). *Camera lucida: Reflections on photography*. New York, NY: Hill and Wang.
Belk, R., & Hsiu-yen Yeh, J. (2010). Tourist photographs: Signs of self. *International Journal of Culture, Tourism and Hospitality Research, 5*, 345–353.
Benjamin, W. (1999). *Illuminations*. London: Pimlico.
Bergson, H. (2004). *Matter and memory*. London: Macmillan.
Bolter, J., & Grusin, R. (1999). *Remediation: Understanding new media*. Cambridge: MIT press.
Caton, K., & Santos, C. (2008). Closing the hermeneutic circle? Photographic encounters with the other. *Annals of Tourism Research, 35*, 7–26.
Cohen, E., Nir, Y., & Almagor, U. (1992). Stranger-local interaction in photography. *Annals of Tourism Research, 19*, 213–233.
Craik, K. H. (1997). On the aesthetics of architecture: A psychological approach to the structure and the order of perceived architectural space – Weber, R. *Journal of Environmental Psychology, 17*, 75–76.
Crang, M. (1997). Picturing practices: Research through the tourist gaze. *Progress in Human Geography, 21*, 359–373.
Crang, P. (1997). Performing the tourist product. In C. Rojek & J. Urry (Eds.), *Touring cultures: Transformations of travel and theory* (pp. 137–154). London: Routledge.
Damasio, A. (1999). *The feeling of what happens: Body and emotion in the making of consciousness*. Orlando, FL: Harcourt.
Dann, G. (1988). Images of Cyprus projected by tour operators. *Problems of Tourism, 3*, 43–70.
Deleuze, G. (2003). *Cinema 2: The time image*. Minneapolis: University of Minnesota Press.
Deleuze, G. (2005). *Cinema 1*. London: Continuum.
Edelheim, J. R. (2007). Hidden messages: A polysemic reading of tourist brochures. *Journal of Vacation Marketing, 13*, 5–17.
Edensor, T. (2001). Performing tourism, staging tourism: (Re)producing tourist space and practice. *Tourist Studies, 1*, 59–81.
Feighey, W. (2003). Negative image? Developing the visual in tourism research. *Current Issues in Tourism, 6*, 76–85.
Foucault, M. (1992). *The history of sexuality: Volume two*. Harmondsworth: Penguin.
Foucault, M., & Rabinow, P. (1991). *The Foucault reader*. London: Penguin.
Garlick, S. (2002). Revealing the unseen: Tourism, art and photography. *Cultural Studies, 16*, 289–305.
Garrod, B. (2009). Understanding the relationship between tourism destination imagery and tourist photography. *Journal of Travel Research, 47*, 346–358.
Griffin, M. (1988). Snapshot versions of life – Chalfen, R. *Journal of Communication, 38*, 174–176.
Haldrup, M., & Larsen, J. (2004). The family gaze. *Tourist Studies, 3*, 23–46.
Heidegger, M. (1977). The age of the world picture. In W. Lovitt (Ed.), *The question concerning technology and other essays* (pp. 115–154). New York, NY: Harper Torchbooks.
Hoskins, A. (2001). New memory: Mediating history. *Historical Journal of Film, Radio and Television, 21*, 333–346.
Hughes, G. (1995). Authenticity in tourism. *Annals of Tourism Research, 22*, 781–803.
Hunter, W. C. (2008). A typology of photographic representations for tourism: Depictions of groomed spaces. *Tourism Management, 29*, 354–365.
Hyman, I. E., & Billings, F. J. (1998). Individual differences and the creation of false childhood memories. *Memory, 6*, 1–20.
Hyman, I. E., & Loftus, E. F. (1998). Errors in autobiographical memory. *Clinical Psychology Review, 18*, 933–947.
Jansson, A. (2007). A sense of tourism: New media and the dialectic of encapsulation/decapsulation. *Tourist Studies, 7*, 5–24.
Johnson, M. K., Oltmanns, T. F., & Maher, B. A. (1988). *Discriminating the origin of information. Delusional beliefs* (pp. 34–65). Oxford: John Wiley & Sons.
Larsen, J. (2006). Picturing Bornholm: Producing and consuming a tourist place through picturing practices. *Scandinavian Journal of Hospitality and Tourism, 6*, 75–94.

Laurier, E., Strebel, I., & Brown, B. (2008). *Video analysis: Lessons from professional video editing practice* [online]. North America. Retrieved January 2, 2011, from http://www.qualitative-research.net/index.php/fqs/article/view/1168/2579
Loftus, E., & Pickrell, J. (1995). The formation of false memories. *Psychiatric Annals, 25*, 720–725.
Lupton, D., (2014). Digital sociology. Abingdon: Routledge.
MacCannel, D. (1979). Staged authenticity: Arrangements of social space in tourist settings. *American Journal of Sociology, 79*, 589–603.
Marks, L. (2000). *The skin of The Film*. London: Duke.
Markwell, K. (1997). Dimensions of photography in a nature-based tour. *Annals of Tourism Research, 24*, 131–155.
Merchant, S. (2011). The body and the senses: Visual methods, videography and the submarine sensorium. *Body & Society, 17*, 53–72.
Neisser, U., & Libby, L. (2000). Remembering life experiences. In *The Oxford handbook of memory* (pp. 315–332). New York, NY: Oxford University Press.
OED. (2011). *Oxford English Dictionary* [online]. Retrieved May 23, 2011, from http://www.oed.com:80/Entry/185321
Pike, S. (2002). Destination image analysis – A review of 142 papers from 1973 to 2000. *Tourism Management, 23*, 541–549.
Pink, S. (2006). *The future of visual anthropology: Engaging the senses*. Oxford: Taylor Francis.
Scarles, C. (2004). Mediating landscapes: The processes and practices of image construction in tourist brochures of Scotland. *Tourist Studies, 4*, 43–67.
Scarles, C. (2009). Becoming tourist: Renegotiating the visual in the tourist experience. *Environment and Planning D: Society and Space, 27*, 465–488.
Slater, D. (1995). Photography and modern vision: The spectacle of "Natural Magic". In C. Jenks (Ed.), *Visual culture* (pp. 218–237). London: Routledge.
Sontag, S. (1977). On photography. London: Macmillan.
Spinney, J. (2006). A place of sense: A kinaesthetic ethnography of cyclists on Mont Ventoux. *Environment and Planning D: Society and Space, 24*, 709–732.
Stallabrass, J. (1996). *Gargantua: Manufactured mass culture*. London: Verso.
Sutton, J. (1998). *Philosophy and memory traces: Descartes to connectionism*. Cambridge: Cambridge University Press.
Tagg, J. (1982). The currency of the photograph. In V. Burgin (Ed.), *Thinking photography* (pp. 110–141). London: Macmillan.
Tussyadiah, I. P., & Fesenmaier, D. R. (2009). Mediating tourist experiences: Access to places via shared videos. *Annals of Tourism Research, 36*, 24–40.
Urry, J. (1992). The tourist gaze "Revisited". *American Behavioral Scientist, 36*, 172–186.
van Dijck, J. (2007). *Mediated memories in the digital age*. Stanford: Stanford University Press.
Wade, K., Garry, M., Read, J. D., & Lindsay, D. S. (2002). A picture is worth a thousand lies: Using false photographs to create false childhood memories. *Psychonomic Bulletin & Review, 9*, 597–603.
Wang, N. (1999). Rethinking authenticity in tourism experience. *Annals of Tourism Research, 26*, 349–370.
Weiser, J. (1990). More than meets the eye: Using ordinary snapshots as tools for therapy. In T. A. Laidlaw & C. Malmo (Eds.), *Healing voices: Feminist approaches to therapy with women*. San Francisco, CA: Jossey-Bass, 83–117.
Williams, L. M., & Banyard, V. L. (1998). *Trauma & memory*. London: Sage.

Immaterial labour in spaces of leisure: producing biopolitical subjectivities through Facebook

Jeff Rose and Callie Spencer

This research critically examines ways in which highly popular yet relatively under theorised leisure experiences inform and are informed by the social and political governance of our everyday lives. Specifically, online social networking, as seen through Facebook, actively produces leisure spaces, even if these spaces are primarily constituted through their discursive dimensions. By introducing the critical lenses of Marx's notion of immaterial labour and Foucault's biopolitics, we describe the ways in which leisure engagement with Facebook produces new forms of often hidden labour from users, thereby further contributing to the biopolitical control over many of our everyday experiences. These increasingly nuanced assemblages of leisure–labour relationships further destabilise any contention that leisure and labour are distinct sociological dimensions in people's lives. We consider ways in which Facebook can counter various problematic hegemonic global structures, incorporating Hardt and Negri's hopeful ideas of the multitude as a form of resistance toward global neoliberal capitalism. From this critical perspective, we explicitly politicise Facebook and layer the ways in which Facebook is currently working (and not working) with Hardt and Negri's ideas of a more-realised democracy in order to illuminate some of the flaws in Facebook's structure and typical operation. Such overtly critical scholarship can contribute to further positioning leisure as a dynamic social institution that constantly becomes conscripted into capitalist structures in increasingly covert ways. Such politicised understandings of leisure, broadly, and individuals' social media experiences, more specifically, offer substantial direction for leisure understanding, scholarship and critique.

> Mr Zuckerberg has attained an unenviable record. He has done more harm to the human race than anybody else his age … It works. Facebook is 'the web' with, 'I keep all the logs, how do you feel about that?' It's a terrarium for what it feels like to live in a panopticon build-out of web-parts … It shouldn't be allowed. We are technologists. We should fix it. (Moglen, 2010)

During a 2010 Internet Society of New York lecture, a crowd of technologists was challenged to address (urgently) the issue of the decaying freedom occurring through Facebook's surveillance and manipulation methods (e.g. Kramer, Guillory, & Hancock, 2014) by designing 'freer' alternatives for public use (Moglen, 2010).

Beyond the issue of 'freedom', what possibilities can Facebook serve in terms of making the world a better place, a more democratic and more just place? Although technologists have an understanding of code and web design, additional knowledge and understanding are needed to address contemporary concerns with Facebook's design (Roberts, 2014). 'Fixing it', in this case, requires a cogent understanding and critique of these online leisure spaces, including their place within the reproduction of dominant discourses and power hierarchies.

As critical leisure scholars, what happens in leisure times and spaces should be thought of as necessary components in making the world a more just place to live (Paisley & Dustin, 2011). In the 'digital age', it has become imperative to ensure that 'not only our physical leisure environments but also our online leisure environments are just' (Spencer & Jostad, 2013, p. 76). The largest online leisure environment and social media site in history, Facebook, has 1.39 billion users and growing (more than one in every seven people on the planet). Facebook is arguably the largest shared leisure space on earth. If Moglen's (2010) claims hold, then the leisure spaces created within Facebook are neither just nor free, and are not organised in a democratic manner. In fact, people's engagements with Facebook can produce biopolitical subjectivities, where leisure and labour become intertwined, where users' lives are the object, subject and site of commodification, commerce and consumption. Leisure scholars are uniquely positioned to study these spaces and bring specialised bodies of knowledge to work with others to create more just leisure spaces (online and otherwise). Leisure scholars should respond to Moglen's (2010) call to 'fix it', articulating the ways in which Facebook shapes and is shaped by our leisure experiences.

We initiate steps toward processes of 'fixing it' by offering a critique of the current structure of Facebook's (online) spaces. Our critiques not only analyse current sociocultural practices of engaging with the online medium, but also offer new avenues for understanding how Facebook shapes our leisure experiences. Further, we consider ways in which Facebook can counter various problematic hegemonic global structures, incorporating Hardt and Negri's (2004) hopeful ideas of the multitude. The multitude provides a helpful – if not fully realised – example of what global democratic governance might look like in a post-capitalist world, with democratically organised practice. The goal is to politicise Facebook and to layer the ways in which Facebook is currently working (and not working) with Hardt and Negri's ideas of a more-realised democracy to illuminate some of the often explicit flaws in Facebook's structure and typical operation (Roberts, 2014), including how resistances are supported or inhibited within Facebook. How does Facebook, as an agency-filled entity *and* as a user-constructed experience, structure its use to facilitate resistance, and simultaneously, how is Facebook using the labour of its users to undermine resistances? In understanding these issues in the structure of Facebook's leisure space, we can partially define our roles as leisure scholars as reshaping (or potentially demolishing and rebuilding an alternative to) individuals' social media leisure experiences. While we avoid offering fixed solutions, the use of Hardt and Negri's multitude provides possibilities for a new global governing order, facilitated and augmented by social media. Leisure scholars should increasingly deploy biopolitics (Foucault, 1979/2008) as an avenue for understanding the collisions, departures and ruptures emerging from a leisure–labour nexus.

To address these goals, we engage with a number of theoretical positions that are rarely taken up in leisure studies scholarship. Specifically, we present Hardt and

Negri's (2004) construct of the multitude as a more just and democratic organisation of, and engagement with, social and political life beyond the control of capitalism's totalising grasp. The multitude, however, operates through the material and discursive regimes of Marx's notion of immaterial labour and Foucault's understanding of biopolitical production. Immaterial labour and biopolitical production are important avenues for engagement with leisure experiences because they both suggest that there are dominant forces subtly informing and often capitalising on people's passive engagement with seemingly innocuous (leisure) experiences. Tracing twenty-first century entanglements of leisure and labour, we consider online social networking as an example of Rojek's (2010) amalgam of the two ever-evolving constructs. Reflecting on the increasing interconnectedness of leisure and labour, we incorporate biopolitics and immaterial labour as critical lenses in analysing online leisure spaces of social networking. Critically, engaging Facebook, as a leisure space that is actively produced and reproduced through social practices and discourses, supports an argument for increased social justice within online leisure spaces. Using direct examples from our critical and reflective engagement with Facebook experiences, we illustrate how Facebook mobilises immaterial labour in increasingly common capitalist processes. By extending our academic understandings of the critical lenses of immaterial labour and biopolitics to leisure experiences and analyses, we can better name, denounce and confront injustices, both overt and covert. Immaterial labour and biopolitics have important ramifications for understanding online social networking and the larger field of leisure studies. Recognising and appreciating produced subjectivities – informed by biopolitics and immaterial labour – provide a useful lens in critiquing labour/leisure and subjectivity production in online leisure spaces and elsewhere.

The multitude, immaterial labour and biopolitical production

In order to position Facebook as a leisure space in need of critical analysis, we contend that people's active engagement with social networking is part of a larger trend of an overall decreasing ability to differentiate leisure and labour in our everyday experiences (c.f. Rojek, 2010). However, before engaging with online social networking, we present the constructs of the multitude, immaterial labour and biopolitical production as critical arenas to situate our leisure argument in a larger global context of capitalist social and political order. This shifting of analytical scales, from the interconnected global to the very embodied local self, is necessary for considering ourselves as biopolitical actors who are intimately involved in labour practices of which we are often not aware. Hardt and Negri (2004, 2009), through close appropriation of Marx and Foucault, provide insightful theoretical engagements that serve as a conceptual basis of our critique and analyses of Facebook.

The multitude

Responding to inherent contradictions in our neoliberal capitalist political economy is one of the primary tasks of critical activists and scholars. A global movement that supports diverse local articulations of this often incoherent movement is perhaps the greatest hope in sustaining such a resistance. As various forms of anticapitalist protests gain steam around the globe (Miller, 2005), social and political groups are increasingly articulating novel forms of dissent and resistance

(Mitchell & Staeheli, 2005; Wainwright & Kim, 2008). Hardt and Negri (2004) articulate these resistances as part of a growing global opposition by presenting *the multitude* as a 'living alternative' to the current global state of capitalist dominance and subjugation of the majority of the population (p. xiii). The multitude can be viewed as an open, diverse and inclusive network in which people or groups retain autonomy, and difference is celebrated and viewed as more of a singularity. This singularity on which the multitude is based is the idea of what Hardt and Negri term 'the common'. The common is produced rather than discovered by the multitude and it is through the common that communication and collaboration is enabled (p. xv). The multitude is striving to realise a new form of democracy that holds peace as its highest value, as its core. Producing this democracy and resisting the global state of war is the 'project of the multitude' (p. 90).

Immaterial labour

In describing the project of the multitude, Hardt and Negri (2004) state that 'capitalist production and the life (and production) of the multitude are tied together increasingly intimately and are mutually determining' (p. 90). The dominant form of the current state of production is *immaterial labour* or 'labour that produces immaterial products such as information, knowledges, ideas, images, relationships, and affects' (Hardt & Negri, 2004, p. 65). Immaterial labour not only produces capital in the form of goods, but also produces social and cultural capital as its structures spill over into other forms of labour. Immaterial labour should not be confused with what Marx (1863) saw as Adam Smith's false distinctions of productive and unproductive labour:

> The determinate material form of the labor, and therefore of its product, in itself has nothing to do with the distinction between productive and unproductive labor. For example, the cooks and waiters in a public hotel are productive laborers, in so far as their labor is transformed into capital for the proprietor of the hotel. (p. 262)

Labourers, as Marx understood, are not to be judged on the materiality of their products, but rather on the social relations existing between the proletariat and capitalist classes.

As a dominant model of politically and socially necessary labour in late-stage capitalism, immaterial labour represents a desired set of productive capacities that supports and extends a version of capitalism that exploits life in its process of working – biocapitalism. In recent manifestations of global capitalism, immaterial labour is increasingly dominant in most advanced capitalist nations (ironically relying on the intensely *material* labour of exploited human and non-human lives in an increasingly unsustainable manner). Immaterial labour differs from traditional labour in that it can be broken down into two principle forms: intellectual or linguistic labour and affective labour. Intellectual or linguistic labour is characterised by 'problem solving, symbolic and analytic tasks, and linguistic expressions. This kind of immaterial labour produces ideas, symbols, codes, texts, linguistic figures, images, and other such products' (Hardt & Negri, 2004, p. 108). Affective immaterial labour requires 'affects such s feeling of ease, well-being, satisfaction, excitement, or passion' (Hardt & Negri, 2004, p. 108). In the necessarily immaterial labour behind immaterial production, production spills over beyond the bounds of the economy traditionally conceived to engage culture, society and politics directly. What are produced in this case are not just material goods, but actual social relationships and forms of life. This biopolitical production highlights how general its products are and how directly it engages social life in its entirety (Hardt & Negri, 2004, p. 94).

Biopolitical production

Hardt and Negri insist that the production of social and cultural capital is 'biopolitical production'. At its core, biopolitics is simply the governance of life itself (Foucault, 1979/2008). Biopower, then, is the control and regulation of forms of life. Since biopolitics governs life, biopolitical control seeks the production of subjectivities (Hardt & Negri, 2009). Foucault's (1979/2008) analyses of biopower are aimed not merely at an empirical description of how power works for and through subjects, but also at the potential for the production of alternative subjectivities. Biopower and biopolitics, then, become a helpful lens of analysis for leisure scholars seeking to better understand the critical ruptures and overlaps occurring between life, labour and leisure (c.f. Davidson, 2014).

While the concept likely preceded him by centuries, the term *biopolitics* originated in the works of Michel Foucault as he examined the ways in which sovereign power changed throughout modernity. Foucault (1979/2008) considered the application of political power (and particularly state power) on all aspects of human life, leading him to arrive at the concept of biopolitics. Foucault saw that biopolitics is always and everywhere in performances of contemporary states. Government constitutes itself in this reflexive processing of both authority and truth, emphasising that 'society must be defended' against all enemies (Foucault, 1976/2003), both internal and external, via the regulation of the body (Foucault, 1990), and therefore, life itself. Regulation also came in the form of political technologies, such as procedures, institutions and legal forms (Lemke, 2001), which support particular political ideologies, and subsequently enable people to be governed as subjects (Foucault, 1988). Foucault understood that bodies were governed through forms of disciplinary power seen in institutions such as prisons, hospitals, factories and schools. Foucault's notion of biopower shifted scales from the individual to power that is organised and directed towards the control and regulation of the population at large. Focusing on Nazi regime as an extreme demonstration of biopolitics, Foucault illustrated the ways in which biopower was embedded in racism and capitalism. Nazi biopower employed race and ethnicity to either enlist individuals into an imperialistic war apparatus or to effectively end people's lives through encampment or death. Under this form of biopower, political practices took the regulation of human vitality to be its goal (Hardt & Negri, 2009). Politics, then, became material in the bodies and the lives of the subjects created. Foucault did not present the Nazi example of biopower as a particularly extreme example or as an anomaly; he contended that contemporary capitalist states exhibit these same inclinations to control and regulate populations in much subtler and less explicitly barbaric formulations. Biopolitics, in more common settings, broadly refers to a type of politics that addresses 'the population as a political problem, as a problem that is at once scientific and political, as a biological problem, as power's problem' (Foucault, 1976/2003, p. 245). Biopolitics, most generally, is a tracing of the movement of sovereign power over life from the one (a king or a ruler, for instance) to a diffuse set of power relations that target and regulate the life of an entire population within the realm of state control.

Contemporarily, as boundaries of states have become more porous through the processes of globalisation and neoliberal capitalism, previous biopolitical spatial confines have been largely dissolved (Hardt & Negri, 2004, 2009). A problematic assemblage of multinational corporations, organising institutions (IMF, World Bank, United Nations, etc.) and even nation states themselves have supported the diffuse reach of global capital through biopolitical instruments. Existing at the productive base of biocapitalism, the types of human and non-human creativity and work taking place in the laboratories, factories and marketing firms are immaterial labour. And, importantly, Facebook, a popular and dominant form of online social networking leisure (Ferreira & du Plessis, 2009), is intricately involved in processes of immaterial labour and the subsequent and interrelated production of biopolitical subjectivities. We underscore leisure's place in our sociopolitical fabric before returning to specific engagements with Facebook and immaterial labour.

Leisure and labour in the twenty-first century

Leisure, in our contemporary sociocultural milieu, is understood at least in part in relationship to labour (Rojek, 1995, 2010). Leisure and work were once thought to be dialectically constituted, where leisure took place in the absence of labour and leisure spaces only could be constructed where there was no labour to be undertaken. Such a simplistic and binaried approach has been significantly altered in contemporary postmodern society. Rojek (2010) contends that processes consonant with modernity have transformed our leisure into a problematic form of labour. Traditional leisure experiences have become rife with the social and emotional imperatives that previously were only associated with one's labour. Leisure's association with freedom and the lack of obligation, therefore, has become significantly compromised.

Leisure remains a rather fluid concept. For Aristotle, leisure amounted to the freedom from necessity to work and was closely linked with knowledge, and, thus, power. *Schole*, a Greek word for leisure, loosely refers not only to the state of being free from necessity to work, but also to time spent in contemplation or search for wisdom. The 'Protestant Ethic' remains a substantial influence on leisure in society, effectively guiding leisure experiences of the masses from the late sixteenth century through industrialization. Work was highly valued and leisure time was shunned unless it was used to worship. Along with industrialization came new thinking on leisure. Termed 'The Leisure Society Thesis', academics largely believed that with the division of labour and the advancements in technology, a new 'leisure class' would arise with all of the extra time that technology and specialisation saved workers (Rojek, 2010). This analysis has yet to emerge and critiques of this thesis abound; however, the efforts of academics during the development of the leisure society thesis continue to broadly shape how we understand 'leisure' as a concept. Although critics (Rojek, 1995, 2010) call for a rethinking of traditional leisure theory for postmodern society, leisure, as an antithesis to the economic function of work, can be categorised into three understandings: leisure as freedom from necessity to work; leisure as a state of mind; and leisure as an activity. Leisure as a state of mind is particularly helpful for our argument concerning social media and the labour it necessitates. Regardless of traditional analyses of leisure's dimensionality, contemporary leisure experiences have become inextricably linked to emotional labour and intelligence. Leisure has become a form of rationalised labour rather than free time, enjoyment and personal satisfaction (Rojek, 2010).

Leisure's relationships with labour are even further from any fixed positionings under the relatively recent neoliberal political economy of the last three decades. Neoliberalism is an advanced form of capitalism featuring a largely decreased government role, except for providing the conditions for a profitable business climate (Harvey, 2005). Contemporary consumer and financial capitalism have sufficiently catalysed a global economy, interconnected in myriad ways, bringing about new ways of doing leisure, as well as new forms of labour, which bring about its subsequent and inherent class conflicts. From the systemization of post-Fordist labour through to the more recent dematerialisation of the service sector, our patterns of working behaviour are constantly being reconfigured.

Class conflict was less complicated before globalisation. Marx and Engels (1848), in predicting the fall of capitalism, declared that 'the bourgeoisie therefore produces, above all, its own gravediggers. Its fall and the victory of the proletariat are equally inevitable' (p. 483). A century and a half after Marx and Engels prophesied the eventual success of capitalism's gravediggers, nearly the exact opposite effect has occurred. The proletariat, still populated with overworked, underpaid labourers, keeps capitalism well afloat for the bourgeois capitalist class. Perhaps ironically, the domination of capitalism globally depends upon the existence of delocalised capitalist enterprises' cheap labour to lower prices and deprive many workers of various human rights. Conflicts between social classes in the twenty-first century involve a massively interconnected web of relationships, commodity flows and capital investments, often pitting working-class resistances against other working-class resistances, in an unpredictable development to Marx's gravediggers assessment.

Beyond class struggle, contemporary Marxist approaches to economic crises have tremendous potential for understanding and appropriately contextualising capitalism's basic struggles and the demands of labour. Zizek (2012) considers the fundamental class antagonism not so much as between the bourgeoisie and the proletariat, but he sees it as being between 'use value' and 'exchange value'. In this light, each commodity has a use value, as demonstrated by its usefulness in satisfying various needs and wants. The exchange value of a commodity, by contrast, is traditionally understood as the amount of labour expended during production. Under our contemporary neoliberal political economy, Zizek (2012) argues, exchange value becomes autonomous and will lead to a revolutionary reordering of global (and local) political economies. Such a post-capitalist society is unlikely to follow historical models of (totalitarian) socialism, but it will, however, necessarily involve a shift from private appropriation to social management on a global scale. The forms it might take and how far it would embody the humanist values of Marx and Engels's liberating vision of communism would depend on the political action through which this change emerged. This scenario is Hardt and Negri's (2004, 2009) multitude, suggesting that our futures depend on the people and our readiness for prolonged struggle in the remaking of capital–labour relationships. Or, as Marx and Engels (1848) famously described at the conclusion of *The Communist Manifesto*: 'Let the ruling classes tremble at a Communistic revolution. The proletarians have nothing to lose but their chains. They have a world to win' (p. 500). But with the confounding intertwinement of labour and leisure, a consistent narrative of resistance to global political economic conditions pits resistance as a form of leisure, and a necessary version as well (c.f. Gilchrist & Ravenscroft, 2013; Mair, 2002).

What, then, is the role of leisure experiences in the production and maintenance of the sociocultural conditions necessary for the proletariat – the multitude – to address the inherent contradictions of capitalism's class struggles and conflation of use value and exchange value? In what ways has leisure been conscripted into the realms of capitalist production and consumption, of profit and loss and of oppression and class struggles? Contemporary leisure experiences, including engaging in social networking on Facebook, often imprison individuals and reinforce conformity, rather than liberating people and releasing creativities and the potential for resistances (Rojek, 1995). Understanding the dimensions of Facebook through an explicit leisure lens provides a context for placing people's engagement with social networking in the realm of immaterial labour and biopolitical production.

Facebook as a leisure space

Facebook is one of many online social networking sites that connect users to one another through postings, photographs and direct messages. Facebook's stated mission is to 'give people the power to share and make the world more open and connected … to friends and family, to discover what's going on in the world, and to share and express what matters to them'. Developed as a social network for elite university students in 2004, it quickly expanded to be accessible to anyone with an internet connection. With more than one billion active users, a wide diversity of individuals, groups and organisations engage with Facebook through both computers and mobile technology, and Facebook is commonly understood as an invaluable marketing tool for businesses, non-profits and other organisations (Treadaway & Smith, 2012). Facebook is both an experience and an institution, meaning that it is both an entity with agency (directed by owners, investors, designers, etc.) and it is controlled by the users contributing to the site in specific ways.

Online social networks, and Facebook specifically, have encountered mixed analyses. Facebook inspires notions of participatory cultures and user-generated materials, often extending many of the positive dimensions of social capital, social networking, activism and compassion (Roberts, 2014). While Facebook provides an effective means of (often global) communication and potentially coordination, it is far from a social or political panacea. Limitations to its potential as an agent of mobilisation are found in Facebook's fragmented and self-selected audiences, its seemingly non-hierarchical structure, the generally weak bonds that Facebook communication generally produces and its near ubiquitous engagement with gatekeepers of corporate advertising (Miller, 2005). There are substantial concerns and campaigns over the protection and use of data, marketing, hate speech, privacy, censorship and surveillance, as well as the psychological and well-being effects in terms of stress-related illnesses, as users compare lifestyles and achievements. However, it remains a 'very valuable means of communicating and coordinating action across space, bypassing the gatekeepers of the corporate mass media' (Miller, 2005, p. 243).

Leisure is freedom from the obligation of labour, a particular state of mind or an activity, and people's engagement with online social networking fits many of these constructions. Facebook has mixed engagement on workers' productivity, but it is largely viewed as something separate from employment (Ferreira & du Plessis, 2009), indicating that many see online social networking as separate from employed labour. Time spent engaging with Facebook can be seen as leisure as a state of mind. Postigo (2003) discusses leisure-labour relationships and evolution of volunteers on

America Online (AOL), noting that when the volunteers saw their role as a freely chosen fun way of creating community, they enjoyed their volunteer experience and viewed it as a hobby or leisure experience. As soon as restrictions were placed upon them and monetary rewards became involved, their mindsets changed, and although they were still participating in the same activity, it was no longer leisure, but labour. Therefore, definitions of leisure as separate from work remain problematic, depending on one's subjectivity (Rojek, 2010). The AOL owners always saw the volunteers as contributing to the company through their free labour, though the volunteers did not see what they were doing as work. Through state of mind, there exists the possibility of an individual experiencing leisure on Facebook. Scholarship has addressed Facebook or online social networking as an explicit activity, indicating increasing trends toward multitasking; Facebook activity intersects with many other leisure experiences that might be taking place simultaneously (Judd, 2014).

Leisure spaces, whether online or otherwise, do not simply exist, but are actively produced and reproduced. In this sense, Henri Lefebvre's (1974) seminal text, *The Production of Space*, illustrates that spaces (of all sorts) are social products, where people's ideas, imaginations, behaviours and representations combine to give space its basic character and functioning. Important to our context, Lefebvre differentiates between 'absolute spaces' (and their material dimensionality) and the more complex and often inexplicit spatialities associated with socially produced significances. These 'social spaces' are produced everywhere, as Lefebvre considered all spaces to be social. As an online medium, Facebook and other online social networking leisure experiences do not require the material spaces (a park, the mall, etc.) traditionally associated with leisure experiences, but still require that the social spaces they occupy are (re)produced through social engagement with the experience. In other words, the social spaces of Facebook clearly would cease to exist without the social engagement of the users themselves, a point we will consider more carefully in the context of immaterial labour and biopolitical production. Leisure spaces, like all spaces, are socially produced through complex assemblages of interaction, meaning making and lived practices. However, Lefebvre, an avowed Marxist, insisted that spaces are constantly (re)produced in tension with the development and expansion of capitalism, threatening their organic and democratic constructions. Power relations remain prominent in the production of space, as hegemonic classes produce spaces that reproduce these relations of dominance. The (re)production of space is fundamental to the (re)production of society, and hence capitalism itself. These (spatial) relations of dominance are under theorized opportunities for engagement from critical scholars and the population at large.

Social justice and democratic (online) space

There is a significant need for a greater focus on social justice in leisure settings and through leisure experiences (Johnson, 2014; Paisley & Dustin, 2011; Parry, Johnson, & Stewart, 2013; Rojek, 2005; Schmaltz & Mowatt, 2014). Social capital, long thought to be one of the enduring products of leisure experiences, requires the creation of space for both consensus and conflict (Arai, 2006). Further, these leisure spaces produce and are products of power and human agency. Socially and materially produced leisure spaces are vital parts of the human condition and leisure spaces have the potential of addressing systemic injustices (Kivel, 2000). Social justice, however, has been widely theorised across disciplines to reference strikingly disparate practices. We understand social justice as a 'process, or work, of infinitely articulating needs and aspirations within a democratically organised social space … Efforts toward social justice actively interrupt systems of oppression that are rooted in culture, history, and economics' (Rose & Paisley, 2012, pp. 139–140). Social justice in traditional leisure spaces is difficult to identify and to apprehend, indicating that social justice within online leisure spaces is even more slippery of a construct (Kahn & Kellner, 2004; Langman, 2005). What does social justice look like in an online setting? How do social media organise and maintain space that is more or less liberatory for users and the non-user populace (Roberts, 2014)? The connections between social justice, online social media and the role of leisure (and labour) are in need of further inquiry.

By employing explicitly critical feminist perspectives in understanding various ethical issues surrounding internet and online research, Morrow, Hawkins, and Kern (2015) identified and analysed the politics and visibility of online spaces, the wavering researcher positionalities that are consonant with online research and the subjectivities and power dynamics associated with online research. The point, however, is that drawing implications from an online medium is not to be taken lightly, and it is increasingly difficult for researchers to claim any sense of sociocultural or sociopolitical objectivity in documenting and analysing online social phenomena. Facebook's potential as a tool for democratic engagement has been critiqued in the context of leisure (Spencer & Rose, 2012) and elsewhere (e.g. Albrechtslund, 2008; Freishtat & Sandlin, 2010). More broadly, cultural texts, such as those found throughout the discursive formations of Facebook, not only provide leisure experiences, but also have the capacity to impart information and meaning in terms of our labour identities through the transmission of cultural values and social norms (Kivel & Johnson, 2009). Many leisure sites and contexts serve as means of consuming a type of media and simultaneously reproducing sociocultural contexts from which leisure participants come (Johnson, Richmond, & Kivel, 2008). Media are not merely neutral vessels of cultural information, but are imbued with sociopolitical ideologies that impact consumers in diverse and poorly understood ways. Media, then, are often the most influential forces in consumers' lives, especially during adolescence and early adulthood. Lastly, critically examining sociocultural perspectives of media moves leisure research scholars beyond the level of the individual leisure experience and pointing towards an analysis of larger social trends that have the capacity to deeply develop social and political change (Arai & Pedlar, 2003).

Having supported the notion that online leisure spaces are both in need of examination and have the potential for greater democratic engagement, we return to immaterial labour and biopolitical production. Leisure, a process, activity and/or state of mind that is now heavily interwoven with labour, is brought into the spaces created by online social networking on Facebook. Here, we analyse Facebook through the lens of Hardt and Negri's immaterial labour to illustrate connections and disjunctures between online social networking as leisure and the commodification of our lived biopolitical experiences in a neoliberal political economy.

Immaterial labour and Facebook

As immaterial labour is labour that produces immaterial products, two different types of immaterial labour are produced within Facebook. The site owners and the site users are *both* involved with the production and consumption of immaterial labour on Facebook. The site owners utilise a 'hegemonic Web 2.0 business model' in which 'they seek to surveil every user action, store the resulting data, protect the data via intellectual property, and mine it for profit' (Gehl, 2011, p. 1). Thus, all of the status updates, photographs, likes and dislikes are archived, becoming the intellectual property of Facebook. This information has a high monetary value to marketing companies as it is a veritable database of popular trends and endless descriptive statistics of a population. Facebook users are not only producing immaterial labour for the benefit of the owners of the site, they are also producing relationships with one another (through Facebook's many options for communication), gleaning information about popular trends (through Facebook's many options for surveillance), working to produce and perform identities and sharing ideas. This form of interpersonal immaterial labour benefits individuals and produces social relationships. Both owners and users are consumers of immaterial labour on Facebook. These two forms of immaterial labour produce immaterial goods on Facebook that are of value to both the individual and the owners of the site; these two forms of immaterial labour are necessarily inextricably intertwined.

Hardt and Negri (2004) identify immaterial labour as having three specific characteristics: (1) mobile and flexible; (2) in the form of networks; and (3) biopolitical and subjectivity producing. The following three examples apply these conceptualisations of immaterial labour to the leisure spaces of Facebook, treating immaterial goods as one good, regardless of the beholder of value.

Mobile and flexible

> I (Callie) opened my eyes this morning and reached instinctually to my bedside table to grab my cell phone, my all-in-one device. I turned off my alarm, checked the weather forecast, then opened my email. Out of 40 new emails, 11 were new messages from Facebook. I had three 'friend requests' that I needed to confirm, a few event invitations, and notifications that a few friends 'liked' my status and posted on my wall. From bed I logged onto Facebook, checked my invites, confirmed the friend requests, and looked to see who 'liked' my status update. I had barely opened my eyes, yet I was actively producing immaterial goods to be mined for profit. I was also building social relationships and laboring to build cultural capital.

As evidenced above, one can produce immaterial labour from their bedroom. As long as internet connectivity is available, physical location has little impact on the ability to produce immaterial labour in these online leisure spaces. Not only is immaterial labour, in this case, extraordinarily mobile, but it is also flexible. An almost innumerable variety of tasks can be accomplished without substantial structural change. As opposed to a factory job producing goods, where one might be strapped in position on the factory line, Facebook users can now 'like', 'dislike', produce text, produce images, share new ideas, comment on blogs and make innumerable connections. They can create knowledge. Users can accomplish a wide variety of tasks relatively quickly and easily.

For Hardt and Negri (2004), the mobile and flexible natures of immaterial labour also serve to blur the lines between labour and leisure. 'There is one tendency, for example, in various forms of immaterial labour to blur the distinction between work time and non-work time, extending the working day indefinitely to fill all of life' (Hardt & Negri, 2004, p. 66). People contribute to Facebook during (traditional) work time and the affective labour we produce in the form of social relationships (discussed in the next section) is sold to marketing companies, furthering the commodification of our leisure experiences and turning those experiences into immaterial labour.

The form of networks

Social networks are integral parts to understanding and analysing immaterial labour. 'Immaterial labour tends to take the social form of networks based on communication, collaboration, and affective relationships' (Hardt & Negri, 2004, p. 66). A popular term in Web 2.0 vocabulary is 'prosumers'. A prosumer both produces and consumes the content for Web 2.0 sites such as Facebook. This process occurs in a bottom-up (rather than top-down) fashion. Thus, the network structure is a constituent part of Facebook's social dominance. This network structure for production works because of a new form of labour discipline: 'Network struggle, again, like post-Fordist production, does not rely on discipline in the same way: creativity, communication, and self-organised cooperation are its primary values' (Hardt & Negri, 2004, p. 83).

This self-organisational discipline is based upon 'affective labour', one of the two broad forms (intellectual labour and affective labour) of Hardt and Negri's (2004) conceptualisation of immaterial labour. Affective labour produces more than just emotions, but reveals 'the present state of life in the entire organism, expressing a certain state of the body along with a certain mode of thinking' (p. 108). Users of Facebook produce and perform affective labour as they express feelings through status updates, messages and photographs. The labour is performed for particular audiences ('friends', for instance), but is also received by Facebook and its corporate backers and advertisers. Just as Hardt and Negri (2004) provide examples of flight attendants who produce affective labour to make the flyer feel safe, happy and comfortable, users of Facebook produce social skills and prosocial behaviour by managing profile appearances and friendships in order to make themselves and their friends feel important and loved.

Facebook users might feel the need to respond to friends' posts, might feel the need to comment or thank their friend for 'liking' their status or they might feel the need to accept a friend suggestion made by one of their good friends. This pseudo self-organised network perpetuates the immaterial labour Facebook users must discipline themselves to produce through increased communication with their many networked connections.

Biopolitical and produces subjectivity

Because immaterial labour is flexible and mobile and in the form of a broad network, thus blurring traditional lines of work and leisure (Rojek, 2010), it is also hegemonic; its structures spread into other forms of labour production. For Hardt and Negri (2004), the diffusion of the impact of immaterial labour does not stop there: 'Immaterial labour is biopolitical in that it is oriented toward the creation of forms of social life; such labour, then, tends no longer to be limited to the economic but also becomes immediately a social, cultural, and political force' (p. 66).

Immaterial labour from the users' perspectives, as well as the site owners' viewpoints, sees labour on Facebook as biopolitical. There are two cyclical patterns. The first such pattern is sociocultural–Facebook–sociocultural: users' social life and culture informs Facebook which thus transforms the users' social life and culture. Users communicate with one another, building connections as well as disseminating information about popular trends and ways of being. Through time spent on Facebook surveilling friends' pages and reading the Facebook news page, users learn how to act in society, how to be an acceptable member. Users learn what is acceptable to discuss and what is taboo. Users are disciplined by others when they step out of line through them 'unliking' status updates or 'defriending'. A second cyclical pattern is economic–Facebook–economic: user purchases inform marketers on Facebook who then inform users on what to buy. As the owners of Facebook store the immaterial goods users produce through affective labour and sell them to marketers, users are then cyclically resold the 'hottest new cool thing' that they have produced through their free labour on Facebook. Users are told about the newest iPad, told that they should value fast, small, abstracted items (a trend that Apple has gleaned from Facebook data trends). These messages come in the form of Facebook advertisements or from friends who have already consumed goods and bragged about features through a status update.

Therefore, in an act of biopolitical production, immaterial labour on Facebook is producing social life as well as culture. 'This is the ultimate role of a hegemonic form of production: to transform all of society in its image, a tendency that no statistics can capture. The real demonstration of this tendency, in fact, is the becoming biopolitical of production' (Hardt & Negri, 2004, p. 115). The becoming of biopolitical production, in its most invasive and effective form, occurs in the production of the subject. 'Ultimately, in philosophical terms, the production involved here is the production of subjectivity, the creation and reproduction of new subjectivities in society' (p. 66). We contend that Facebook, through the immaterial labour that is contributed to it through our online leisure experiences, is actively producing new biopolitical subjectivities that are different in quantity, intensity and kind. These networked relationships can produce a new political subjectivity as well as a new conception of difference, where Marx's viewpoint on political subjectivity requires 'not only self-representation but first and most fundamentally internal communication' (p. 123). The immaterial labour produced through networked communication on Facebook is producing such subjectivities.

In 2012, one of the most memorable viral Facebook videos was the controversial Kony 2012 video and ensuing conversation streams. This viral sensation has largely come and gone in its online presence, even if the material conditions it references remain unchecked. Tens of millions of viewers had seen the YouTube video depicting horrors the Ugandan warlord Joseph Kony was inflicting on local children. The video urged the public to get involved by raising awareness by plastering Kony's name everywhere, hoping that by making Kony famous, he would be captured and the suffering would be alleviated. While the video has many sympathisers, it simplifies the issues and places focus on uneducated outsiders trying to be 'heroes' who 'rescue' African children. Facebook saw a second wave of responses posting an image stating: one does not simply destabilise a Ugandan warlord by liking a status. These rejoinders indicate sharp differences between the immaterial labour that Facebook users (perhaps benevolently) commit and the lack of material change that follows.

This scenario brings into question the type of (bio)political subject Facebook might be producing, perhaps critiqued as 'slacktivism', where critical action is supplanted by clicking a button. Individuals then feel as if they have contributed, done their duty and participated in activating change through their 'vote'. The narrowness and banality of this biopolitical subjectivity is hardly an articulation of the multitude and does not address basic (Marxist) contradictions existing in the class struggles of contemporary neoliberal capitalism. However, this immaterial labour not only engages with various social movements (Kony, the Arab Spring, Occupy, etc.), but also commonly is deployed in favour of the profit-minded investors and advertisers who see users' immaterial labour as a wellspring of not yet fully tapped capital. Facebook can be leveraged in more productive ways and the roles of social media leisure experiences need further investigation.

A role for leisure scholars

We have purposely taken this argument to its logical extreme to incite imagination and questioning into what does happen and what could happen in the various leisure spaces of Facebook and in similar online social networking spaces. Our immaterial labour through online social networking can produce subjectivities and these subjectivities serve to (horizontally) connect us to greater and more diverse people, while also (vertically) integrating us into existing power structures that are commensurate with contemporary neoliberal capitalism. Acknowledging that our immaterial labour and biopolitical production on Facebook can produce such subjectivities is a step towards progressively understanding the possibilities of leisure scholarship in contributing to a more fully realised global movement of Hardt and Negri's (2004, 2009) multitude.

From a critical perspective, the power to guide the production of subjectivities should never be in the hands of the few and should be horizontally or flatly distributed among a seemingly limitless number of interested parties (Hardt & Negri, 2004). When Facebook became a public company, Zuckerberg (2012) wrote a letter to future shareholders asserting that 'giving people control over what they share is a fundamental principle of this rewiring'. He continued, explaining that rewiring was for a more realised democratic space and that for change to happen, concerns communicated to the government must be 'raised directly by all their people rather than through intermediaries controlled by a select few'. However, as indicated by our examination of immaterial labour and biopolitical production on Facebook (which is controlled/owned by Zuckerberg and stored in warehouses full of servers), control over the people's or multitude's voice (control over the common) is by the few.[1]

Looking at production in this fashion elicits an analysis of Facebook being top-down, controlling, manipulating and exerting panopticism on an unknowing and/or uncaring user base. The affective labour produced by the user is stored in digital archives that are out of users' control. As Hardt and Negri (2004) suggest, this scenario is an unwelcome condition of immaterial labour: 'When our ideas and our affects, or emotions, are put to work, for instance, and when they thus become subject in a new way to the command of the boss, we often experience new and intense forms of violation or alienation' (pp. 65–66). Feelings of alienation in our labour are not conducive to the existence and thriving multitude and are in fact a condition prescribed by Marx. Therefore, the structure of Facebook may have to change to look more democratic in order for it to be fully utilisable as a tool for the project of the multitude. In concert with necessary structural changes from vertically oriented to more horizontally oriented, the coming of the multitude demands that users recognise our often passive envelopment into the capitalist system that underscores our interactions with Facebook and many other online social networking experiences. In what we commonly consider to be our leisure experiences and leisure spaces, we are also performing the affective, immaterial labour that further renders ourselves as biopolitical subjects.

Currently, technologists are working on building alternative more free and user-controlled social networks, with interesting ramifications for leisure. Two popular options are the 'Federated General Assembly' and 'Diasopora' (Pinto, 2012). These new networks are described as 'radically democratic' as they are 'horizontal and decentralised' (FGA-information stored locally by community servers) and 'open-source, controlled by users, respectful of privacy' (Diaspora-information stored locally by users) (Pinto, 2012, p. 19). For decades, leisure scholars have studied physical aspects of leisure spaces, have studied the social aspects of leisure spaces and the central role of leisure in building healthy (local and global) communities. With this great wealth of theory and knowledge, leisure scholars are well positioned to respond to Moglen's (2010) call to help fix problems with Facebook. For years we have imagined and created leisure spaces for social networking that do not come with the price tag of the exploitation of personal information and constant surveillance, and instead contribute to a world that is less aggrieved and more socially and environmentally just. Further, it is becoming increasingly clear that leisure and politics are not (necessarily) distinct social domains. Leisure scholars:

> ... have to do more than report events and practices, by acknowledging the particular and political forms that constitute the event, and how one shares in the ethical and political values that leisure practices encode ... Leisure does more than reflect our political sympathies and values; it actively engages in them. (Gilchrist & Ravenscroft, 2013, p. 51)

While Mair (2002) understands leisure broadly and equates it with classical ideals of freedom, democracy and citizenship, Rojek (2010) suggests that leisure – an always contested construct – is an essential site of emotional labour, where one develops both social competence and credibility. Leisure, then, in addition to all of its social and social-psychological dimensions should be critically examined as a site and space for biopolitical engagement, with all of the associated strengths and pitfalls that come with the subjectivity of the self to the various state apparatuses in our leisure lives.

Rojek (2013) showed Marxism's short-lived influence upon leisure studies, despite leisure and allied disciplines being ripe arenas for Marxist analysis. And despite leisure scholarship's apparent shyness towards Marxist analysis, we remain unable to escape an understanding of leisure that does not complicate and implicate the role of our own biopolitical productions of immaterial labour in many of the leisure practices we undertake; in the case of Facebook and social networking, it is a leisure experience that is engaged at massive rates, with many unexamined and poorly understood consequences. A history of capital–labour–leisure relationships is also a history of the institutions that support it, including the (institutionalised) scientific discourses of in areas such as health, planning, family, education and others, the very essence of Foucauldian biopower. An important component of Foucault's work on this subject is that 'his analysis of biopower are aimed not merely at an empirical description of how power works for and through subjects but also at the potential for the production of alternative subjectivities' (Hardt & Negri, 2009, p. 59). The accumulation of capital, as well as the spread of capitalism as a reproducing process, requires the accumulation of normalised individuals and the accumulation of knowledge about the sociopolitical processes of capital and the populace. Leisure scholars should be well positioned to inform these emerging and ever-dynamic discourses.

Disclosure statement

No potential conflict of interest was reported by the authors.

Note

1. While Facebook is a public company, Zuckerberg owns 28.2% of the total shares. Over 60% of the company is owned by five individuals and two investment companies.

References

Albrechtslund, A. (2008). Online social networking as participatory surveillance. *First Monday, 13*(3), 1–11.

Arai, S. (2006). Where does social control end and social capital begin? Examining social space, conflict, and the politics of difference. *Leisure/Loisir, 30*, 329–339.

Arai, S., & Pedlar, A. (2003). Moving beyond individualism in leisure theory: A critical analysis of concepts of community and social engagement. *Leisure Studies, 22*, 1–18.

Davidson, J. (2014). Racism against the abnormal? The twentieth century Gay Games, biopower and the emergence of homonational sport. *Leisure Studies, 33*, 357–378.

Ferreira, A., & du Plessis, T. (2009). Effective online social networking on employee productivity. *South African Journal of Information Management, 11*(1), 1–11.

Foucault, M. (1976/2003). *Society must be defended*. New York, NY: Picador.

Foucault, M. (1979/2008). *The birth of biopolitics: Lectures at the college de France, 1978–1979*. New York, NY: Palgrave Macmillan.

Foucault, M. (1988). Technologies of the self: A seminar with Michel Foucault. In L. H. Martin, H. Gutman, & P. H. Hutton (Eds.). Amherst: University of Massachusetts Press.

Foucault, M. (1990). *The history of sexuality: An introduction*. New York, NY: Vintage.

Freishtat, R. L., & Sandlin, J. A. (2010). Shaping youth discourse about technology: Technological colonization, manifest destiny, and the frontier myth in Facebook's public pedagogy. *Educational Studies, 46*, 503–523.

Gehl, R. (2011). The archive and the processor: The internal logic of Web 2.0. *New Media & Society, 13*, 1228–1244.

Gilchrist, P., & Ravenscroft, N. (2013). Space hijacking and the anarcho-politics of leisure. *Leisure Studies, 32*, 49–68.

Hardt, M., & Negri, A. (2004). *Multitude*. New York, NY: Penguin Group.

Hardt, M., & Negri, A. (2009). *Commonwealth*. Cambridge, MA: Harvard University Press.

Harvey, D. (2005). *A brief history of neoliberalism*. London: Oxford University Press.

Johnson, C. W. (2014). 'All you need is love': Considerations for a social justice inquiry in leisure studies. *Leisure Sciences, 36*, 388–399.
Johnson, C. W., Richmond, L., & Kivel, B. D. (2008). What a man ought to be, he is far from: Exploring collective meanings of masculinity and race in media. *Leisure/Loisir, 32*(2), 1–28.
Judd, T. (2014). Making sense of multitasking: The role of Facebook. *Computers & Education, 70*, 194–202.
Kahn, R., & Kellner, D. (2004). New media and internet activism: From the 'Battle of Seattle' to blogging. *New Media & Society, 6*(1), 87–95.
Kivel, B. D. (2000). Leisure experience and identity: What difference does difference make? *Journal of Leisure Research, 32*, 79–81.
Kivel, B. D., & Johnson, C. (2009). Consuming media, making men: Using collective memory work to understand leisure and the construction of masculinity. *Journal of Leisure Research, 41*, 109–133.
Kramer, A., Guillory, J., & Hancock, J. (2014). Experimental evidence of massive-scale emotional contagion through social networks. *Proceedings of the National Academy of Sciences, 111*, 8788–8790.
Langman, L. (2005). From virtual public spheres to global justice: A critical theory of internetworked social movements. *Sociological Theory, 23*, 42–74.
Lefebvre, H. (1974). *The production of space*. New York, NY: Wiley.
Lemke, T. (2001). 'The birth of bio-politics': Michel Foucault's lecture at the Collège de France on neo-liberal governmentality. *Economy and Society, 30*, 190–207.
Mair, H. (2002). Civil leisure? Exploring the relationship between leisure, activism and social change. *Leisure/Loisir, 27*, 213–237.
Marx, K. (1863). Chapter IV: Theories of productive and unproductive labor. In *Theories of surplus value*. Retrieved from www.marxists.org
Marx, K., & Engels, F. (1848). Manifesto of the communist party. In R. Tucker (Ed.). (1978). *The Marx-Engels reader* (2nd ed., pp. 469–500). New York, NY: W. W. Norton.
Miller, B. (2005). Spaces of mobilization: Transnational social movements. In C. Barnett & M. Low (Eds.), *Spaces of democracy* (pp. 223–246). Thousand Oaks, CA: Sage.
Mitchell, D., & Staeheli, L. (2005). Permitting protest: Parsing the fine geography of dissent in America. *International Journal of Urban and Regional Research, 29*, 796–813.
Moglen, E. (2010, February 5). *Freedom in the cloud-NYU lecture* [Video file]. Retrieved from http://www.youtube.com/watch?v=QOEMv0S8AcA
Morrow, O., Hawkins, R., & Kern, L. (2015). Feminist research in online spaces. *Gender, Place, & Culture, 22*, 526–543.
Paisley, K., & Dustin, D. (Eds.). (2011). *Speaking up and speaking out: Working for social and environmental justice through parks, recreation, and leisure*. Urbana, IL: Sagamore.
Parry, D., Johnson, C. W., & Stewart, W. (2013). Leisure research for social justice: A response to Henderson. *Leisure Sciences, 35*, 81–87.
Pinto, N. (2012). Rise of the Facebook killers: At the pinnacle of the social network's success, its critics are busy building its replacements. *City Weekly, 28*, 17–20.
Postigo, H. (2003). Emerging sources of labor on the internet: The case of America online volunteers. *International Review of Social History, 48*, 205–223.
Roberts, J. M. (2014). *New media and public activism: Neoliberalism, the state and radical protest in the public sphere*. Bristol: Policy Press.
Rojek, C. (1995). *Decentring leisure: Rethinking leisure theory*. London: Sage.
Rojek, C. (2005). An outline of the action approach to leisure studies. *Leisure Studies, 24*, 13–25.
Rojek, C. (2010). *The labour of leisure: The culture of free time*. London: Sage.
Rojek, C. (2013). Is Marx still relevant to the study of leisure? *Leisure Studies, 32*, 19–33.
Rose, J., & Paisley, K. (2012). White privilege in experiential education: A critical reflection. *Leisure Sciences, 34*, 136–154.
Schmaltz, D., & Mowatt, R. (2014). An introduction to the special issue: The unsettling nature of prejudice. *Journal of Leisure Research, 46*, 245–251.
Spencer, C., & Jostad, J. (2013). Facebook's status in the lives of generation Y: Exploring power structures in an online leisure space. In K. Schwab & D. Dustin (Eds.), *Just leisure: Things that we believe in* (pp. 75–90). Urbana, IL: Sagamore.

Spencer, C., & Rose, J. (2012). The democratizing potential of an online leisure space. *International Journal of Virtual Communities and Social Networking, 4*, 59–75.

Treadaway, C., & Smith, M. (2012). *Facebook marketing: An hour a day* (2nd ed.). Indianapolis, IN: Wiley.

Wainwright, J., & Kim, S. (2008). Battles in Seattle redux: Transnational resistance to a neoliberal trade agreement. *Antipode, 40*, 513–534.

Zizek, S. (2012). *Less than nothing: Hegel and the shadow of dialectical materialism*. Brooklyn, NY: Verso.

Zuckerberg, M. (2012, February 2). *Letter to shareholders from Mark Zuckerberg*. Retrieved from http://www.ft.com/cms/s/2/a2109a54-4d88-11e1-b96c-00144feabdc0.html#axzz1odkrubG3

Afterword: a new digital Leisure Studies for Theoretical Times

Steve Redhead

It is a pleasure to write this Afterword to an excellent special issue on young people's everyday lives and digital leisure cultures. I commend it to readers in the strongest possible terms. The special issue is not just for those interested in digital leisure and young people's everyday lives, as there are implications in these important papers for Leisure Studies in general – for the 'digital' and 'digital age' in Leisure Studies. There are a number of high-class articles in this special issue pushing at the shifting barriers of the discipline of Leisure Studies and of youth studies within Leisure Studies. Empirically and theoretically, they are directly relevant to the debates in the discipline right now, and indeed beyond the discipline. Work in these articles on digital citizenship, online fitness, video games, health promotion, sporting celebrity and sexuality, their myriad links to Facebook, Instagram, Snapchat and Twitter and their refraction through the high theoretical maze of Foucault, Hardt and Negri, Zizek, Deleuze and others, shows the diversity, sophistication and the intellectual rigour of Leisure Studies as an academic discipline which has come of age. The dark side of digital leisure is also drawn attention to in work on abuse of young athletes via Twitter and the widespread discrimination evident on the basis of image, looks, sexuality, gender and race. The idea that digital leisure for young people is a bed of roses is rightly subjected to pulverising critique. The papers in this special issue also problematise digital methodologies.

Digital Leisure Studies

Nevertheless, stimulated as I am by these fascinating studies with rich data I cannot help feeling that we need to push harder at the barriers of the discipline – we might call them barricades even. We need to ask the hard question, where is international Leisure Studies going? Most of my academic work, which began in sociology of law and criminology and broadened out over the years into the interdisciplinary study of popular culture and leisure, has, over decades, had some connection to a fairly stable and well-defined area of study called Leisure Studies with all its accoutrements of professional organisations, journals, activities and so on. However, the field, like many others, now feels like it is on the brink of a new era. This structure of feeling I am alluding to is due not just changes in the examples of new digital leisure we see all around us brought about by global phenomena like Nintendo's Pokemon Go, updating the analogue treasure hunt for the digital age. It is more of a conceptual change, riding the tectonic shifts brought about by globalisation, digitisation and neoliberalism in the last 20 or 30 years, leaving us bereft of satisfactory resources to explain what is going on and where we are all heading. But hope is on the horizon. After pioneering work on the nature and contours of 'digital sociology' by far-sighted academics such as Deborah Lupton, it is possible to envisage what I see as an emerging Digital Leisure Studies. I have written essays and given talks in the last few years arguing for this perspective to be taken seriously, and trying to sketch out what it might look like. Others have taken up the call and pushed the whole thing forward. For present purposes it is worth emphasising two essential points. As academics in this discipline, or for that matter any other, we are ourselves increasingly digitised – we have web profiles, we blog, we tweet, we write for online journals, we publish *e*-books and *e*-journals, we podcast and vodcast, we supervise students through Skype. Secondly, what we are studying in our respective disciplines is increasingly digitised. The fine special issue contained in these pages is a particularly good example of this object of study – everyday lives of young people and digital leisure. These digital leisure cultures are the 'real' of our discipline, its object and subject, and no longer are we, if indeed we ever were, in the misleading binary realms of the real and the virtual. New directions in digital leisure cultures are necessary in my view because the present routes forward are often confused and unsatisfactory, reflecting a more general concern in the population as a whole about our digitised world and how to come to terms with the effects of it on global citizens as authoritarian populist politicians dominate the global air waves. The basic question – is the internet a good or a bad thing? – structures the debates but urgent questions on digitisation remain unanswered, as they do on new technology, climate change, globalisation and the seemingly long-lasting predominant idea of the free market as sacrosanct. Specifically, as far as digital leisure cultures are concerned, the crucial question is what are gigabytes doing to us and how can we explain in detail, as it unfolds in front of our eyes at breakneck speed, these complex and disturbing processes of technologically driven digitisation and globalisation? Echoing Manchester United fans' chant about former player and assistant coach Ryan Giggs 'Giggs Will Tear You Apart' (aimed at opposing fans and based on Joy Division's classic track 'Love Will Tear Us Apart') I am asking in these essays and talks, whether will these 'gigs' tear us apart? We have certainly become so addicted to the hyperspeed of electronic digital connection that we all feel the familiar sickening stomach churning while we wait for our screens (on whatever myriad digital platforms) as almost a global cultural condition, yet we heartily binge watch whole series of our favourite TV shows in an afternoon once the connection is eventually made a few seconds later. Speed of new technology is so pervasive and its effects so widespread that we can be said to be 'post-TV' such is the change in our watching and listening habits and the platforms available at the touch of a button. Further, these shifts are so great that we are back in the realms of asking whether we are at long last now living today in the post-work futurist 'leisure society' predicted for us in the 1980s, enabled now it is said by the combination of forces I have already identified in this Afterword: namely, globalisation, neoliberalism and digitisation.

Meanwhile, specific sub-areas of study and approach are accorded solid status quite quickly. For instance, Physical Cultural Studies and Deviant Leisure are making their mark in debates about the same basic area that Digital Leisure Studies stakes out. Also, there is some excellent work now around what have been labelled digital football cultures. Stimulating studies all over the globe are being undertaken to capture the changes taking place in 'digital football'. These changes are due to and part of digital leisure cultures being produced and regulated and have far reaching social and economic consequences. For example, contemporary football culture is permeated by discussion and critical debate about amongst other contemporary news stories as professional footballers' digital resistance to Louis van Gaal's digital daily stalking of his players while he worked as Manchester United football manager, whether football stadia should have Wi-Fi, why Juventus fans can watch the game on TV screens in the back of the seats in front of them and how the Red and Black Bloc (RBB) ultras of Western Sydney Wanderers organise protests against the Football Federation of Australia (FFA) through their smart phones and tablets. Recent developments in digital leisure cultures like these reflect the delayed effects of a global financial crisis which still permeates our globe in unforeseen ways. As I have emphasised in this Afterword the essays in this special issue are all provocative and extremely interesting explorations of digital leisure cultures. We do, though, all of us need to embark on something of a further journey to sort out what exactly it is that has changed in digitisation – in other words we need to produce sustained theorising of the 'digital turn' in Leisure Studies and with it more satisfactory theoretically informed empirical studies of digital leisure cultures.

Theoretical Times

But there is an even more pressing reason for developing, urgently, a new Digital Leisure Studies. We are living to some extent in new times, an era which I call (slightly tongue in cheek) Theoretical Times. I am currently writing a book on the phenomenon called Theoretical Times, which is partly being constructed through blog posts on my personal website, twitter conversations, Facebook posts, Skype meetings, vodcasts, podcasts and other social media links – it is effectively being written in instalments in and through social media, taking into account wide-ranging feedback. The various digital platforms used have ensured many tens of thousands of downloads in global audiences. The bibliographical research was undertaken partly by tweeting references to the theorists' writings, and writings about them, and subsequently archiving the material on the tweets. Many of these practices and platforms are what constitute my, and others, leisure practices and they are invading work practices. I am myself partaking in digital leisure cultures in the labour of writing of the academic book itself. In this Afterword I want to indicate some relevant aspects of these Theoretical Times to emphasise the urgency of our task. We live I think, interestingly, in Theoretical Times. Previously, we lived, theoretically, in interesting times. Study has attached itself to 'theory' and 'theorists' as never before. And 'high theory' at that. But there has also been a delve into 'the popular' of culture as never before, too – both high and low popular culture. Digitisation itself has been absolutely critical in this process but it is a part of an advanced global capitalism not something which simply comes out of the air. Of course there has been an academic celebrity intellectual culture in the past, but I would contend that this time it is different. The maturity of the systems of theoretical thought on offer is worth taking seriously as a whole. Entire areas of study are on the verge of being replaced or displaced by systems of thought devoted to singular theorists. In the case of my book on Theoretical Times the theorists Paul Virilio, Jean Baudrillard, Alain Badiou and Slavoj Zizek have been particularly singled out, partly because of the production over their lifetimes of systems of thought which are capable of capturing the new times we are entering in this digital leisure age, and partly because they are the foremost theorists of an advanced global capitalism within which the digital leisure cultures of our everyday lives are being transformed.

There is not space here in this Afterword for detailed analysis of the ground laid out in the book Theoretical Times but I want to indicate some of the salient points in the argument, and especially the overall links to digital leisure cultures. For instance, the specific celebrity intellectual culture which has developed over the past few years has produced open access online journals devoted to theorists such as Jean Baudrillard, Alain Badiou and Slavoj Zizek making the work of these theorists ever more accessible around the globe. The *International Journal of Baudrillard Studies* began in 2004, the *International Journal of Zizek Studies* began in 2007 and *Badiou Studies* began in 2012. In some cases the open access journals overlap: for instance, in 2016 the *International Journal of Zizek Studies* published a special issue on Slavoj Zizek and Jean Baudrillard around the theme 'Before Zizek – There was Baudrillard'. In 2016 Badiou Studies hit the headlines for having to retract their acceptance (and publication in Vol 4 No 1) of an article purportedly by a single author which turned out to be a hoax by two authors writing about Alain Badiou, raising comparisons with a similar hoax by Alan Sokal in the mid-1990s which supposedly sought to expose postmodernism. In the 2016 case, however, the digitisation of online journals meant that once the hoax was discovered all that remained to be done was the deletion of the offending hoax article. Furthermore, the European Graduate School where most students study remotely features people like Paul Virilio, Badiou and Zizek as star professors whose lectures are then posted on YouTube. Jean Baudrillard who died in 2007 is still featured prominently after his death. YouTube promotes hour plus long presentations by theorists such as Zizek and Badiou as if they were rock or pop stars like Bruce Springsteen or Lady Gaga giving extended shows, an essential part of 'showbiz' academia, making themselves indistinguishable from all other performers. It has rather cynically been suggested in some quarters that this intellectual movement, especially that variant around the Badiouian notion of the 'communist hypothesis', is reflective of the values of capitalism in an attractive brand name or even a company label, the exact opposite of the 'communist idea' that they seek to promote. These theorists are also hailed as some classic throwback to earlier times, even earlier centuries. Alain Badiou himself has been seen as our Lenin or Marx and Slavoj Zizek has said of his friend Badiou that a figure like Plato or Hegel walks amongst us.

Post-disciplinary theory

Certainly, theorists today are sitting astride the globe like giants while whole disciplines wither on the vine. In some senses, disciplines have been superseded. We have become post-disciplinary in our trans or cross or interdisciplinarity and devoted in our studies to the life and work of singular theorists. Entire dictionaries have been produced concentrating on theorists such as Virilio, Baudrillard, Zizek and Badiou in the intellectual space where whole disciplines would have featured in the past.

It is only recently that the full extent of this change in global theory has become apparent and with it the radical implications for disciplines. The global financial crisis of 2007–2008 was followed by a brief global Keynesianism before a return to business as usual and an even more brutal neo-liberalism raging throughout the globe with endless war, mass random killings, mobile mass migration and massive social and technological change on the horizon as far as we can see. Discipline after discipline in the academic world has since agonised over whether the tenets of yesteryear still hold good after the earth shattering events of 9/11 and 2007/8 which play out ever more widely today as the recent global stock market and currency market 'wobble' after the Brexit vote in the United Kingdom to leave the European Union has demonstrated. These processes have, for instance, already begun to re-energise the field of contemporary political economy which attempts to demystify finance and show how finance exploits us all. In turn, after cultural studies lost its way as some have known it its founding fathers have asked, agonisingly, the question what is the future of cultural studies? Further, criminology has charted new directions away from both neo-liberalism and liberal postmodernism and towards a new 'ultra-realism' and a new conceptualisation of harm. In turn, legal studies has renewed its call for a new interdisciplinary legal studies, incorporating new critical legal theory and the rediscovery of critical legal thinkers and for law and critique and critical legal studies as never before. Even economists, largely in thrall to neoliberalism in the first place, have been forced to ask whether there is anything left of economics after the crisis while all the while regenerating neo-liberal economics. Economics students at the University of Manchester in England even set up a Post-Crash Economics Society to demonstrate their vehement displeasure at the modern university curriculum seemingly devoid of explanatory power and contemporary relevance. Pyschoanalysis, once again, has renewed its love/hate relationship with Jacques Lacan's life and work in an attempt to find its way out of its own disciplinary despair. Theology has moved beyond its previous terrain to look at God in Pain and a materialist Christianity, whereas philosophy has returned to Hegel, German idealism, Marx and dialectical materialism to forge a transcendental materialism. Political theory, too, has mused about whether it still has the power to explain contemporary events like the 2011 riots in the UK and the various aspects of the Arab Spring in the way that, for instance, Karl Marx and Friedrich Engels once analysed the revolutions in Europe in 1848. Leisure Studies cannot escape such soul searching in the post-crash digital age. Calling out in the dark for a Digital Leisure Studies is one way of provoking debate about the crises in these other disciplines as well as the field of Leisure Studies.

These brief comments in this Afterword are a part of a much larger long-term work on theory, and the history of theory in the post-crash global condition and the narrow theoretical ledge we now inhabit in its wake. Although couched in general terms, the book Theoretical Times concentrates on the work of Paul Virilio, Jean Baudrillard, Slavoj Zizek and Alain Badiou both in terms of taking seriously their theoretical analyses for our sometimes profoundly untheoretical times and their participation in the hyperreal world of 'theory' today. Theorists like Alain Badiou, Paul Virilio and Slavoj Zizek have become integrated into a form of 'hyperreality' which Jean Baudrillard when he was alive has theorised and, for a brief fleeting moment, enigmatically captured. Debates and controversies have presented these theorists either as gods or charlatans and they have felt the full brunt of the consequences, and the reach, of social media in celebrity intellectual culture. Alain Badiou, for example, has been subjected to an internet hoax which declared that he was, at 79 years of age, dead and stimulated thousands of his 'fans' to write in obituary mode on facebook. Indeed such 'theory' fandom in celebrity intellectual culture has become a phenomenon worthy of study in its own right. I look in the Theoretcial Times book at the idea of hyperreality and related concepts in the recent development of theoretical and empirical work, especially since the global financial crisis of 2007–2008, the effects of which still permeate our fractured globe. The aim is to produce better theorising of these concepts in theory and ultimately better empirical work on our rapidly digitising world in its wake. In other words, to answer the question: what critical theoretical resources can we turn to?

Theory and theorists, are no longer optional or marginal: they are central to reconstruction – political, economic, cultural, social – in so-called 'postmodern capitalism'. Theoretical Times is the moniker I have given to a continuing project looking at the way in which certain theorists have begun to displace academic disciplines in the contemporary post-crash world, and how we might generate more more meaningful and appropriate concepts and theories for the contemporary globe. Part of the reason for stressing the singularity of our Theoretical Times is that there are theorists who are not usually utilised in this field of Leisure Studies, and the study of digital leisure cultures, that we can and should turn to. For example, French urban theorist of speed Paul Virilio has claimed that we are moving from cosmopolis to claustropolis. Building on this idea I have argued that my concept of 'claustropolitanism' (the feeling that we want to escape the planet because we are now so foreclosed) is fast becoming a reality – a post-crash cultural condition spreading globally on a daily basis. For Virilio, who is actually claustrophobic, Joy Division's mantra in Digital 'feel it closing in, day in, day out' is personal, but the consumers of mediatised global sporting culture are also experiencing the same structure of feeling. Football and social media is a specific area which illustrates this claustropolitan tendency. In my recent work in this area, I am trying to tease out the theoretical implications for the study of digital leisure cultures in general. They point in the direction of the need for a new Digital Leisure Studies. The aim is to produce better theorising of these concepts and tropes of Digital Leisure Studies in leisure theory and ultimately better empirical work on our rapidly digitising world in its wake. What we require is a shift in our thinking – a Digital Leisure Studies. Digital Leisure Studies with hyperreality incorporated? On the brink of a Digital Leisure Studies what critical theoretical resources can we turn to?

Digital leisure cultures as a term is fraught with difficulty. But I would argue that it covers some of the following technologies and practices which have built cultures around them: namely, apps (applications), smart phones, online games, interaction on some form of social media and the downloading of films, live televised sports events and music. Traditional notions of legal intellectual property have been thrown into disarray by these developments in digital leisure cultures. Entertainment and Sports Law has become an important part of the legal curriculum worldwide. Digital fan cultures in sport and music have subsequently developed and been an object of study – witness academic work on fan forums and fan identities. Sports personalities have also featured strongly in the new celebrity culture promoted by social media. However, in cyberculture there are video gamers *and* cyber football hooligans, and there are campaigners for social justice *and* hate crime promoted by trolls and cyber bullies. Although we may not have labelled them in this way, digital leisure cultures have been around for at least some of the last 15 years since the millennium but the years between the global financial crisis of 2007/8 and today have been fundamental in the digital turn, especially in their inexorable speeding up. In my work I call this widening process accelerated culture and have developed a theoretical framework for explaining its development more generally in our contemporary society drawing on theorists such Paul Virilio and Jean Baudrillard and Alain Badiou and Slavoj Zizek. Certainly, there is a global recognition that we are living through significant changes, but there is uneven social and technological development and a critical questioning of globalisation as a consequence. Academics and commentators unfortunately write as if everybody in the world is digitally connected when there is massive unevenness in the form and content of connection. A technological determinism is abroad too. Some have argued that the development of tablets, streaming video and music along with the emergence of social media between 2009 and 2014 will be seen as a key moment when we come to look back on the contemporary capitalist present in the future. A technologically driven future, full of digital leisure cultures driven by an 'Internet of Things' is hailed by many even as the globe hurtles towards new uncertainty. This imagined reality of coming decades, combined with the astonishing acceleration of high-end computing, is a modern technological revolution in anyone's language, and one occurring in a very short space of time, but there is little sense of what it actually mean for us as digital leisured citizens. Are the internet and the web part of a sinister movement from the dark side designed to enslave us in what the Slovenian Lacan Slavoj Zizek has called a 'new dark ages', or are they instead somehow hiding in the light. Leisure Studies' study of leisure, and digital leisure cultures, has in some ways come late to this debate about the good and evil sides of digitisation. In Theoretcial Times, I identify Paul Virilio, Jean Baudrillard, Alain Badiou and Slavoj Zizek as theorists who may illuminate the path ahead (though they are not without their own flaws). They are a necessary if insufficient resource.

Digital Leisure Studies and critical theory

The idea of a Digital Leisure Studies requires critical theory, and critical theorists, to sustain it is it is not to fall by the wayside as is often the case with new labels or designations of trajectories of study. In the book Theoretical Times, it is the theory built by four critical theorists that I largely draw upon for the generation of my own concepts such as accelerated culture, claustropolitanism, foreclosure and bunker anthropology. Theorists mentioned in this Afterword are in many ways on opposite sides of the debate about the good and evil narrative in studies of digitisation and Digital Leisure Studies. Slavoj Zizek, for example, has occasionally lauded the internet and its supposed associated postmodern freedoms where everyone gets a chance as part of a neo-communist future which he has promoted with fellow new 'new left' theorists like Alain Badiou. Furthermore, Zizek has sometimes reflected on the rapidly changing internet and its promotion of postmodern leisure pursuits. Zizek, especially muses on the acceleration of digital leisure cultures and the attendant homogenisation, miniaturisation and digitisation. For Zizek, though he is a fan of the digital world, there is a perceived danger in the speed of change in this digitised world – homogenisation, monopoly and standardisation in the internet and the web are double edged in his view. He worries openly about the consequences of the standardisation in a world of massification. In general, though, despite his misgivings, Zizek is in favour of the accelerated culture that is being generated by these technological changes. On the other hand, self-styled left-wing militant Christian Paul Virilio is more pessimistic and sceptical, envisaging the high-speed accidents of technology as 'events' as part of the dangers of what he calls the futurism of the moment where wars (real on battlefields and digital on gamers' screens) are fought at the speed of light. Virilio in particular, has seen events in our digitised world as partially, the result of what he describes as an automatic speculation in the futurism of the instant. For Virilio the aim of shrinking time and space has arrived in the modern world, but his own avowed political economy of speed is often flawed, with surprisingly little empirical evidence brought forward to support his aphoristic commentary. The accelerated culture of the past four decades which Virilio occasionally obliquely captures in his uniquely singular way, is, though, absolutely at the heart of the crisis of our post-crash condition. Virilio is on the more cynical side of the argument about the merits of digitisation, despite celebrating the city of the instant which the online world has supposedly brought us – that is 'live' broadcasting, with everyone watching at the same time, of, for instance, the Euro 2016 Championships in France replacing the real community of the past with a digitised community of today. For the anarchistic Christian Paul Virilio, there is a communism of affect in the city of the instant so there is a hopeful, optimistic side to his thought too. Although politically on different parts of the left, and on different sides of the good and evil of digitisation debate, both Zizek and Virilio suffer sometimes from a pervasive libertarianism which is part of the contemporary politics of digital leisure cultures and the questions of identity and community which accompany this politics. It certainly mirrors the free market dominance of neo-liberalism in the wider world and it is this aspect of political economy rather than a spuriously attributed 'postmodernism' that matters. Paul Virilio's friend and colleague, the late Jean Baudrillard, as critical commentators have noted, casts a more complicated shadow over the good and evil narrative conflicts over digitisation, and on the ideas of postmodernity and postmodernism. Baudrillard often endured a reading of his work which highlighted 'postmodernism', (and also ideas like 'simulation' and 'hyperreality'), whereas 'impossible exchange', 'dystopia' and 'apocalyptism', conditions more attuned to the 2007/8 global financial crisis, were actually much more commonly applied in Baudrillard's work. Such concepts were used explicitly and implicitly by Baudrillard in the few years before his death much more than the more commonly attributed ideas of postmodernism, simulation and hyperreality. As reinterpreters of Baudrillard and his global significance have rightly pointed out, the term 'postmodernism' is not an accurate portrayal of Baudrillard's work or of Jean Baudrillard himself. Baudrillard utterly rejected it in many interviews over his lifetime. Regarding digitisation, Jean Baudrillard has distinguished himself from Paul Virilio on the specificity of 'digital' virtualisation. Baudrillard, who died from cancer in 2007 but left several important works to be published posthumously, argued that his friend Paul Virilio was correct in seeing great risks in developing the internet but that there were a more complex series of questions at play in what Baudrillard saw as the 'radical uncertainty' of the contemporary world. Baudrillard argues for seeing a radical uncertainty in the world which is not just about good or evil, dark side or bright side. The fourth theorist I cite in the book Theoretcial Times in this debate is Alain Badiou. For Badiou, who was a student of Louis Althusser's in the 1960s and for a time a committed Maoist, the debate about the global digitised society is a matter of seeing the potential in global and local organisation for a neo-communism of the future which the internet provides, and indeed he envisages nothing less than a global 'resurrection of communism' with an organised global politics to sustain it. For Badiou, interested in universalism rather than the failed experiment of 'globalisation' and there is a lot to report on and talk about if we are to enter a new era of politics that isn't a politics of representation. Whether or not he is fully aware of it Alain Badiou is actually describing, quite powerfully, some political and social aspects of the contemporary internet and social media – universal and full of potential for radical change, in amongst the ubiquitous trolling, bullying and outright discrimination, a 'duality' which this special issue examines in minute detail as far as digital leisure cultures and young people's everyday lives is concerned. Sustained by these unlikely critical theorists, Digital Leisure Studies is a label which may help us to move onto new and fertile ground, and which may help us shift gear in a time of great global upheaval, social and economic. The post-disciplinary and cross-disciplinary future we face leaves us in radical uncertainty as Jean Baudrillard has described it, but it should not leave us, at least in Leisure Studies, unprepared.

Disclosure statement

No potential conflict of interest was reported by the author.

Index

Note:
Page numbers in *italic* type refer to figures
Page numbers followed by 'n' refer to notes

www.ingramcontent.com/pod-product-compliance
Ingram Content Group UK Ltd.
Pitfield, Milton Keynes, MK11 3LW, UK
UKHW051830180425
457613UK00022B/1190

* 9 7 8 0 3 6 7 5 8 4 9 7 9 *